September Evening

The Life and Final Combat of the German World War One Ace Werner Voss

BARRY DIGGENS

GRUB STREET · LONDON

Published by
Grub Street
4 Rainham Close
London SW11 6SS

Reprinted 2012

British Library Cataloguing in Publication Data
Diggens, Barry
  September evening: the life and final combat of
  the German World War One ace Werner Voss
  1.Voss, Werner, 1897-1917 2. Fighter pilots, German – Biography
  3. World War, 1914-1918 – Aerial operations, German
  I. Title
  940.4′4944′092

ISBN 1 904010 47 4

Typeset by Pearl Graphics, Hemel Hempstead

Printed and bound in Great Britain by
the MPG Books Group, Bodmin and King's Lynn

**For three of God's little miracles, my grandsons
James, Samuel and Benjamin**

CONTENTS

FOREWORD

There have been a number of works published on the life and death of the First World War German fighter pilot Werner Voss; most have appeared as short articles in journals and magazines, and as an occasional chapter in the memoirs of old-time aviators. However, there are three books dedicated to the subject that are worthy of note: the first, Rolf Italiaander's seminal German account *Pour le Mérite Flieger mit 20 Jahren*, is useful in as much as a good deal of the narrative can almost certainly be attributed to Oberleutnant Karl Bodenschatz, who served with Voss in 1917 and bore witness to his prowess in the air. Unfortunately this work is laced with a liberal helping of Nazi idealism that detracts somewhat from its worth as a serious study of the German ace. Almost a quarter of a century later, in 1962, the author-historian Walter Musciano offered *Lt. Werner Voss, Germany's Greatest Teenage Ace*, which in parts follows Italiaander's work, but also includes the service record of Voss, and a fairly accurate victory list, both published for the first time. Last, and by no means least, Dennis Hylands presented the aviation fraternity with what is arguably the best short vignette: *Werner Voss*, a scholarly work developed from an original article he wrote for the celebrated aviation journal *Cross & Cockade* (Great Britain), volume 6#3 (1975). These three works are important in their own right, and yet none ran to more than 7,000 words, and all contradict each other in matters of detail. The explanation for this is quite straight-forward, as the authors were not only breaking new ground in terms of original research, they were also bogged down by sifting fact from fiction, which was no easy task at the time. Werner Voss was something of an enigmatic figure, he was undoubtedly a loner, and very little is known of his early life, other than the fact that he was the son of a middle-class industrialist. In his short flying career, however, he came closest to outstripping Manfred von Richthofen as Germany's greatest ace.

From the British standpoint the circumstances surrounding the final combat between the Royal Flying Corps' 56 Squadron and Voss on the evening of Sunday 23 September 1917 are well documented. Several renditions of the action are to be found in the combat reports of those British pilots who took part in the fight, the publications noted above, private correspondence and the eyewitness account of arguably Britain's most famous fighter pilot, James McCudden, who wrote *Five Years in the Royal Flying Corps*. In the main, these accounts all provide substantially similar scenarios, yet all contain inconsistencies concerning aspects of that remarkable final combat that have been questioned over the last eighty odd years by eminent historians worldwide: vacillations and niggling doubts gave rise to a diatribe that continues to this very day. The German view is somewhat different, and in recent years there has been much pondering over the possibility that Voss actually survived the action and evaded his opponents, only to be shot down some time later that same evening. Unfortunately, what very little verifiable evidence there is to support such a theory, be it German or otherwise, is sadly fragmented. In part this is due to the fact that important documents relating to the life and death of Werner Voss have been lost: between August and November 1918 many units of the Luftstreitkräfte (the Imperial German Air Service) destroyed their records in the field, lest they fell into the hands of the advancing Allies. Accordingly, by the time those documents that did survive found their way to the German Reichsarchiv at Potsdam they were already seriously depleted. More than this, although it was fashionable for middle-class families to treasure personal correspondence in that bygone era, whatever Voss family papers there may have been were either destroyed in the Allied air-raids on Voss' Rhineland hometown of Krefeld in 1943, or lost among the effects of close relatives in more recent times. Likewise, a number of official German documents relating to operations on the Western Front, among them many of the scarce war diaries and record books deposited at Potsdam, were destroyed during the bombing of the archive in 1944, else they were looted by elements of the Red Army after they blasted their way through the ruins of Berlin in the spring of 1945.

All told, this scarcity of corroborated evidence from the German side makes producing a well-balanced study of Voss an almost impossible task, and accounts for several highly romanticised incidents surrounding his life being published in books and journals in the last century that left much to be desired.

Sadly, gaps in the fabric of evidence were all too often replaced by conjecture, supposition and what can only be termed unmitigated fictions, simply in order to pad-out an otherwise brief story. This has led to several inaccuracies being accepted as gospel in recent years. The net result is that present-day aviation enthusiasts are left with only thumbnail sketches of Voss' early life, his enlistment in the military, his service on the Eastern Front, his period as a probationary pilot, and finally his untimely death at the age of twenty. An approach to the truth was certainly achieved by the authors noted above, because they took the trouble to do their homework, yet incredibly, whilst researching the subject several important pieces of the jigsaw puzzle were overlooked, forgotten or simply filed away for future reference. My own research has uncovered a scattering of these pieces that in some small measure brings us a little closer to the ultimate goal of presenting a factual rendition of the Voss saga.

Having said this, I make no claim to have produced a definitive study on the life and death of the young German ace, nor due to its incompleteness, can this work be classified as a biography in the truest sense of the word. Not long after beginning this project I came to the conclusion that I would only be able to offer a series of observations and commentaries on often controversial events that took place more than eighty years ago, events that nonetheless have become legendary in the annals of aviation history. If anything the purpose of this present study is to examine the fictions and get a little closer to the truth, to animate a new generation of enthusiasts and to stimulate further research on the subject. I am assured by friends and colleagues that fresh and recently rediscovered evidence presented within these pages will cause consternation among those who think they know all there is to know about the subject. Be that as it may, I ask only that my readers keep an open mind, and to those that will insist on nit-picking I say be my guest, find the inevitable errors that must occur here: infallibility is not among my gifts, so right the wrongs and add fuel to the debate. This will serve my purpose admirably, for I am mindful that this offering raises more questions than any answers it could possibly impart.

Responsibility for the text and my findings, including all errors and any grammatical nonsense, remains mine, but it would have been truly impossible to produce a work of this nature without the help and encouragement of many respected historians and friends. First and foremost I offer my sincere thanks to the eminent author-historian Alex Revell, who not only corrected my manuscript but also provided many photographs and kindly allowed me access to his personal correspondence with the late Douglass Whetton. Thankfully this saved me many months of painstaking detective work, and by giving me his permission to quote freely from his two great labours of love, *Brief Glory* and *High in the Empty Blue*, I was able to draw on facts and figures that had taken him many years of laborious research to accumulate. Others that have also contributed much include my friend Dennis Hylands who wrote the work that inspired me to tackle this subject from a different angle. A special thanks also goes to Aaron Weaver, who put me on to the recently discovered Rüdenberg papers and sought out several unique photographs that are here published for the first time. I must also acknowledge the help of the aviation historians: Terry Treadwell who provided more photographs; Alex Imrie, who kindly gave me permission to quote from his definitive work *The Fokker Triplane*, and also provided photographs from his extensive private archive; Norman Franks, Hal Giblin, Frank Bailey, Russell Guest and Christopher Shores, better known as the Grub Street crew, and of course their publisher, Grub Street, who allowed me to quote freely from their scholarly reference works: *Above the Trenches*; *Over the Front*; *Above the Lines* and *Under the Guns of the German Aces*.

I am also deeply indebted to the author Evan Hadingham who now lives in the United States, but as a fifth-form English schoolboy wrote *The Fighting Triplanes*, a study that has become an essential work of reference for aviation enthusiasts. While on a rare visit to his old home in the historic Gloucestershire town of Cheltenham, Hadingham dug out his yellowing Collishaw papers and graciously made them available to me, in the certain knowledge that I would question his findings. In consideration of this unselfish act I have entitled my work *September Evening*, the original heading of his chapter on Werner Voss.

Others, unconnected with aviation matters, made my hectic life easier by turning incomprehensible scribble into readable type, researched overseas, or simply sweated it out at the PRO in London and other dark dungeons because I couldn't make the journey. These include my sister-in-law Jenny Donoghue who endured months of typing and corrections to my many drafts; Gunnar Söderbaum, who found a rare copy of Italiaander's book in Sweden; Thorsten Pietsch and Gretchen Winkler, who rummaged through the dusty files at the Stadtarchiv in Krefeld for Voss material and discovered much; Paul-Günter Schulte and Claudia Bloemer of the Stadtarchiv, who managed to cut through miles of red tape and finally provided copies of several original photographs that have not seen the light of day for almost eighty years; Urban Kühl, who so expertly translated German Gothic script; Carole Thomas of the University of Texas at Dallas; David Parry, Colin Bruce and Chris Hunt of the Imperial War Museum; Barbara Pessina and her resourceful niece from Boston, who did some incredible detective work in the USA, and last but by no means least my long-suffering wife Sheila who, when I jumped out of bed in the middle of the night to write down an important thought, patted me on the head when I got back and sleepily asked if it was really worth all the trouble – I like to think it was and I hope my readers will think so too.

And finally, lest we forget:

This study is set against the back-drop of the ground fighting on the Western Front, which serves to remind us that air war casualties were relatively light compared to the many millions who were killed or horribly maimed in those blood-sodden trenches of France and western Flanders so many years ago.

INTRODUCTION

On 16 November 1916 five Royal Flying Corps DH2 Scouts of 29 Squadron were patrolling their sector of the Western Front, between the River Ancre and the medieval city of Arras. Shortly after chasing off a German two-seater reconnaissance machine near Blairville, they spotted a lone Halberstadt fighter being 'Archied' over the village of Humbercamps, just west of Monchy-au-Bois and well inside the British lines. The flight commander promptly turned the patrol to engage the enemy machine, which appeared to be flying in circles, ignoring the desultory anti-aircraft fire, and simply enjoying the scenery. Sacrificing height for speed, one member of the RFC patrol, Sergeant Pilot James T.B. McCudden, put his machine into a shallow dive to position himself below and slightly east of the German, blocking off any escape route.

McCudden watched from below as his comrades surrounded the Halberstadt like a swarm of angry bees and began shooting for all they were worth. To their amazement, between throwing his machine all over the sky and flying rings around the DH2s, the German pilot fought like the devil, and was shooting back at everyone in turn. The fight lasted for some four or five minutes, then, suddenly, just when the British pilots thought they had him, the German dived under them and headed east. McCudden was there, waiting for the Halberstadt, latched onto its tail and began shooting from a range of less than fifty yards, but with no effect. Another member of the patrol then joined him and the pair continued firing at the German, who was now weaving left and right, unerringly making for home. Streams of bright orange tracer bullets chased after the departing Scout, though not a single round was seen to be on target. McCudden alone fired off four drums of Lewis gun ammunition, but time and again he was frustrated as the very agile Halberstadt was put through what must have been its complete repertoire of evasive manoeuvres, never holding a straight line for more than a second. It wasn't long before McCudden was out of ammunition. He could then but watch as the enemy turned directly across his bow at less than twenty yards distance. Incredibly, he noticed the pilot was grinning like a Cheshire cat. The German made good his escape and, nearing the lines, turned on full power to zoom away. McCudden later wrote: 'What he was doing over our lines I do not know, but he was a very cool and experienced hand, for I must admit he made us all look fools. . . . Anyhow, I give that Hun full marks.'

This particular incident never warranted so much as a mention in the RFC Communiqué for the day, and McCudden never found out who the impudent Hun was, but after the war it was widely believed it could only have been nineteen-year-old Werner Voss, who, at that early date, actually had little experience of flying fighting Scouts and was in fact a probationer awaiting secondment to Jagdstaffel 2. This has never been verified, but if it be true, it is entirely in keeping with his impish character to have found the failure of five RFC pilots to nail him most amusing. Voss never shunned a fight, was reckless and impetuous in action, thought nothing of taking on overwhelming odds – and consistently got away with it. This audacious behaviour was to earn him the respect of friend and foe alike. Ten months after the Humber-camps fiasco, on an evening in late September 1917, James McCudden, now a captain and flight commander in 56 Squadron, ran into this dashing young man again. On that occasion the outcome was to prove entirely different. In 1918, when commit-ting Voss' final combat to paper, McCudden, himself acknow-ledged as one of the greatest fighter pilots of the war, penned what must be the most poignant epitaph to any airman living or dead: 'As long as I live I shall never forget my admiration for that German pilot, who single-handed fought seven of us for some ten minutes, and put bullets through all of our machines. His flying was wonderful, his courage magnificent, and in my opinion he is the bravest German airman whom it has been my privilege to see fight.'

Not only was Werner Voss acknowledged as an exceptional pilot who displayed skill and daring whenever and wherever he met the enemies of his country, there are those who claim he falls into that rare category that epitomise the chivalrous image of the air fighter. His shooting is said to have been every bit as good as his flying, and it has been reported that on more than one occasion he brought down an enemy machine by aiming only for its engine rather than its occupants. This last accolade probably has little or no foundation in truth as it is difficult enough to hit a moving target in the air, let alone aim for a vital spot such as the engine. However, it is generally accepted that his exploits in the skies over France and western Flanders, whether real or imagined, became truly legendary. Conversely, there is conclusive evidence to prove he often strafed his helpless victims on the ground. Hardly a chivalrous act by any standards!

This statement should, however, be taken in context. Instances of the practice were common to all sides during the first air war, and rarely considered an act of wanton barbarism. On at least one occasion the highest scoring British ace, Edward 'Mick' Mannock, was guilty of repeatedly attacking a defenceless enemy on the ground, and was soundly admonished by his flight commander for doing so; but that was as far as it went. Voss was very much a man of his times, and the times called for the defeat of the enemies of his country by whatever means – fair or foul. Yet recorded instances of his attacks on downed enemies on the ground relate solely to two-seater observation and photo-reconnaissance machines, which minutes earlier had been either photographing or ranging artillery fire on German positions. It is now widely accepted that the first duty of a Scout pilot was to prevent reconnaissance machines returning with information to their home bases at all costs. Therefore, utterly destroying them and their precious intelligence, either in the air or on the ground, was considered justified. In a letter home Voss once touched on the unhappy plight of Allied two-seater crews, revealing that he was not without a degree of compassion. He referred to them as 'Verachtliken' – poor devils – adding: 'I know how they felt. I have flown in such a type. They must be destroyed because they spy out our secrets but I would prefer to shoot down fighters.' In this respect Voss was the antithesis of Manfred von Richthofen, Germany's highest scoring ace, who many historians now argue habitually sought out lame-ducks and the often vulnerable reconnaissance machines rather than chance a full-blooded encounter with a highly manoeuvrable Allied Scout. In truth this is a little uncharitable. Richthofen was undoubtedly a very brave man and an exceptional leader of men – however, the methods he employed to destroy his enemies are another story.

Voss' career as a fighter pilot lasted ten short months. At the time of his death he was credited with forty-eight victories and was running a close second to Richthofen and, had fate not played its fickle hand, it is entirely possible he would have overtaken 'The Red Air Fighter' by the early months of 1918. Voss was also acknowledged as the greatest exponent of Germany's much acclaimed wonder weapon and the best known of all German fighters, the Fokker Triplane, the first examples of which arrived at the Front in late August 1917. Its sleek lines and incredible performance was what every German fighter pilot dreamed of. Though relatively slow for the period it had few equals in a dogfight, and what it lacked in speed was more than compensated for by its incredible manoeuvrability and amazing rate of climb. Voss tested the prototype V4 triplane at the Fokker factory at Schwerin in mid-summer 1917 and immediately fell in love with it. Once in the air he and this superlative example of a fighting machine became as one – a formidable, singular entity, ready to take on anything the Allies could throw at it, including the much vaunted SE5s and Sopwith Camels that were then arriving on the Western Front in ever increasing numbers. Few doubt that his boundless enthusiasm and glowing report on the triplane were instrumental in convincing Richthofen and the office of Kommandierenden General der Luftstreitkräfte, (General in Command of the German Army Air Service – commonly abbreviated to Kogenluft) that this was the machine that could help maintain German air superiority.

Over a period of twenty days in September 1917, and whilst flying one of the first pre-production triplanes, Voss shot down ten Allied machines, and still managed to squeeze in a leave that covered at least eleven of those heady days. In the same period Richthofen accounted for two, his sixty-first and sixty-second victories. Due in part to an enforced leave, it was to be two months to the day since Voss had been killed before Richthofen scored again. He then took seven long months to reach his final total of eighty. Moreover, by the end of the war only two other German pilots had surpassed the tally notched-up by Voss: his fellow Jasta 10 comrade Eric Löwenhardt, who was killed shortly after downing his fifty-fourth, and the diminutive Ernst Udet, who survived the war and was credited with sixty-two victories. [Recent research now suggests that Joseph Peter Jacobs, who finished the war as commander of Jasta 7, actually equalled the score of Voss.]

Ironically, few historians have offered more than a chapter or two on the short life of Werner Voss. Yet his prowess as a flying tiger, the forty-eight confirmed victories that finally placed him fourth among the list of elite German fighter aces, and his incredible encounter with 56 Squadron RFC on the evening of 23 September 1917, must rank him high among the leading fighter pilots of that first great war in the air.

CHAPTER ONE

LEUTNANT DER RESERVE WERNER VOSS

(13.04.1897 – 23.09.1917)

Werner Voss was born on 13 April 1897 in the Rhineland mill town of Krefeld. Long famed for its quality silk and velvet manufacture, this ancient town still boasts a number of factories that continue a tradition of textile finishing that can be traced back to an influx of Mennonite cloth weavers who settled in the region during the 18th century. Some time in the 1890s, Max Voss, a wealthy industrialist and one of the town's most respected citizens, married his childhood sweetheart Mathilde Pastor; a staunch Evangelical Lutheran who took her faith seriously. It has been intimated in several histories that the Voss family were non-practising Jews, but this has no foundation in truth, and though there was at least one Jewish family of the same name living in Krefeld during the 1930s they were not related to the subject of this book. Voss is a very common name for the region, and at the time of writing the Krefeld directory lists no less than eighty-five telephone numbers for residents named Voss.

Shortly after their wedding Max and Mathilde moved into a large, well-to-do house on Blumenthalstrasse, then a pleasant tree-lined avenue that like most of the town was sadly destroyed by Allied bombing during the Second World War. But before the turn of the century the couple had produced five lively children, two girls Margrit and Katherine, and three boys Werner, Otto and Max. Mother saw to it that they were brought up properly; church on Sundays and Bible readings before bedtime. As might be expected the Voss children enjoyed all the comforts of an affluent background. Their fortune stemmed from a highly successful cloth dyeing business, then situated on Geburstsstrasse, that still exists to this day, though now merged into a larger concern trading as Voss-Biermann Lawaczeck GmbH.

Werner was happy and carefree as a child, and often displayed a natural wit that was popular with everyone, but at times he could be headstrong and impetuous – characteristics that came to the fore during his military career. Afforded a good education at Krefeld's Real Gymnasium, he did well as a student and passed several examinations with distinction. As the years passed he grew into a handsome young man of slim build, topped off with a mop of dark hair. Though not over tall, he had captivating blue eyes that from his early teens won the hearts of many a young Fraülein he chanced to meet in and about Krefeld. Unfortunately, the clouds of war arrested any possibility of his casual liaisons blossoming into long-term relationships, although there was talk of a young lady named Doris, who at some time may have figured large in his life and wrote a touching yet thought provoking letter to his mother in June 1918.

It was intended that the Voss boys would join the family business after completing their education, and no doubt they would have done so, but like so many impressionable young men of that hapless generation they were caught up in a wave of nationalistic fervour that swept through Europe like a tidal wave just prior to the outbreak of the Great War. In April of that fateful year of 1914, notwithstanding German conscription laws, Werner volunteered for his local militia, Ersatz Eskadron 2, a replacement unit for Westfälische Husaren-Regiment Nr. 11, then stationed at Paderborn. At the time the great alliances of Germany and Austria, opposed by Russia, France, and a less enthusiastic Great Britain, were busily stockpiling the powder kegs of war – and looking for an excuse to light the fuse. In April the French Ambassador to Austria wrote: 'Feelings that the nations are moving towards conflict grow from day to day.' In May a US envoy reported to President Woodrow Wilson: 'Militarism runs stark mad . . . It only needs a spark.' The spark came in June when a young Serbian anarchist assassinated the heir to the Austrian throne during a state visit to Sarajevo. Heated diplomatic exchanges flew back and forth between the capitals of Vienna and Belgrade and Austrian accusations were followed by demands, which in turn were followed by an impossible ultimatum to Serbia. Self-righteous Austria demanded retribution – but was refused. On 28 July 1914, with the full support of Imperial Germany, the Austro-Hungarian Empire declared war on the tiny Balkan state. Within a matter of days the continent of Europe became irrevocably embroiled in the greatest conflict the world had ever known.

When Germany mobilised Werner Voss was still only seventeen years old, but this did not stop him taking full enlistment in his active service regiment on 16 November 1914. Two weeks later Hussar Regiment No. 11 was ordered to the Eastern Front where, in contrast to fighting in the west, a war of movement was still being fought. However, like so many cavalrymen of that era, the young Rhinelander soon found himself fighting on foot. The battle fronts settled down, and as static warfare spread from the Baltic Sea to far off Galicia, the opposing armies were forced to dig-in. Unpleasant, muddy trenches, constantly swept by shell-fire and flying bullets, were not to his liking at all. Inclement weather only added to his misery and with the onset of that chilling winter of 1914 life in the firing line became particularly arduous. As on the Western Front, the war in the east degenerated into localised acts of attrition that daily took their toll on the men in the trenches. Despite the hardships, and no doubt fortified by the invulnerability of youth, Voss did his duty and distinguished himself in action on more than one occasion. On 27 January 1915 he was promoted to Gefreiter and by May he had been awarded his first decoration for bravery, the Iron Cross 2nd Class, which was quickly followed by a second promotion to Unteroffizier. But after ten months at the front, and by now feeling there could be no glory dying in a sea of mud far from home, he applied for a transfer to the Imperial German Air Service and was accepted. It is entirely possible that he actually engineered this move by getting himself classified as 'unfit for further infantry and cavalry duties.'

His discharge from the Hussars finally came through, and on 1 August 1915 Voss reported to Flieger-Ersatz-Abteilungen Nr. 7 stationed at Cologne. FEA-7 was a training and replacement depot where recruits were put through a stiff induction course and assessed. Within a month he was recommended for pilot training and on 1 September presented himself at the conveniently located Fliegerschule at Eglesberg field – a wind-swept hill just outside his hometown of Krefeld. Here he proved to be an exceptional pupil, and after completing the course was returned to Cologne on 12 February 1916 to await posting to an operational unit. During the war, German aircrews underwent training at flying schools in Germany and were then returned to their depots for an orientation course that normally included several flights over the battlefront. They were then sent to an operational unit where they were expected to complete a certain number of combat sorties before being awarded their pilot's badge. Werner Voss was no exception, though while languishing at the depot, eagerly awaiting his posting, he was employed as an instructor and at the tender age of eighteen had the distinction of being the youngest in the service.

Voss didn't have too long to wait for the posting to come through. On 2 March he was promoted to Vizefeldwebel, and on the 10th assigned to a newly-formed fighting section, Kampfstaffel 20, which came under the aegis of Kampf-geschwader IV. The Kasta became operational on 28 March and he began his flying career as an observer on two-seaters in the Verdun sector. Here he was employed on bombing sorties, spotting for the artillery, and photographic missions that involved flying over one of the bloodiest killing-grounds in France: Mort-Homme, Fort Douaumont, Poivre Hill, and the dark waters of the Meuse as they gently meandered through the valley of the Argonne. It was a hot place to receive his initiation. General Philippe Pétain, then Commander of the French Armies of the Centre, charged the Aviation Militaire to clear the skies above Verdun; no German could be allowed to cross the lines. But constantly being harassed by anti-aircraft fire, and the often maniacal attacks pressed home by French fighting Scouts, soon taught Voss how to survive in the air. Finally, on 28 May, he received his coveted pilot's badge and the Kasta was hurriedly moved up to the rolling downland of the Somme in preparation for the expected British offensive launched there on 1 July. Voss was glad to get away from the hell of Verdun, but there was to be no respite; he and his Kasta comrades experienced a harrowing time during the opening days of what was to be the long drawn out Battle of the Somme, a gargantuan struggle for a few yards of rain sodden French soil that lasted seven long months and claimed the lives of over half a million men. German observation and photo-reconnaissance machines took a terrific beating from the Royal Flying Corps during the early weeks of the struggle, and by the end of July the nineteen-year-old Vizefeldwebel was noted as the only original member of his unit to survive the intense air offensive mounted by the Allies.

Shaken by two-seater losses, Voss applied for a commission and was posted to the officer training college at Lochstadt Camp on the North Sea coast of East Prussia. Again, he did well and received his advancement on 9 September 1916. As a newly commissioned Leutnant der Reserve he was soon posted to the single-seat pilot's training school, (Einsitzerschule) at Grossen-hain in Saxony, where he converted to fighting Scouts. His service record and family correspondence reveal that in early October he was then sent on a flying visit to Bulgaria, though the purpose of his brief stay there has never been explained.

On 21 November Voss was officially transferred to the most celebrated German fighting squadron of the day, Königliche Preussische Jagdstaffel Nr. 2, then stationed at Lagnicourt-Marcel on the Somme. This posting seems surprising. Jasta 2 had been formed in August 1916 under the leadership of the great Oswald Boelcke, an inspirationalist, brilliant tactician and experienced fighter pilot who, along with his contemporary Max Immelmann, became a national hero and one of the first great aces of the war. The son of a Saxon schoolmaster, Boelcke was known to his men as the 'Master' and eventually to the general public as the Father of the German Air Service. His series of critical reports, and an assessment of the air war prepared for Chef des Feldflugwesens (Chief of Field Aviation) Major Hermann von der Lieth-Thomsen, was instrumental in bringing together the most experienced pilots and loosely grouping them into single-seat fighter detachments known as KEKs (Kampfeinsitzer-Kommandos). Their brief was to achieve air superiority over hotly contested areas of the Front and to clear the skies of their Allied opponents in order to allow bombing and photo reconnaissance groups to go about their business unmolested. Although the concept was experimental, the outstanding success of the KEKs led to the formation of the first all single-seat fighter units, the Jagdstaffeln, seven of which were raised in the autumn of 1916. The Jagdstaffeln, commonly abbreviated to Jasta or Staffel, soon had at their disposal the most formidable German fighting Scout to come off the production lines, the Albatros D I, and shortly thereafter the variant D II. Power provided by a 160 h.p. Mercedes D-III engine enabled this relatively heavy aircraft to carry greater loads aloft than any other fighter of the day and also its two hard-hitting Spandau machine guns that were to reap a grim harvest among Allied two-seater crews in the spring of 1917.

For the most part, Jasta 2 pilots were handpicked, many by Boelcke himself. In the main they were either known to him personally or had been recommended by trusted friends and, without exception, were all men of experience or recognised fighting potential. Within weeks Boelcke had forged them into an elite, and the most successful fighting group at the Front. But by the time Voss arrived the 'Master' had been dead for just under a month, killed in an aerial collision with one of his own men on 28 October 1916. So, had the new commander of Jasta 2, Oberleutnant Stephan Kirmaier, chosen Voss, a young pilot with little experience on single-seaters, or was he previously known to

Boelcke? This is a question that may never be resolved, though it is interesting to note that between March and July 1916 Boelcke had been on the Verdun Front with one of the first KEKs equipped with the infamous Fokker Eindeckers that had given the Allies considerable problems in the winter of 1915-16. Boelcke's KEK had been stationed at Sivry in the Consenvoye sector, some three kilometres behind the lines, and was assigned the task of escorting two early bomber groups, BAO and BAM, acronyms for Brieftaube Abteilung Ostende and Brieftaube Abteilung Metz, better known as The Carrier Pigeons. The incongruous cover names were intended to fool the Allies into thinking these units were simply concerned with intelligence gathering, but it wasn't too long before their true purpose was established. Voss' own bombing group was attached to BAM during March and May, and Boelcke's Eindeckers often flew with them. Which begs the question, did they actually meet, or was the Master simply apprised of Voss' two-seater exploits by friends in Kampf-geschwader IV? The inclusion of a signed Boelcke portrait photograph among the few Voss papers that survived the Allied bombing of Krefeld in the Second World War, now held in the town's Stadtarchiv, suggests that they did know each other.

Stephan Kirmaier succeded Boelke as Staffelführer on 30 October, but survived only twenty-five days before being shot down over Lesboeufs by DH2s of 24 Squadron RFC – one day after Voss was officially assigned to the Staffel. The burden of leadership was then thrust upon Hauptmann Franz Josef Walz, an experienced thirty-one-year-old pre-war military pilot who took command of the unit on 29 November. Although recognised as a born leader by his superiors Walz was no Boelcke, and it wasn't long before his ability to command the unit effectively was brought into question. In the meantime, Voss slotted comfortably into the flight commanded by one of the Master's star pupils, an up-and-coming aristocrat and former Uhlan cavalryman, Leutnant Manfred Freiherr von Richthofen – and from this point their careers became inextricably linked.

Although the two airmen were at opposite ends of the social spectrum they soon became friends, for if nothing else Richthofen judged a pilot by his flying ability and fighting spirit and not by his station in life. It has been intimated in several histories that Voss and the soon to be christened 'Red Baron' never got on, and that this led to antagonism. This is improbable. There was indeed a certain rivalry between them, but this could only have been professional – or at worst one-sided. Though he was never in awe of the man, Voss respected Richthofen as a leader and accomplished tactician, and for his part Richthofen recognised a born air-fighter when he saw one. In this respect their abilities complimented each other: Richthofen went on to become a great leader of men and Germany's highest scoring ace, but was never considered a great pilot – and while Voss went on to become possibly the greatest German fighter pilot of them all he was, by his own admission, never a great leader.

By mid-1917 the pair were household names, idolised by the German public, and unlike their British counterparts whose daring exploits were rarely publicised due to the RFC's rigid policy of anonymity, they were fêted by the press and treated almost as equals. Although, after witnessing one of Richthofen's victories over an outclassed two-seater, which had taken 600 rounds of precious ammunition to bring down near Givenchy-en-Gohelle, Voss wrote: 'He is a great fighter and has done wonderful work for the Fatherland, but I do not believe that he is better than I am.' It was said without undue pretension, as the cloth dyer's son was well aware of his own limitations. There is no question that Voss thought Richthofen a close friend, and it is known that Richthofen reciprocated in some measure. Their friendship extended to sharing an interest in photography, and on more than one occasion they took leaves together that included visits to the Voss family home in Krefeld. Moreover, Richthofen had an open invitation to use the family's hunting lodge in the Black Forest whenever he found time to indulge his passion for the chase – hardly a courtesy to be extended to someone disliked.

After the death of Voss, Richthofen continued his relationship with the family and there was talk that he and Werner's younger sister Margrit were more than just fond of each other. It is possible that she (among other candidates) was the mysterious young woman who regularly wrote voluminous letters to Richthofen up until the time he was killed in April 1918. Lothar von Richthofen, Manfred's younger brother, also kept in touch and regularly corresponded with Voss family members until after the war, as did other pilots and personnel of Jagdgeschwader Nr. 1. That Richthofen genuinely liked Werner Voss may be another matter. Curiously, he was seemingly kept at a distance, and Richthofen never mentioned his demise in any official capacity, yet he fairly eulogised two other star pilots of JG1: Karl Allmenröder, who in four months shot down thirty enemy machines but was killed in June by a pilot of the Royal Naval Air Service (RNAS), and the thirty-three-victory ace Kurt Wolff, who was shot down in one of the first Fokker Triplanes to see service at the front – eight short days before Voss met his own nemesis. It is well known that Richthofen cultivated few real friendships during his career and that he remained aloof even to those he gathered around him. No doubt this was due to the realisation that friendship, like life itself, could be all too brief at the Front, and, having seen too many good men go west, he allowed few to get close to him. Voss and Richthofen were undoubtedly friendly rivals, but perhaps an element of jealousy had crept in somewhere, and this is possibly why he made no great play about the death of the young contender. Whatever the real reason, their true relationship remains something of a puzzle.

Hauptmann Walz followed the example set by Boelcke to the best of his limited abilities. Abilities that in fairness were only limited by the fact that he had little or no experience of commanding a fighter squadron – in reality he was a dyed-in-the-wool two-seater man with over 300 reconnaissance sorties under his belt. But now at Pronville, to where the Jasta had moved in December, he was like a fish out of water and found it difficult to adjust. Not unexpectedly his cautious behaviour and lacklustre battle tactics perplexed his pilots. Even so, he gave them a considerable degree of latitude, favouring personal initiative rather than regimented discipline, and allowed the more experienced to make lone forays across the lines. Scores continued to climb and, just a week after joining the squadron, Leutnant der Reserve Werner Voss began his mercurial rise to fame, fame that spread to both sides of the lines.

CHAPTER TWO

'A DAREDEVIL FIRST CLASS'

(27.11.1916 – 23.09.1917)

By the autumn of 1916 aerial combats were commonplace, more so than in the previous two years of the war, and in the heat of battle it was not always possible for pilots to observe details of either the aircraft they were engaging or the results of a fight. This is illustrated by the intriguing controversies that surround Voss' last combat. Conclusive proof of the outcome of engagements depended on witnesses, either in the air or on the ground. In fact the German criterion was particularly rigorous. Pilots were expected to provide a minimum of three corroboratory statements before victories could be confirmed by the office of Kogenluft and entered into the Abschusse, and even when such evidence could be produced errors inevitably occurred. On occasions this resulted in fanciful reports being accepted and recorded.

Understandably, in a full-blooded dogfight, a Scout pilot's life depended on his ability to perform a continuing series of unpredictable turns and zooms, dives and banks; never holding to a straight line for more than a second. As the war progressed and more and more aircraft were pressed into service aerial combats often became a kaleidoscope of whirling machines darting about the skies missing each other by scant feet or even inches. In a dogfight there was ever present the dreaded possibility of a mid-air collision, which usually proved fatal. Allied airmen were denied the use of parachutes, and only in the last few months of the war were they employed by the Germans. In consequence, a pilot needed to have his wits about him just to avoid crashing into friend or foe, and once involved in a mêlée there was no time to take stock of aircraft as they flashed past, nor to note type or markings. There was but a moment to identify an opponent and to shoot as opportunities presented themselves. Unless a machine actually broke up in the air or burst into flames – definite proof that it would crash – there was little time to watch an aircraft falling out of control.

Confirmations were more of a problem for the Allies than the Germans. They were in fact at a considerable disadvantage. From very early on Allied pilots were charged to take offensive action on all occasions, a directive that was even extended to the hapless two-seater crews who rarely flew machines capable of a chase, much less a dogfight. Whereas, as a matter of policy the Jagdstaffeln, often equipped with superior aircraft, all but occasionally remained east of the lines in strategic defence. Not surprisingly, the majority of combats took place over German territory, euphemistically known to the British as Hunland, and this could be fifteen miles or more beyond the front lines. An added problem for the Allies was drift – something the Germans used to good effect – for on average eight days out of ten the prevailing winds blew out of the west. Embroiled in a fight, British and French pilots regularly found they were steadily drifting eastwards, whilst at the same time being drawn deeper and deeper into the German hinterland by their better-trained and often more experienced opponents. In these situations a pilot's only course of action, if at all possible, was to disengage and head west, but it was doubly difficult for a damaged fighter or reconnaissance machine to reach the distant front lines and safety. In fights deep within their own territory the Germans had little difficulty establishing claims as they could usually rely on troops in the back areas and flak batteries that regularly reported combats and crash sites; whereas Allied pilots could only hope their comrades would be able confirm a 'kill'. Not surprisingly, 'Out of Control' is the commonest statement found in early Royal Flying Corps official communiqués, while the Aviation Militaire, perhaps more judiciously, adopted the more positive term 'Probable'.

For the most part, historians are in agreement about the details of the victories credited to Werner Voss. And yet occasionally opinions differ, as a number of discrepancies on dates, timings and locations creep in that may never be resolved. In the main, two authoritative 'Victory Lists' have been consulted and are cited in this book. Alex Revell and Douglass Whetton compiled a fairly accurate list in the mid-1970s; this was then revised and added to by Norman Franks and Hal Giblin in 1997. Producing these 'definitive' lists was no easy task. Like many dedicated aviation historians before them the authors embarked on a labour of love that involved hundreds of painstaking hours spent researching often difficult archive sources. Their efforts are to be commended, if only for the wealth of information afforded modern aviation enthusiasts, historians, and of course readers of this work.

A similar and much greater problem exists for German aviation sources. In the last days of the First World War many front line units destroyed their records in order to prevent them falling into Allied hands; all other records of the former Luftstreikräfte that did survive were subsequently deposited in the Reichsarchiv at Potsdam. During the inter-war years, when the prime concern of governments was the mammoth task of rebuilding a devastated Europe, there was little interest in war aviation and few historians bothered to consult what was actually available. In the final phases of the Second World War the Reichsarchiv was bombed and partially destroyed by fire. As a result, many of the scarce Jagdstaffeln war diaries and important documents relating to air operations on the Western Front were lost. Fortunately, in the late 1950s and 60s, when many former first war airmen were still alive, there was a resurgence of interest in the subject and enough material in the form of eyewitness accounts, newspaper reports, personal diaries and other private documents was steadily uncovered by historians. Other details of the Voss victories were gleaned from the book written by Oberleutnant Karl Bodenschatz, *Jagd in Flanderns Himmel*, an all too idealistic but important history of the Richthofen Squadrons. Bodenschatz, a twenty-six-year-old former Bavarian cavalryman, was adjutant of JG1 throughout the war and kept the Combat Wing War Diary. Although the diary only covers Voss' victories between 31 July and 23 September 1917, and is not without errors, it does help corroborate the more exact English lists.

By far the greater part of Voss' victories were scored over RFC machines and very few over those of the Aviation Militaire – in fact he was credited with bringing down only three French machines, and one of these is questionable. The reason for this is two-fold: first and foremost the Jagdstaffeln to which Voss was seconded were stationed mainly on the British Front in hotly contested northern France and west Flanders; secondly the Germans recognised the RFC as being by far the greater threat throughout the entire war. In his memoirs, when commenting on the resurgence of RFC fortunes in late 1917, Luftstreitkräfte Commanding General Ernst von Hoeppner had this to say of the British and the deployment of his forces: 'Because of their number and their sporting audacity, the English continue to be our most dangerous adversaries and, as before, the major part of the German air strength was concentrated against them.' This does not mean the French did not play their part. During the war French aircraft factories produced some outstanding fighter aircraft: the highly manoeuvrable Nieuport Scouts that held the Germans at bay when the British had very little to offer; and the very successful Spad variants, that given the right conditions could more than match the German Albatros in a dogfight. And of course there were several famous French aces whose names are synonymous with the first air war: Georges Guynemer, René Fonck, Charles Nungesser, Jean Navarre, and the diminutive pre-war exhibition pilot Roland Garros, who became one of the first aces and was instrumental in developing a functional yet primitive means of firing a machine gun directly through the arc of an aircraft's whirling airscrew without shooting the blades off, an innovation that electrified the Germans into producing the first operational fixed machine-gun interrupter gear.

At this point, it should be noted that throughout the war there was normally a one hour difference between British and German time. This actually varied according to the year, but for the better part of the period concerned with here German time was one hour ahead of British time, and only coincided for the brief three-week period between 25 March and 15 April 1917, after which the hour difference was reinstated. In order to avoid confusion, where timings given below relate to Allied reports British time is given, and German times are used when reports emanate from or refer solely to original German sources. It should also be noted that wherever the term 'British' is used in relation to aircrews and ground forces it is deemed to include men of the British Empire that flocked to the aid of the mother country between 1914-1918: in the main only the cream of Australian, Canadian, New Zealand and South African volunteers came to the RFC. In fact, more than one-third of all RFC aircrews hailed from Empire dominions and other colonies and so many volunteered it was impossible to accommodate them all. Yet those that did manage to get in included several of the top Allied aces, among their number men who became legends of the first great war in the air: Billy Bishop, credited with shooting down seventy-two German machines; Raymond Collishaw sixty; William Barker fifty; Anthony Beauchamp Proctor fifty-four; Keith Caldwell twenty-five and Roderic Dallas thirty-two, to name but a few.

There was also a good measure of Americans who either from ties of blood with the old world, or a simple sense of duty to the cause of liberty, crossed the Atlantic to join the French Aviation Militaire, or whenever possible the Royal Flying Corps. In the early months of the war it was far easier for American volunteers to get into the Aviation Militaire via the French Foreign Legion than into the RFC, which already had more volunteers than it could handle. There was not only the tricky problem of compromising US neutrality to consider, but also Americans joining any branch of the British Armed Forces were obliged to swear an oath of allegiance to the British Crown, thus jeopardising their US citizenship, whereas by joining the Legion they were only obliged to swear obedience to their French officers. Even so, more than 200 Americans managed to get into the RFC, and what later became the Royal Air Force, during the course of the war. Notable among them: Howard Boyson, who flew with 66 Squadron and shot down five Germans; Frederick Libby, who downed ten and was the first American ace in any air service; Wilfred Beaver who got nineteen, and Frederick Gillet who flew with 79 Squadron and downed twenty. But before many of these Yanks had even seen the cockpit of a fighting Scout a young man from the German Rhineland was well on his way to becoming a legend in his own lifetime.

Werner Voss opened the floodgates on 27 November 1916 with the first of several doubles, downing a French-built Nieuport 17 of 60 Squadron RFC in the morning, and what was probably a two-seater Royal Aircraft Factory FE2b of 18 Squadron in the afternoon. Both losses were confirmed in the RFC Communiqué for this date. The Nieuport fell behind the German lines near Miraumont, just west of Bapaume, and its pilot twenty-four-year-old Captain George A. Parker was reported missing in action. The remains of Parker and that of his Nieuport were never found. The FE2b was recorded in the Jasta 2 War Diary as a 'Vickers'. At the time, the Germans generally referred to all British pusher types as such, being more familiar with the early Vickers Gunbus than the FE variants that appeared later on: these lattice tail machines were in fact all of strikingly similar configuration. The FE attacked by Voss burst into flames after he poured a stream of tracer bullets into it over Ginchy, it then crash-landed on the 5th Army front behind the British lines. The observer, Air Mechanic Oliver F. Watts, was killed in the air and his wounded pilot, Lieutenant Frederic A. George, was lucky to survive the terrifying ordeal of bringing his burning machine down. Although unfit for further flying duties, George remained in the RFC until the end of the war and in later life became Chairman of the North of England Ship Owners Association.

For this double success Voss was awarded the Iron Cross First Class, confirmed by the office of Kogenluft on 19 December 1916. But after a promising start it was to be almost a month before he scored again.

Voss next chanced on a BE2d of 7 Squadron spotting for the artillery over Beaucourt on 21 December. The BE, another product of the Royal Aircraft Factory, and the bulwark of RFC reconnaissance squadrons, was shot down between the lines near Miraumont – the only recorded RFC loss of that day. Lieutenant Darol W. Davis survived the crash but was badly wounded. Unable to move, and in terrible pain from his injuries, Davis lay beside his wrecked aircraft and the lifeless body of his observer, Second Lieutenant William M. Cotton, for almost three days before being found by a German infantry patrol. He spent many weeks in hospital and was subsequently sent to the POW camp in Voss' home town of Krefeld. After the war he recalled his teenage victor had visited him twice during his captivity, once in the hospital and later at the camp where he was presented with his victor's calling card.

January of 1917 passed without Voss scoring at all: a spell of leave, intermittent rain, strong winds and occasional snow showers all conspired to curtail his activities over the Front. On 11 January Richthofen left Jasta 2 to take command of Jasta 11, and faced a daunting task. The unit was not doing well, in fact it was woefully inept and the least distinguished of any Jasta attached to the German 6th Army. It had failed to score even a single victory since its formation in September 1916, and required considerable coaxing to bring it up to anything like the standards achieved by Jasta 2, which by Imperial Decree had now been renamed Jasta Boelcke, in order that the name and example of its first great leader be perpetuated. Yet, despite getting to grips with sole command of a fighting Jasta, and trying to whip its apathetic pilots into shape at the same time, Richthofen continued to score. He was already well ahead of Voss and by the end of January was credited with eighteen victories. But the young Rhinelander was trying hard. In February he produced a total of eight, including two more doubles: two Airco DH2s on the 25th and two BEs downed on the 27th.

The first of his New Year harvest fell to his guns on 1 February 1917. Captain Albert Peter Daly of 29 Squadron, flying a DH2, arguably the best British pusher type fighter in service at the time, was chasing an Albatros of Jasta Boelcke over Achiet-le-Grand when Voss appeared from nowhere and attacked from astern. Firing short accurate bursts, he peppered Daly's machine and disabled the engine. As he turned the crippled DH2 to get out of the way Daly ran straight into a line of murderous fire, was hit in the shoulder and lost control. The aircraft went into a steep dive but the plucky RFC pilot managed to pull out at 3,000 feet and put his machine into a long, shallow glide heading west, though by now he was already too low and well behind the German Front. Without power, and struggling against a stiff headwind, Daly realised there was no hope of escape and, despite the pain of his wound, had the presence of mind to keep the nose of the DH2 down in order to maintain air speed. He then began circling, looking for a suitable place to land. At every turn he was losing height, so kept flattening out every few seconds to keep in the air as long as possible. Finally, dangerously close to stalling, he picked out a large field and put his crippled machine down close to the village of Essarts where he was subsequently taken prisoner by ground troops. Voss again visited his victim in hospital, and this time, as well as leaving his calling card he also took a gift of cigars and, rather pretentiously, presented Daly with a signed photograph of himself.

Voss almost certainly learnt an important lesson from the engagement with Daly, a lesson that was to stand him in very good stead throughout his career. It was widely accepted that the best way to shoot an opponent down was to get in as close as possible in order to be sure of hitting the target. This is a reasonable course of action if attacking from astern or below. But it was no mean feat to hit a moving target from a machine that was often going in the opposite direction or coming in from the flank. Captain Daly had unwittingly turned into Voss' line of fire, and thus fell victim to a deflection shot, a method of shooting not widely appreciated during the first air war: by aiming well ahead of an enemy moving across the bow, then holding the course while firing at the same time, the target would run straight into the stream of bullets. This usually resulted in riddling an opponent from end to end. Although a number of pilots understood the laws of deflection, the shot wasn't easy to master; the trick was to calculate how far in front to aim and how long to hold the course, and all but a chosen few failed to achieve this. Possibly the greatest exponent of the deflection shot was Edward 'Mick' Mannock, the British ace of aces, who amassed seventy-four victories before being shot down in July 1918. But during his first tour of duty in France Mannock was a very nervous pilot, and considered less than mediocre by his squadron mates. Some said he was gun-shy, others less charitable called him a coward, but at thirty-four years of age it wasn't easy for an old dog to learn new tricks. In fact, it was several weeks before Mannock found his form, conquered his fear of death, and mastered the deflection shot, then there was no holding him back. Voss, being much younger, was quick to learn, and in action he soon developed an economy of style that can be only be described as both cold and calculating.

Voss' fifth customer was a BE2d of 16 Squadron that crashed in flames behind the British lines near Givenchy on 4 February. The pilot, Second Lieutenant Herbert Martin-Massey, although badly burned, survived the crash and in the next war rose to the rank of group captain. His observer, Second Lieutenant Noel Vernham, was not so lucky. The RFC Communiqué for this day reported that artillery officers at the front stated (in error) that the German machine involved was also brought down in this combat.

Voss added another DH2 to his score on the 10th, which he claimed as 'downed behind the British lines' southwest of Serre. In fact this machine, flown by Captain Leslie Aizlewood of 32 Squadron, though badly shot about, returned to its base at Lealvillers and landed safely. The RFC Communiqué for 10 February naturally makes no mention of any battle damage to Aizlewood's machine but does report that he engaged and drove down a German aeroplane, which was seen to have fallen out of control, although this could not have been the machine flown by Voss.

On the 25th Voss found himself up against McCudden's old unit, 29 Squadron, and in a hard fought skirmish he claimed the second double of his career. Around noontime, six Albatros Scouts of Jasta Boelcke bounced a flight composed of six DH2s over Arras. The two formations immediately broke up and machines began tail-chasing each other all over the heavens. Individual combats ensued, and Lieutenant Reginald Lund foolishly tried dogfighting the Albatros flown by Voss. He was severely wounded in the encounter and crashed his machine into the British lines near Arras. Minutes later the German blazed away at another DH2, flown by Captain Harold Payn, who put his machine into a steep dive to try to escape the onslaught. Fortunately two comrades came to his aid and promptly attacked the young German, causing him to break off the pursuit and dive into a nearby cloud. Voss claimed and was credited with both DH2s, although Payn, an experienced fighter pilot, who could boast McCudden among his many friends, managed to nurse his badly damaged aeroplane back to his airfield where he was able to make a very passable landing. The Jasta Boelcke War Diary records three DH2s claimed in this engagement, but RFC records reveal only one had actually been shot down. This was Lund, who, although wounded, survived the crash and eventually rose to the rank of captain. The third machine, flown by Lieutenant J.H. Sutherland, observed by German ground troops as 'diving into the lines', had dropped out of the fight with a bad gun stoppage and smashed rudderpost. Sutherland also landed safely.

Jasta Boelcke was eventually fully equipped with Albatros fighters, but in early 1917 it still had the odd Halberstadt Scout at its disposal. It was whilst flying one of this type that Voss downed his ninth victim, a BE2c of 16 Squadron. This crashed just north of Arras on 26 February. In his pursuit of the Englishmen Voss made a ferocious and prolonged attack that continued almost down to ground level, clearly in an attempt to utterly destroy the reconnaissance machine at all costs. Both occupants survived but were severely wounded. The pilot, Lieutenant Harry Bagot, recovered but never flew again, whilst his unfortunate observer, Second Lieutenant Robert Jack, died of his wounds the next day.

Voss' tenth and eleventh victories came on the 27th. There was no need to chase the first one down. This was a BE2e of 8 Squadron, surprised over Arras whilst ranging for the artillery. Flown by Second Lieutenant Edwin Pope, he and his observer, Second Lieutenant Hubert Johnson, made a brave attempt to fight the German off. But it was a one-sided encounter that lasted for brief seconds. The BE's petrol tank was punctured in the first burst of fire. The British gunners for whom the airmen had been ranging could only watch in horror as a hideous conflagration, trailing a long plume of oily black smoke, plummeted to earth close to their emplacements near Blairville. The second victim of the day was a BE2c of 12 Squadron, caught in the late afternoon in almost the same location as the first. This crashed behind the British lines at St. Catherine, a leafy suburb on the western outskirts of the city. Its crew, Captain John McArthur and Private James Whiteford were also killed.

Fire in the air was the recurring nightmare of pilots on all sides. The petrol tank of tractor type aircraft (where the engine was in front of the pilot) was positioned either behind the engine in front of the pilot, else the pilot actually sat directly over it. A single tracer bullet in the right place usually exploded the tank, showering the crew with liquid fire – and from 12,000 feet it could take two minutes or more before a stricken aircraft crashed to earth, finally ending the torture of falling in flames. But few pilots talked about this horror. Many years after the war Arthur Gould Lee, a 46 Squadron pilot, who ended his flying career with the rank of air vice-marshal, recalled: 'There were few flyers with any experience of air fighting who were not obsessed to some degree, though usually secretly, with the thought of being shot down in flames.' The officially recommended practice was to try side-slipping the machine, in order to keep the flames away from the cockpit, but this rarely worked. Once their aircraft began to burn many pilots, realising there was no hope of surviving the ordeal, chose to jump rather than roast to death, whilst others carried a revolver with them at all times – it had but one purpose. Edward Mannock, who hated all Germans with a passion, was obsessed by thoughts of such a death and habitually carried a pistol. Conversely, when recounting victories to his squadron mates he invariably imitated the path of a 'flamer' by theatrically twirling a finger down through the air, and then finished the tale with 'sizzle-sizzle wonk' and a demonic smile. Mannock was to suffer death by fire in July 1918, though mercifully he was shot down from a very low altitude.

As an aside to this most grisly of spectres, it is interesting to note another problem often faced by two-seater crews flying the outmoded BEs. The lumbering reconnaissance machines credited to Voss on 27 February were two of three BE losses on the Arras Front recorded by the RFC that day. The third was a 13 Squadron BE that was surrounded by a flight of six hostile aircraft – possibly the same Jasta Boelcke Scouts that had been patrolling the sector that day. The pilot, Second Lieutenant H.F. Mackain was killed when one of the Germans (who has never been identified) dived on the BE with both guns blazing. Mackain's observer, Second Lieutenant J.A.E.R. Daly fired at the Scout as it flashed past. The German then continued on in a long, shallow dive, heading east. Daly was watching as it went down, wondering if his aim had been true, when he suddenly felt the otherwise stable BE begin to stagger into a sickening sideslip. Realising that it was out of control, and that the pilot was either dead or wounded, Daly climbed out on to the port wing and dragged himself into the rear cockpit. Half sitting on the dead pilot's lap, with his left foot still out on the wing, he righted the BE and, to his intense relief, was able to make a passable landing in the biggest field he could find.

4 March was a day of intense air activity over the Front and, all

told, more than a score of aircraft were shot down on this day: eight hostiles were confirmed by the RFC, with nine others claimed as driven down out of control; while the Germans were known to have brought down eleven RFC machines, including four that were first posted as missing. But the only victory of the day for Werner Voss was an 8 Squadron BE2d that fell to his expert marksmanship less than an hour after leaving base. His attack was again sickeningly brief. The inexperienced crew, Sergeant Pilot Reginald Moody and probationary observer Second Lieutenant Edmund Horn, could hardly have known what hit them. One long burst of tracer at close range was enough. Within seconds, their outclassed aeroplane tumbled out of the sky, engulfed in flames, to crash south of Berneville, again near the city of Arras. Both crewmen were killed. This 'kill' is often confused in aviation histories with Manfred von Richthofen's twenty-second victory. However, as with several Richthofen claims, the details he gave are somewhat nebulous and the location of the crash site is erroneously given as 'one kilometre from Loos, near the German Trenches.' The RFC report on the only BE loss of the day confirms that 'it fell in flames within our lines', undoubtedly the machine flown by Moody and Horn.

The sight of BE 'Tommy Cookers' falling in flames may have disturbed Voss, for he left the 'poor devils' alone until the 18th, but on 6 March he scored a 32 Squadron DH2, downed near Favreuil north of Bapaume. There were no Allied witnesses to this combat and the RFC simply reported the machine as missing. Its pilot, Lieutenant Herbert Southon, was severely wounded in the engagement but did manage to crash-land his machine behind the German lines and was taken prisoner. In late December 1917 he was among a group of disabled airmen exchanged – via the Red Cross – into Switzerland. RFC losses on this and days immediately preceding it were such that no further casualty lists were included in the Official Communiqués after 10 March. This proved to be a prudent decision – the period known to the British as 'Bloody April', when the RFC lost more aircrews in a single month than at any other time during the war, was just around the corner.

On 11 March Voss was credited with another double: his fourteenth and fifteenth victories. In the morning he shot-up an FE2b of 22 Squadron which crash-landed at Combles. The pilot, Second Lieutenant Leslie Beal was unhurt and his gunner/ observer, Air Mechanic F.G. Davin, was only slightly wounded, but their FE was a complete write-off. A week before their encounter with Voss, Beal and Davin had narrowly survived being shot down in flames by another German ace, Leutnant Renatus Theiller of Jasta 5. On that occasion the two RFC men had managed to put the fire out before it took hold, but their machine was completely wrecked in a forced landing. The luckless Beal was brought down for a third and final time on 26 April 1917. Although, again, managing to put his FE down behind the British lines he was severely wounded and subsequently invalided out of the Flying Corps.

In the afternoon two Nieuport 17s of 60 Squadron, acting as escorts to a BE working over the lines near Arras, sighted a formation of six German Scouts 1,000 feet below them. Impetuously, Lieutenant Arthur Whitehead dived to attack. He fired thirty rounds into an enemy machine that promptly fell away to port, apparently out of control. As he lined up a second German, he was suddenly attacked by Voss, who riddled his Nieuport from end to end. During the vicious onslaught a bullet smashed into the cockpit coaming, went through Whitehead's left knee and came out via his right thigh. The shock and pain of this double wound caused him to momentarily lose control and the Nieuport spun down. After losing considerable height he managed to pull out of the dive, levelled out, and made for the British lines. Within seconds Voss was on to him again. This time he shot the engine and elevator controls to pieces and the Nieuport fell in a spinning nosedive. Whitehead struggled to regain control, but to no avail. Between 3,000-4,000 feet he finally fainted from shock and loss of blood; then, by some miracle, the well-balanced Nieuport crash-landed itself. It was a week before the young RFC pilot regained consciousness, only to find himself under guard in a German hospital at Douai. Due to the severity of his injuries, which included a fractured skull sustained in the crash, Whitehead spent many painful weeks in hospital and was eventually repatriated to Switzerland in January 1918.

Six days after bringing down the Nieuport and the FE, Voss scored two more victories. These came on 17 March – both within ten minutes of each other. The first was another FE2b of 11 Squadron that came down close to the village of Mory, just north of Bapaume. Here its crew, Second Lieutenant Russell Cross and Lieutenant Christopher Lodge, were taken prisoner. Minutes later, nine Albatros Scouts of Jasta Boelcke ran into twelve DH2s from 32 Squadron. A fierce dogfight ensued, but although the DH2s fought like hell-cats they were no match for the faster enemy machines. Voss latched on to the tail of Lieutenant Theodore

Cooch and jockeyed for position. The weaving DH2 was no easy target, but by deft handling of the controls Voss stuck like glue. As the DH2 centred on the cross hairs of his gun sights the Rhinelander squeezed the triggers on his twin Spandaus and a maelstrom of bullets flew into the British machine that sent it down to crash northeast of Warlencourt, behind the British lines. Cooch survived the nerve crunching experience but spent many months in hospital. He returned to the service in 1918 and ended the war as a captain, only to be killed in a flying accident on 17 September 1919 – one day before being demobilised from the RAF.

With seventeen victories under his belt Voss was now well into his stride. He scored yet another double the very next day, again within the space of a few minutes. The first was a BE2e from 8 Squadron, caught whilst dropping bombs on Beaurins south of Arras; the second was a BE2d of 13 Squadron that came to earth near to the village of Boyelles. The crew of the wretched 8 Squadron machine, Lieutenant Charles Dougall and Second Lieutenant Sydney Harryman had a bomb hung-up and were desperately trying to release it when Voss and four other Jasta Boelcke Scouts suddenly attacked them. Dougall was hit in the legs and Harryman was fatally wounded in the back. The BE began to smoke and shortly after caught fire, but Dougall skilfully brought his burning machine down behind the German lines. Despite his own wounds, he was able to drag his unconscious observer from the blazing wreck before the flames reached him. Unfortunately, Harryman died five days later and Dougall spent the rest of the war in a prison camp.

Thirty-five-year-old Captain Guy Thorne was an experienced pre-war pilot who had learnt to fly at his own expense. At the time he met Voss he was in temporary command of 13 Squadron and, rather than detail anyone else to the task, personally made what was considered a very dangerous but necessary reconnaissance over Fampoux, a village northeast of Arras in the valley of the Scarpe. All went well until he and his observer, Second Lieutenant Philip van Baerle, were on their way back. As they approached the lines, they were attacked from astern and Thorne was hit in the back by what was thought to be an explosive bullet. The purpose of explosive ammunition, phosphorus rounds known to the Germans as Ph-Munition, was the destruction of observation balloons. Characteristically, a small lead plug at the base of the bullet was forced forward on impact. This ruptured the casing and showered the target with burning phosphorous to good effect.

Such ammunition was supposedly only to be loaded when a balloon was the target, and their use in any other circumstance was considered unlawful. But as the British were the first to include Buckingham incendiary for the same purpose, the Germans felt justified in matching like for like: both types were equally deadly. Their all too frequent use was governed by the terms of the 1908 Hague International Convention, which called for written authorisation to be carried by the pilot, stating that his mission was solely to attack enemy balloons. However, it should be noted that the Germans were not signatories to the Convention, and in any case the rule was flawed, it never allowed for the fact that pilots were liable to be attacked by enemy Scouts during the course of such missions and would almost certainly fire back in defence; but then it should also be remembered – Werner Voss was never a balloon buster.

Despite his horrendous wound, Captain Thorne managed to make something of a landing behind the German lines at Henin sur Cojeul, close to the village of Boyelles, before slumping into unconsciousness over the controls. By some miracle van Baerle was uninjured but taken prisoner. Later that day his captors informed him that the courageous Thorne had died of his wound. For van Baerle the war was over; he spent the next twenty-one months in captivity at Karlsruhe and was not released until mid-December 1918. On his return to England he bitterly recalled Voss had fired on the BE2d after their forced landing.

There is a sequel to this somewhat unpalatable incident of the Great War that in part owes its origins to Manfred von Richthofen. It became part of aviation folklore after the Red Baron recounted it in his autobiography *Der Rote Kampfflieger*, published in 1918. There is of course no mention of explosive bullets, strafing an aircraft on the ground or the horrible death of Guy Thorne. According to Richthofen the encounter took place shortly after the Germans had retired to the Hindenburg Line and Voss had brought down the British machine in No-Mans-Land. He wrote: 'During a pursuit flight with Jagdstaffel Boelcke, Leutnant Werner Voss was victorious in aerial combat with an Englishman. He had forced him to land in neutral territory between the lines. We had of course already abandoned this position, but the enemy had not yet occupied it. Only patrols, English as well as German, were in this unoccupied zone. The English plane landed between the lines, and the Englishman probably believed that this territory had already been occupied by his own forces, an assumption in which he was justified. But Voss was of a different opinion. Shortly thereafter he decided to land near his victim. With great haste he loaded the enemy machine gun and other useful parts from the enemy's aircraft into his own. Then he put a match to the enemy machine and in a few moments it went up in bright flames. A moment later, he was up in his victorious charger smilingly waving to the Englishmen then gathering on all sides below.'

Richthofen is notoriously fanciful throughout his auto-biography, yet there is some truth in his rendition of the incident. Shortly after bringing down the 8 Squadron BE over Beaurins, Voss attacked and shot Thorne and van Baerle down close to Boyelles. At this time the village was very close to the front line, but there is a question as to whether it was still on the German side or not; the German withdrawal to the Hindenburg Line commenced on 16 March, but was not completed until the 29th. During this period the front lines were still being strongly held, some sectors in considerable depth. Voss landed near to the machine in order to retrieve its twin Lewis guns and destroy its secrets, not to prove a claim: on the day he was accompanied by Leutnant der Reserve Hans Wortmann, who habitually flew with the young ace during his time with Jasta Boelcke. Other Jasta comrades followed at a distance.

Rolf Italiaander repeated the story in his *Pour le Mérite Flieger mit 20 Jahren*, and may be forgiven for spicing it up a little; after all his publication was aimed at a new generation of idealists – Adolf Hitler's National Socialists. But unlike the author William E. Barrett, who also included a hyped-up version of the story in an article that appeared in the 1963 booklet *Sky Fighters of World War I*, Italiaander undoubtedly had the benefit of being apprised of the incident by Karl Bodenschatz, and was able to quote from Voss' Jasta 2 combat report for that day. Thorne and van Baerle are not named as the crew but are positively identified from the details given in the combat report: Voss gave the correct date, time and place the BE2d was brought down, and correctly noted its serial number as 5770. He reported that after a curving and spiralling descent it had made a heavy landing and broke up. However, from van Baerle's post-war statement it is clear Guy Thorne was in no position to have made for the safety of the British lines as recorded by Barrett: he was unconscious and near to death. Interestingly, Voss stated that he handed over the twin Lewis guns to a patrol from Jäger Regiment 107 for safekeeping; he never loaded them onto his aircraft as claimed by Richthofen and Barrett. After setting fire to the BE, Voss returned to Jasta

Boelcke's new airfield at Eswars, northeast of Cambrai. He gave no clues as to the fate of Thorne and van Baerle, which suggests they had been whisked away before he landed, one to die of a terrible wound, the other to spend the rest of his war in captivity. Nor did he mention Englishmen gathering on all sides, or anything to do with taking off again amid a hail of bullets.

Richthofen's hyped up rendition of the incident was endorsed by Italiaander and further embellished by Barrett; and is a typical example of a story that grows with the telling. Actual facts are inflated, and an interesting, yet fairly commonplace, occurrence of the war becomes the stuff of legend. Putting down close to the site of a crashed foe was not uncommon. Whenever conditions were favourable pilots on all sides did their utmost to land beside their victims or at least visit the crash site from the ground; it was actually considered a great challenge to obtain a souvenir and perhaps even meet an enemy face to face – if he was lucky enough to survive the combat. Voss did it several times. Paul Baümer, a Jasta 5 pilot who survived the war with forty-three victories to his credit, noted one such occasion. He recalled watching Voss attacking a formation of Allied aeroplanes in June 1917 and shooting one down within sight of the squadron's airfield at Boistrancourt-Suererie. Baümer and others drove to the crash site in a car. On making enquiries they were told that two enemy aeroplanes had actually come down in the area and a German Scout had landed near to one of them. At the scene of the crash the party found Voss, busily unscrewing the dashboard clock from the enemy machine and answering, in a very offhand manner, questions posed by a high ranking army officer. Finishing his task, and with but a cursory salute to the officer, he took off and returned to the airfield. Arriving back at Boistrancourt, and asking for Voss in order to congratulate him on his victory, Baümer and his companions were told that the young ace was in the hangar working on his machine. There they found him, wearing an oily old drill jacket, busily filing, screwing and hammering away in expert fashion. Some recently arrived mechanics of the Jasta actually thought that he was one of them, and were addressing him in the familiar language of the ranks.

There was nothing vainglorious about his behaviour, in fact Voss was simply taking no chances, he knew only too well that life in the air depended on the reliability of his machine and that sloppy workmanship could prove fatal. He also knew that a gun-stoppage at the wrong moment could be equally deadly so, like many other great pilots of the war, he personally inspected every round of ammunition he used before it was loaded. Yet he had another side to his character. When flying he usually wore his best tunic and a non-regulation silk shirt, so that he could – as he cheerfully said – play the gentleman with the girls in Paris if he should have the misfortune to be shot down and captured. In fact the silk shirt was probably not for the benefit of the girls in Paris. Woollen or cotton shirts and scarves tended to irritate and chafe the neck, they also wore out fairly quickly when every few seconds a pilot's neck was being turned about in the cockpit looking for an opponent approaching from above or behind. Whereas silk, a very pliable and much hardier material, withstood the rigours of these constant neck exercises.

The Royal Aircraft Factory's RE8 was a two-seater reconnaissance machine that came into operational use during the latter part of 1916. Unfortunately, it fared little better than the ageing BE it was intended to replace, and many squadrons continued to fly the earlier type. They also had two very good reasons for not wanting to fly the newer model. The RE8s had a preponderance to spin at low speeds and almost always caught fire in a crash and the main fuel tank, positioned directly behind the engine, invariably ruptured on impact. To RFC aircrews the RE8 was 'affectionately' known as the 'Harry Tate', named after a popular music hall comedian of the day. Needless to say, it was indeed a farcical machine, but it had few comic attributes and aircrews quickly developed a healthy dislike for the type. Even so, it was better armed than the BE, sporting a Vickers machine gun mounted on the engine cowling and one Lewis gun, sometimes two, mounted on the rear cockpit Scarff ring for use by the observer. On occasions, given the right conditions, it was able to give a good account of itself but, like its primogenitor, inherent stability in flight prevented fast manoeuvring and it was considered slow compared to the high performance German fighters of the time.

59 Squadron had recently been re-equipped with the RE8, when on the morning of 19 March two aircraft were despatched to reconnoitre in the vicinity of St. Léger. One machine, flying slightly higher than the other, acted as escort, whilst the lower, crewed by Captain Elred Bowyer-Bower and Second Lieutenant Eric Elgey did the recce work. Voss, accompanied by another Jasta Boelcke pilot, Fritz Otto Bernert, who attained high honours during his career, spotted the RE8s at work and fell on them from above. Bernert got the escort, to be credited as his eighth victory, and Voss shot down the recce machine. The German pilots made

the mistake of identifying the RE8s as Sopwiths, and as such they are recorded in the Abschusse. The luckless crews of both machines were reported as 'Missing in Action.' Three men were actually killed in the engagement; one of the escort crew survived and was taken prisoner. Bowyer-Bower and Elgey crashed behind the German lines near Croisilles and their smashed bodies were hurriedly interred by troops in the locality. During the Battle of Arras the Germans were pushed back from their original front line positions leaving the two shallow graves in No-Man's-Land. As the British advance crossed the relinquished wasteland a party of Royal Engineers, commanded by Captain Thomas Bowyer-Bower, the father of Elred, found the two graves marked by pieces of a wrecked aeroplane. The bodies were exhumed and Bowyer-Bower Senior was able to inform his grieving wife that the remains of their lost son had at last been found.

The last two victims sought out and downed in March fell on the afternoon of the 24th, to be credited as Voss' twenty-first and twenty-second victories, though there is some dispute as to exactly who they were. The first was almost certainly an FE2b of 23 Squadron, flown by Sergeant Pilot Edward P. Critchley, with Air Mechanic Frank Russell acting as his observer/gunner. Voss was again out with his friend Bernert when they came across the photo reconnaissance FE. Voss attacked and killed Russell outright in his first pass. Critchley was also wounded, but despite being attacked again managed to make a forced landing on farmland near Achiet-le-Grand, southeast of St. Léger on the British side of the lines. Critchley recovered from his wounds and was commissioned as a second lieutenant in November 1917. He was wounded once again in 1918 but survived the war and was demobilised in 1919. Although some historians believe Voss' first victim of the day was Lieutenant J.R. Middleton of 11 Squadron, flying an FE2b, with Air Mechanic Gosney acting as gunner, recent research reveals this may be an error as RFC records indicate 11 Squadron losses all occurred in the morning.

Voss' second victory of the day, and his last for the month of March, came some twenty minutes later. This was definitely a BE2d of 8 Squadron flying a photographic mission over Boyelles. The pilot, Lieutenant Hugh Norton and his observer, Second Lieutenant Reginald Tillett, died when the machine crashed southeast of Mercatel, a hamlet close to the village of Boyelles. At the time of his death Tillett was just three days off his twenty-third birthday. Whilst during his secondment to the RFC, Norton had clocked up forty flying hours and had been in France only three weeks before the encounter with Voss. Ironically, at this period, three weeks was the average time newly seconded RFC aircrew could expect to survive at the Front.

Manfred von Richthofen had been awarded the Orden Pour le Mérite on 16 January 1917 and was given command of a Jasta. At the time his score stood at seventeen confirmed victories; by mid-March it had risen to twenty-five, and he had been promoted to the rank of Oberleutnant. By the end of March Werner Voss had scored his twenty-second victory and could expect a similar reward; on the 27th he became the recipient of the Order of the Knight's Cross with Swords of the Royal House of Hohenzollern – a prestigious though lesser decoration, normally awarded shortly before the Pour le Mérite.

The Pour le Mérite, an impressive Maltese cross lavishly enamelled in royal blue and edged in gold, with four golden eagles displayed between the limbs, was the highest decoration awarded for gallantry to German forces in the field during the Great War. It was primarily a Prussian order, founded as the Brandenburg Ordre de la Génerosité in 1667 by Frederick I of Prussia. Apart from its early years, its distribution was somewhat limited, and awards were quite rare; it was then revived by Frederick II in 1740 and renamed the Orden Pour le Mérite. Originally awarded for both civil and military distinguished service, by 1810 the criterion had changed, and it was reserved solely for military distinction. Although other duchies, principalities and kingdoms within the German Federation had their own decorations and similar orders, it was generally accepted that a Pour le Mérite was the finest of them all. During the course of the First World War, eighty-one German airmen received the award, including one balloon observer. In a ceremony that took place at Douai on 12 January 1916, Max Immelmann and Oswald Boelcke were both invested with the coveted Pour le Mérite. As the medal was fastened around Immelmann's neck it is said the winter sunlight caught its bright enamel and cast a blue reflection on his pale countenance. Thereafter it was known throughout Fliegerkorps as 'The Blue Max'.

Captain Arthur Meredith Wynne and probationary observer Lieutenant Adrian Somerset Mackenzie had the dubious honour of becoming two of Bloody April's first RFC casualties. On the first day of the month, at 0930 hours British time, Wynne and Mackenzie headed their 15 Squadron BE2e out over the Front on an artillery-observation mission, and were soon engrossed in their work. Two hours later, and close to shutting up shop for the day, Wynne, a pre-war pilot of 1912, was circling the BE between Ecoust and St. Léger when Voss emerged from a low cloud bank and attacked from above. His first burst of fire wounded the pilot, who immediately began weaving the outclassed BE for all he was worth. Mackenzie stood up in the observer's cockpit and made a brave attempt to fight back with their Lewis gun – he had little more than seconds to live. Voss zoomed to regain the advantage of height, and on his next pass shot Mackenzie through the heart killing him instantly. Despite his wound, Wynne finally managed to edge the badly shot up machine back across the British front lines, crash landed beyond the trenches, and was unceremoniously thrown out of the cockpit on impact. This added mishap proved to be fortuitous, for as the injured pilot painfully dragged himself away from the crash Voss came in low and poured a hail of bullets into the wreck. Arthur Wynne lived to fight another day, was awarded the Air Force Cross, and in the war of 1939-45 served in the RAF Volunteer Reserve.

6 April proved to be another day of intense air activity over the Front. The British were about to open their expected offensive in the Arras sector; this was to include a major attack on part of the Hindenburg Line, and aerial reconnaissance was stepped up accordingly. On this day Voss brought down his twenty-fourth victim near Lagnicourt at 0930 hours British time. This was almost certainly a BE2e of 15 Squadron out photographing enemy positions around Bullecourt. Second Lieutenants Albert H. Vinson and Everard Champion Gwilt were going about their business when six Jasta Boelcke Scouts suddenly appeared from nowhere and bounced them. Gwilt, the observer, cocked his twin Lewis guns and let rip at every enemy machine as it came into his line of fire. Five of the Germans promptly broke off, climbed away and began circling above. But Voss was made of sterner stuff. He pressed home his attack and a storm of tracer bullets slammed into the BE. Vinson immediately put the machine into a near vertical crash-dive that was so sudden it dislodged the twin Lewis guns from the Scarff ring mounting and they promptly fell overboard. Gwilt, now reduced to a spectator, could only clasp his hands in prayer as he watched Voss turn for his next attack. Vinson, who had been slightly grazed by three bullets, pulled the totally defenceless BE out of the dive and headed west in a desperate attempt to reach the safety of the British lines. But Voss remained in close pursuit and continued pouring shots into the battered reconnaissance machine. Though Vinson weaved and dodged to throw off his

aim, Voss kept his guns on target and before long he had holed the fuel tank. A long white stream of vaporising petrol escaping from the tank punctuated the BE's painfully slow progress across the bright blue sky. Luckily, there was no fire and Vinson finally touched down beyond the lines near Lagnicourt. Once on the ground the crew leapt out and took cover in a nearby shell hole. Voss then came in low to rake the crippled machine, but enraged British soldiers in the trenches put up such a fusillade of rifle and machine-gun fire that he was forced to break off the attack and rejoin his comrades circling above. German artillery then ranged on the crash site and shells soon began raining down. At great personal risk, Vinson broke cover, raced back to his aircraft and retrieved the exposed plates from the camera. These plates subsequently produced excellent views of the Hindenburg Line and the area surrounding Bullecourt that was soon to be attacked.

Shortly after shooting down the 15 Squadron BE, Voss attacked a Sopwith Pup flown by Second Lieutenant R.M. Foster of 54 Squadron. The Pup, an agile lightweight single-seat fighting Scout, was armed with one synchronised Vickers machine gun firing through the propeller arc. It had been in service since December 1916, and with its exceptional ability to maintain height in a dogfight, it could just about hold its own against the heavier Albatros D III. Though on this occasion, after a short but frantic fight, Foster's machine was crippled and he was obliged to make a forced landing close to where the BE crew had just come down near Lagnicourt, but on the German side of the lines. Surprisingly, on this rare occasion, the German ace was unable to obtain confirmation for the victory, however there exists a photograph of Voss' Jasta 2 comrade Fritz Otto Bernert standing before Foster's Pup (A6165) at Lagnicourt shortly after it had been repaired and given German iron cross markings; this indicates that it was almost certainly brought down by a pilot of Jasta 2, and subsequently commandeered by the unit. Voss may not have been credited with the Foster victory but his disappointment was short-lived, and more than compensated for on 8 April 1917, when he was finally awarded the prized Orden Pour le Mérite.

As a recipient of Imperial Germany's highest award for gallantry, and in keeping with practice, Voss was granted home leave. The award could not have come at a more opportune moment – the leave, which covered Easter and what remained of the month, allowed him to celebrate his twentieth birthday at

home. After half a hundred combats, Voss was finally able to
wash the smell of the Front out of his hair and indulge himself.
There was a large family gathering, at which many photographs
were taken, but most of the leave was spent simply relaxing
about the house and in the leafy garden of 75 Blumenthalstrasse
enjoying the early spring sunlight and the company of family
and friends; among them, perhaps, the mysterious young lady
named Doris, who has never been positively identified. On one
special day he kept an appointment with a local photographer to
sit for his Pour le Mérite portrait, a likeness that has appeared
in many publications over the years. For the rest of the time he
tinkered with the motorcycle given him by his parents on an
earlier birthday; it was one of the latest machines and,
engineering wise, state of the art for the time. At full power it
roared like a lion, and he tore through the peaceful country
lanes and byways about Krefeld and the lower Rhineland like a
man possessed. But all too soon the leave was up and on 5 May
1917 the youngest Air Service recipient of the Blue Max
returned to the Front. He arrived back with a swagger and
something of a pinched smile: he had every reason to feel
proud, as Germany's most coveted award now hung from his
slender neck by its black and silver ribbon. Voss was itching to
get back into the air, but he had missed the killing times of
April, there was never to be a trip to Paris, and there was to be
no further advancement in rank during his all too short career.

On Easter Monday, 9 April, just two days after Voss had
commenced his leave, four Canadian Army Divisions stormed the
heights of the most strongly held German bastion on the Western
Front: the infamous Vimy Ridge. The attack on the ridge, carried
out in a blinding snowstorm, was the opening gambit in the Battle
of Arras, the first full scale British offensive of 1917. One of the
main objectives of the battle was to draw German reserves away
from the French, who were preparing to launch a major attack a
few days later in the Chemin des Dames sector further south. As
ever, the intention was to strike a hammer blow that would finally
break through the German lines and end the war. From the
comfort and safety of magnificent chateaux in the rear, well-
heeled and often over-fed French generals urged the army to make
one last great effort for France. The men in the trenches were told
it was the best planned attack of the war. Every German strong
point, trench, and machine-gun post had been carefully registered
by the artillery and would be pounded into oblivion long before
zero hour; moreover every effort would be made to keep

casualties to a minimum. The attack could not fail! In the event it failed miserably, as weeks earlier the Germans had got wind of the plan and withdrew their front line forces many miles east to newly prepared positions. At the appointed hour eighty French divisions crossed No-Man's-Land in a steady downpour of rain and icy snow squalls into what, until recently, had been the German front line; here they were cut to pieces by one of the most intense artillery cannonades of the war. The attack was more than just a costly debacle. Not only did the French suffer horrendous casualties, more than 50,000 killed and wounded on the first day, morale now slumped to an all time low, and this coupled with the staggering losses at Verdun – 450,000 killed and wounded in a little over six months – was all too much for the war-weary poilu. Those holding the line simply could not take any more, and by mid-May there were widespread mutinies throughout the French army affecting more than fifty elite divisions: thousands of men simply threw down their arms and refused to return to the trenches. Luckily, the Germans never got wind of this before order and discipline had been brutally restored.

The British had fared somewhat better on the ground further north, at last capturing the important high ground around Vimy, yet their air offensive was an unmitigated disaster. From the outset of the battle the RFC outnumbered Luftstreitkräfte by almost two-to-one in men and machines, but the Germans possessed superior fighter aircraft, flown by experienced and well-trained pilots. In consequence, the RFC lost almost one-third of its front line forces in a little over four weeks: ten machines and their crews being the daily average. In terms of both men and machines it proved to be the most costly month of the war, in fact so costly it was christened 'Bloody April'. Thanks to Richthofen's inspiring leadership, Jasta 11 had been well and truly whipped into shape and accounted for an incredible eighty-nine Allied aircraft during the month. Richthofen was personally credited with just under a quarter of this total, downing twenty-two, whilst the pilots of Jasta Boelcke managed only twenty-one, two of these being credited to Werner Voss before he went on leave.

Although it came too late to make any significant difference to the outcome of the air fighting in April, by the time the young man from Krefeld returned to the Front the long awaited SE5 had finally arrived in France. The SE5 and variant SE5a were undoubtedly the best fighters to come out of the Royal Aircraft Factory at Farnborough and rank alongside the Sopwith Camel as the best British fighters produced during the entire war. Armed with two guns, a belt-fed Vickers firing through the propeller arc and a drum-fed Lewis mounted on the top wing, the SE5 was to prove more than a match for what had become the backbone of the German Air Service: the Albatros D III and variant D V. The first operational unit to be equipped with SE5s was the newly formed 56 Squadron; just out from England. It was first stationed on a wind-swept field at Vert Galant Farm, a little south of Doullens, ten miles behind Albert, and almost directly opposite Richthofen's JG1 airfields. With experienced pilots like 'Duke' Meintjes, Albert Ball, Cyril Crowe, and others of similar mettle leading young but enthusiastic pilots, 56 was to become the most successful RFC squadron to serve on the Western Front, accounting for more than 400 enemy aircraft by the war's end. Firmly believing it had been formed for the sole purpose of destroying their illustrious leader, pilots and personnel of JG1 dubbed 56 the anti-Richthofen squadron.

Ironically, it was a 56 Squadron pilot who was to claim the life of Werner Voss later in the year. But it was still early days, and on the evening of 7 May, just two days after returning from leave, Voss chanced on his first SE5. Second Lieutenant Roger Chaworth-Musters of B Flight had joined the RFC straight from Eton College. He had been at the Front with 56 Squadron for little more than a month. On the last patrol of the day he spotted an enemy Scout through a chink in the cloud over Bourlon Wood. Without waiting to alert his flight commander, the courageous but inexperienced pilot dived towards the cloudbank and gave chase. Sometime later, at about 1925 hours German time, Chaworth-Musters, a boy less than three weeks away from his nineteenth birthday, was shot down and killed by Voss. The Old Etonian's SE5 was reported falling north of where he was last seen by his comrades. Subsequently the wreckage was located from the air near to the little village of Etaing, just south of Douai on the German side of the lines.

The RFC Communiqué for 7 May 1917 reveals that although the morning was crisp and clear, heavy thunderclouds developed over the Front in the afternoon. A big storm was in the offing that would normally have prevented much aerial activity after the morning patrols, but towards evening a good deal of fighting did take place between the SE5s of 56 Squadron and enemy aircraft. The communiqué also records the squadron claimed two enemy machines destroyed and two others driven down out of control. What it doesn't mention is the fact that the squadron suffered perhaps its greatest loss: Captain Albert Ball VC, DSO and two bars, MC, did not return from this patrol. At the time the indefatigable young man from the historic city of Nottingham had forty-seven victories to his credit and was the RFC's top scoring ace. It was later confirmed that Ball, known to the Germans as the 'English Boelcke', had crashed close to the village of Annoeullin, north of Lens on the German side. Interestingly, after Chaworth-Musters chased after the enemy Scout, 56 tussled with a number of hostile formations during the late afternoon, then ran into a patrol of Jasta 11 aircraft led by Manfred von Richthofen's younger brother Lothar. During what proved to be an epic fight between nearly two dozen machines, Ball disabled the younger Richthofen's Albatros forcing him to make a hasty landing in a field behind the German lines. Minutes later Leutnant Georg Simon, flying a red and green Albatros D III, put a lucky shot through the water jacket of Arthur Rhys Davids' engine, then in a series of climbing and diving attacks proceeded to shoot his stricken SE5 to pieces. Unaccountably Simon, who was only credited with one victory during his flying career, failed to finish the job; as quickly as he had appeared he suddenly dived away east, leaving Rhys Davids to wrestle with the badly shot about controls of his machine and wonder at his luck. Though considerably ruffled by this unnerving experience, the plucky nineteen-year-old pilot eventually managed to put his badly damaged SE5 down on friendly territory close to the village of La Hérlier. Karl Allmenröder and Werner Voss both claimed the SE5 flown by Chaworth-Musters, but after considering both their reports and hearing eyewitness evidence Richthofen awarded the victory to Voss.

The Germans subsequently issued an account of this important fight, claiming Ball had been shot down by the junior Richthofen, though research proves almost beyond doubt that Ball's death was due to a technical quirk of fate, and that Lothar's claim owes more to German propaganda than fact. The English ace was last seen by a squadron mate, Captain Cyril Crowe, who witnessed Ball chasing an Albatros into an extremely dark thundercloud; minutes later four German officers on the ground, among them Leutnant Franz Hailer of Flieger Abteilung 292, saw Ball's machine materialise out of the cloud at about 200 feet. He noted it was in an inverted position, with the engine off and the propeller stopped. Hailer stated the British machine then dove straight into the ground. On inspection of the wreckage, he and his comrades came to the conclusion it had not been shot down in combat or by anti-aircraft fire: there were no wounds on Ball's body and little evidence of any battle damage to the SE. In an interview with the aviation historian Alex Revell, H.N. Charles, 56 Squadron's engineering officer, gave the probable cause for the crash. He recalled that the early SE5 could not sustain inverted flight. The large float-chambered carburettor on the 150 h.p. Hispano-Suiza engine was prone to fill with petrol if the aircraft was flown on its back. This glut of fuel flooded the air intake, thus choking the engine, which would suddenly stop. By the time Ball's machine broke through the cloud Lothar von Richthofen, who in his combat report actually claimed a triplane, was already on the ground a few miles from the scene probably thanking his lucky stars he was still in one piece. There was no hidden machine gun in the clock tower of the little church at Annoeullin as proclaimed by the author Arch Whitehouse, a prolific writer of the 1960s, whose fanciful tomes sold thousands of copies to spread, among several other myths of the air war, the story that Ball had been brought down by ground fire. The truth is all too simple: cloaked deep within the dark thundercloud Ball was flying blind, and became completely disorientated. Then, either the turbulence experienced within the cloud inverted the aircraft; else in a state of confusion the English ace inadvertently turned the SE onto its back and the engine stopped. (Unexpectedly turning upside down in dense cloud was a phenomenon not unknown to aviators in the early days of flying.) As he suddenly broke through into daylight there was no time to right the powerless, diving fighter, and seconds later Ball crashed near the church and died almost instantly.

In many respects Werner Voss and Albert Ball were much alike. Although worlds apart ideologically, both hailed from historic mill towns; had similar comfortable, middle-class, semi-religious backgrounds; took a keen interest in all things mechanical and displayed a passion for flying. Both were loners, not shy and retiring but instilled with enough self-confidence to prefer hunting alone. Each took incredible risks in a fight, and as exceptional pilots and expert marksmen they never missed a chance to attack their enemies on sight – no matter what the odds. Yet both had a side to their character that has never been widely publicised. Unlike McCudden and Richthofen, who shepherded those under their command like babes-in-arms, responsibility never came easy to men like Voss or Ball. Their actions reveal they had scant regard for the men they led into the air, often leaving new and inexperienced pilots to fend for themselves while they flew off to attack their enemies. In so doing, they were guilty of impetuous recklessness bordering on the very edge of reason; recklessness that to many seemed like some demonic death wish that could have only one end. And for this there was a price to pay: in combat they consistently excelled and showed no fear, but on the ground, and secretly at night, like so many front line pilots they suffered the trauma of nervous strain – strain that eventually took its toll. In July 1916, during his first tour of duty in France, Ball, who had already amassed a creditable score and had just been awarded the Military Cross, told his commanding officer, Major T. Hubbard, he needed a rest and had the temerity to request a few days off. Hubbard forwarded this unusual petition to Wing HQ, but instead of sending him to Paris or home on leave, Brigadier-General J.F.A. Higgins, furious at receiving such a solicitous appeal from a junior officer, posted him to a two-seater squadron employed on dangerous bombing missions. Werner Voss suffered similar pressures, though in early May it was not that apparent. But on a day in mid-September, after surviving a very close shave at the hands of an experienced British pilot the young ace, by now a Staffelführer, landed back at Heule field and hastily wrote out his own leave warrant.

Two days after Ball was killed Voss scored the first of his two hat-tricks. In the early afternoon of 9 May he came across a BE2e of 52 Squadron spotting for the artillery over Metz en Coutre. Lieutenant Rowland Humphrey Coles and his observer, Second Lieutenant Charles Sigismund Day, encountered the methodical Rhinelander and never knew what hit them. After being struck by a sudden deluge of fiery shots from the guns of Voss the outclassed BE broke up or exploded in the air. The wreckage fell over a wide area, so wide in fact it was impossible to determine the crash site, but as most of the fuselage fell close by Havrincourt around 1300 hours British time, this is given as the position. Both crewmen were killed.

After returning to Pronville to re-arm and re-fuel Voss was up again looking for customers within the hour. This time he was leading six Jasta comrades. They shortly came across a flight of FE2bs of 22 Squadron, out on a photographic reconnaissance for the 4th Army. On this occasion the FEs were escorted by Sopwith Pups from 54 Squadron. Ignoring the escorts, the German Scouts dived into the FEs over Hesdin, but while his comrades dealt with the reconnaissance machines Voss attacked a Pup at close range, riddling it from end to end: tracer strikes danced all over the top planes and about the cockpit coaming causing splinters of wood and torn fabric to fly off into the slipstream. The pilot, Lieutenant

George Copland Temple Hadrill, put the machine into a sickening corkscrew-spin in an attempt to throw Voss off, though with his petrol tank holed and his engine threatening to pack up at any second, he could do little to avoid the chase down. Voss hung on to his tail and continued firing until he thought the Pup was done for. Although badly wounded, Hadrill flattened out at treetop height and put his machine down in a field. After gathering his wits he dragged his battered body out of the wrecked Pup and was desperately trying to set fire to it when he was captured by ground troops. Hadrill spent the rest of his war in a prison camp.

Voss then climbed back to the fight and singled out an FE2b of 22 Squadron. This was crewed by two second lieutenants: Charles Mackenzie Furlonger, the pilot, and Charles William Lane. Lane had joined the squadron only one day before this action and was acting as Furlonger's observer/gunner. Their machine was the formation's Tail-End-Charlie, lagging well behind the others and inviting attention. By now the fight was down to 2,000 feet and the leading FEs had formed a circle in order to defend each other against the experienced German pilots. As their comrades continued their climbing, diving and head-on attacks on the leading FEs, Voss and two wingmen jockeyed for position on Furlonger and Lane. Voss finally lined up his Albatros and poured a withering fire into the tail-ender. Twin converging streams of tracer bullets slammed into the FE's engine and within moments it stopped. At his de-briefing after the war, Furlonger reported his machine had been damaged by anti-aircraft fire prior to the attack and that it had fallen far behind the others before the German Scouts put in an appearance. Without power, he had no choice but to spiral down to land in a cabbage field at Bel Aise Farm, close to Le Bosquet. Unhurt, but extremely shaken, the two crewmen jumped out and, unlike Hadrill, did actually manage to set fire to their machine before being taken prisoner. They then had to wait until early January 1919 before being repatriated. Lane left the service three months after his return to England, but twenty years later Furlonger answered the call to arms once again. In 1939 he rejoined the RAF, fought throughout the Second World War, and rose to the rank of squadron leader.

However, Jasta Boelcke didn't have things all their own way that day, as evidenced by RFC Communiqué No. 87. It reveals that the FEs of 22 Squadron, and the escorting Pups of 54 Squadron had a 'big fight' with seven German machines. The Communiqué reads: 'Capt. C.M. Clements & Lt. M.K. Parlee, 22 Squadron, drove down one H.A. [hostile aircraft] out of control and then dived at three others that were following one of our Sopwiths down. They were unable to get there in time, however, and the Sopwith Scout was forced to land in a field [this was Hadrill], but they succeeded in engaging one H.A., which crashed quite near to the Sopwith. Second Lieutenant M.B. Cole, 54 Squadron, fired at a large white two-seater, which was seen to crash by other pilots. Lt. E.J.Y. Grevelink, 54 Squadron, drove down a black and white German Scout which was also seen to crash, [black and white were the colours of Jasta Boelcke]. A third H.A. was destroyed by Lt. M.D.G. Scott of the same squadron.'

At this point events began to unfold that had a significant effect on the career of Werner Voss. The entire scene was changing, the air war was hoting up and towards the end of May there was something of a resurgence in the fortunes of the RFC, albeit transient. Front line squadrons were being re-equipped with new fighter types: the SE5, the Sopwith Camel and the very successful two-seater Bristol Fighter – all machines capable of holding their own against the ubiquitous Albatros. There was also another machine that had held the Germans in awe since its arrival at the Front in February 1917; this was the Sopwith Triplane, flown by pilots of the Royal Naval Air Service. When, in late 1916, the Germans got wind of a triplane fighter being developed by the British they considered its potential, thought it could be promising, but rejected the idea on the grounds that it was but a passing phenomenon that would make no significant difference to the outcome of the air war. In the event they were right, but the Sopwith outclassed the Albatros in all respects, it was an extremely agile little fighter that could dive like a comet and climb like a monkey. If the powers that be had allowed it to be fitted with two Vickers guns instead of just the one it could have made a difference. Unfortunately only 150 models were ever built and relatively few saw action during Bloody April, but those that did certainly stirred the imagination of the opposition. When an intact example of the British triplane was forced to land behind the German lines on 6 April [thought to be close to Mons-en-Chaussée, then a front line German airfield near St. Quentin] it was immediately shipped off to the aviation testing grounds at Adlershof for evaluation. German pilots who flew it there were most impressed with its handling and performance, and Kogenluft was forced to take a fresh look at the tri-wing configuration.

As May dragged into June the British ground offensive of 1917 was centred further north, away from Vimy and the ugly slag heaps surrounding the dirty mining town of Lens, and into the Ypres Salient, reputedly the most dangerous place on the Western Front. For the French it was the hell of Verdun, for the Germans 'Das Blutbad' of the Somme, but for the British it could only be Ypres, the graveyard of the old regular army that had fought the enemy to a standstill outside the ancient cloth weaving town in 1914. To 'Private Thomas Atkins' it would remain forever 'Wipers' simply because the common soldier could not get to grips with its tongue twisting Flemish and French pronunciations. Three years on, and the very thought of Ypres struck fear into the heart and soul of every British infantryman; a shiver ran down the spine and hair on the neck stood rigidly to attention at the very mention of its name. In the southern sector, six miles from the ruins of this once prosperous Flemish town, the Salient was dominated by the long sweep of the Messines-Wytschaete Ridge, curving from southeast to north around the town. Little more than a hump, and no higher than sixty metres above sea level, it dominated the shell-torn Flanders Plain that stretched out before it to the Channel ports. The ridge now stood sentinel over the labyrinth of British trenches that criss-crossed the cratered landscape below, and nothing could move in or out of the sector during the hours of daylight without being seen from its heights. Messines had been held by the Germans since October 1914 and between the lines literally hundreds of rotting corpses lay unburied, mute testimony to a dozen or more Allied attacks that had failed – but it now had to be taken whatever the cost if the war was to be won.

Throughout 1916 a series of tunnels, dug from the British trenches, were pushed out below the crest of the ridge. Their galleries ended abruptly in cavernous halls directly beneath German front line positions, some up to half a mile away from the tunnel entrances. In all, twenty-two galleries were completed by the first week of June 1917, and most were packed to capacity with ammonal, a high explosive three times more powerful than TNT. One of the longest tunnels, pushed out to the great German redoubt at Spanbrokmolen, held a massive explosive charge of over forty tons, but none of the others held less than twelve. At zero hour on 7 June 1917 British army engineers detonated nineteen of these gigantic mines and within moments an estimated 10,000 Germans were either blown to pieces or buried alive. In the immediate area the explosions caused an earthquake of considerable magnitude. The citizens of Lille, more than twelve miles away, were said to have been literally thrown out of their beds by the shock waves, thirty miles back men working in the docks at Calais felt the ground tremble beneath their feet, whilst an audible rolling thunder could even be heard on the English coast more than fifty miles distant. (One mine was discovered by the Germans and neutralised, two others were not fired at the appointed hour; the war moved on, and the two charges lay forgotten until one mysteriously exploded in July 1955 – the other still sleeps deep within the bowels of the ridge somewhere close to Ploegstreete Wood.)

Weeks prior to the detonations aerial activity over the Salient had been stepped up in preparation for the great attack and German losses began to rise, for by now the RFC had the measure of Luftstreitkräfte tactics. Ever increasing numbers of reconnaissance machines and fighting Scouts were crossing the lines into German airspace, seemingly at will and often without hindrance. Something had to be done about the situation, and it had to be done quickly. After one or two successful experiments, the original idea of forming small fighter sections into the Jagdstaffeln was recycled and Kogenluft ordered a number of select Jastas to be formed into larger defensive groups. Operated under a single command, these groups were known as Jagdgeschwadern (roughly comparable to Royal Flying Corps fighter wings). Each Jagdgeschwader was composed of four top Jagdstaffeln, and could collectively muster up to fifty fighting Scouts. Their brief was to dominate airspace above 12,000 feet and provide top cover for units operating at lower levels. Richthofen was of course the logical choice for such a command. In early June he was promoted to Rittmeister and on the 23rd he was given the honour of leading Germany's famous Jagdgeschwader Nr. 1 into action.

The appointment naturally came as no surprise to Richthofen, he had long advocated the use of large fighter groups and was in favour of in-depth defence. While German fighter pilots were fairly chafing at the bit to take the war to the Allies, Richthofen was far more pragmatic. He understood the utter frustration of his 'Gentlemen', as he was wont to call all those under his command, but he accepted that it was the job of reconnaissance machines to operate beyond the lines, with or without escorts, and that the responsibility of the Jagdgeschwader was to stem the rising tide of Allied aircraft crossing into German territory. When referring to RFC incursions, he once cheerfully told his men: 'It is better if the customers come to the shop', making it quite clear to them that they should remain east of the lines as directed by Kogenluft, but he revealed his admiration for his British opponents by adding: 'They are brave, but it is bravery that has a touch of foolishness about it.' And as an afterthought, and with a rueful smile, he curtly dismissed the Aviation Militaire with: 'In a Frenchman, bravery is quite exceptional and if you do meet it, it is like a glass of lemonade and very soon goes flat.'

After some experimentation with its formation Jagdgeschwader Nr. 1, commonly known as JG1, was finally composed of four leading Jagdstaffeln: Nos. 4, 6, 10 and 11. Within weeks pilots of the RFC had christened it the 'Travelling Circus' because of its seemingly nomadic ability to appear up and down the Front at will. Contrary to popular belief, JG1 was not known as the 'Flying Circus' until sometime later, and only then by those who thought the Wing's multi-coloured aircraft reminded them of gaily painted circus clowns. During the course of the war the Red Baron's famous combat wing was to prove most emphatically that it was no circus act: by the time of the Armistice in November of 1918, it had accounted for more than 600 Allied aircraft.

Rittmeister Manfred Freiherr von Richthofen relinquished command of Jasta 11 on 25 June and was succeeded by one of his star pupils, twenty-one-year-old Karl Allmenröder. But Allmenröder had little chance to shine as a Staffelführer, he was shot down and killed just two days later, near to Klien-Zillebeke; his days of glory ended by a lucky, extreme-range shot from the Vickers gun of a Sopwith Triplane from Naval 10. In later life, Raymond Collishaw, Britain's third highest scoring ace, readily accepted the possibility that he had been the triplane pilot, but this has never been authenticated. Richthofen was visiting his brother Lothar in Hamburg when the news of Allmenröder's death reached him, so he was unable to attend his protégé's funeral, but he did write to the boy's father: 'I myself could not wish for a more beautiful death than falling in aerial combat; it is a comfort to know that Karl felt nothing in the end.' The Rittmeister had then to organise a speedy replacement for the unfortunate Allmenröder, and there was no time to worry about the problems of units outside his direct sphere of influence. As a matter of urgency he arranged for the immediate return of Kurt Wolff to Jasta 11. Wolff was another rising star and personal friend who, like Allmenröder, had been tutored by Richthofen during their early days with Jasta 11. Such was Wolff's success he had been given command of Jasta 29, but with Allmenröder out of the picture, he was returned to the fold and took on the mantle of its leadership. This left 29 without a competent commander.

Meanwhile the reputation of Voss, now an established ace and recipient of the Pour le Mérite, was blossoming within the air service – nor had his fame gone unnoticed across the lines. As a flight commander his aggressive tactics had done much to elevate the already exalted standing of Jasta Boelcke, but at the tender age of twenty he still had the mischievous bearing of youth, and his successes in combat owed nothing to his behaviour on the ground. Voss openly consorted with lower ranks and was on first name terms with his two mechanics, Gefreiter Christian Rüser and Flieger Karl Timm, who dutifully followed him on his several moves. Moreover, he made no secret of the fact that he had little confidence in the abilities of his immediate superior Hauptmann Walz. Unfortunately, these improprieties did not escape the attention of Luftstreitkräfte Commanding General, Ernst von Hoeppner, another former Uhlan cavalryman and a strict disciplinarian.

It has been intimated in several histories that because of his 'outrageous' conduct Voss fell foul of von Hoeppner, who viewed the Rhinelander's attitude to authority and lack of military discipline with considerable displeasure. Whether this is true or not, at some point Voss and a fellow Westphalian Hussar, Leutnant Rolf Freiherr von Lersner, contrived to have Hauptmann Walz removed from command – because they firmly believed Jasta Boelcke needed a more daring leader. When this act of sedition eventually came to light Walz, an honourable man, felt obliged to request re-assignment, but in the event it was the conspirators who were removed first. Lersner was posted to a bombing group, where he was killed just a few weeks later, and on 20 May 1917 Voss was appointed acting Staffelführer of Jasta 5, which came under the aegis of Jagdgruppe 2, based at Gonnelieu.

Opinions differ, but some historians believe that this and following moves were a form of punishment, and that Voss was deliberately being kept in the shade because of the Walz incident. There is no concrete proof of this. In fact, at the time of his transfer, Jasta 5 had almost ninety victories to its credit, and was one of the leading front line fighter units. More probably the changes affecting Voss were simply echoes of the enforced reshuffle that took place within the Jagdstaffeln due to the disproportionate losses of key personnel. Jastas 5 and 29 were both well established and more than holding their own against the Allies, and as a flight comander in one of the most successful units at the Front, Voss was the logical choice for a command appointment. Accordingly, the transfers can hardly be considered punishment, although they may have been part of a rehabilitation process. Other writers have intimated that von Hoeppner placed obstacles in the way of the young ace in order to slow his progress, thus preserving the reputation of his star performer Richthofen: far better to keep a Prussian aristocrat in the public eye than the son of a nouveau riche industrialist! But again this is doubtful. Werner Voss was an exceptional fighter pilot who fought the enemies of his country whenever and wherever opportunities arose and by now he was more than just a national hero idolised by the press and public at home, he was a valuable asset to the air service and excelled during his short appointment to Jasta 5 by adding six more victories to his tally.

A two-seater FE2b of 18 Squadron was to be Voss' first victim as a Staffelführer. It took off at 11.45 hours British time on 23 May as part of the escort to a flight of 20 Squadron photo-reconnaissance machines working on the 5th Army Front. A little under two hours later, in the area of Havrincourt, the flight had the misfortune to run into seven Jasta 5 Scouts. After some pretence of tail chasing, Voss singled out the ageing FE and shot it down into the front line trenches. The crew, Second Lieutenant Wilfred Ferguson Macdonald and Lieutenant Frank Shackell, were both killed.

Voss clocked up his thirtieth 'kill' on the 27th. This was a Sopwith Pup of 54 Squadron flown by twenty-one-year-old Second Lieutenant Mortimer George Cole. Cole had been in France since early March and had served his apprenticeship flying Nieuports with 1 Squadron. There he was credited with downing two enemy aircraft before being transferred to 54, one of the first RFC squadrons to take delivery of the Pup in October 1916. Voss had previously accounted for two 54 Squadron Pups before he came across Cole. Now protected by five of his comrades, Voss swept in and got on to the Englishman's tail. He then commenced pouring a terrific volley of shots into the Sopwith, shooting away its control wires and wounding Cole in the thigh. The machine went in to a dive and crashed between the British support and front line trenches near Gouzeacourt. Cole miraculously survived the crash and soon recovered from his wounds, but never flew again. After the war he obtained a publicans licence, and for the next thirty odd years played the convivial host in a number of small hotels and wayside inns dotted around the West Country.

The next day, 28 May, was relatively quiet; few machines were up and about. Even so, four FE2ds of 25 Squadron were ordered out on a long reconnaissance covering the sector triangle: Douai

– St. Amand – Orchies. All went well until they were attacked by a gaggle of Jasta 5 Albatri over Lomain. Three of the FEs immediately went into a tight defensive circle, flying around each other in order to afford protection from all sides. Keeping formation they fought off their attackers and gradually edged themselves back towards the British lines. Eventually all three made good their escape, but the fourth machine was lagging well behind and never made the circle, it was picked off by Voss, who expertly shot the engine to bits on his first attack. Without power and far from home the pilot, Captain Aubrey de Selincourt was forced to put his aircraft down behind the German lines between Douai and Lomain. He and his Canadian observer/gunner, Lieutenant Henry Cotton, were taken prisoner and were forced to sit out the rest of their war in a prison camp; both were repatriated on 14 December 1918. Selincourt, a classical scholar, returned to his studies at University College Oxford, obtained his degree, and was subsequently appointed Senior Classics Master at the Dragon School. In later life he became a prolific writer, wrote several scholarly books and regularly contributed to the famous *Times Literary Supplement*. Cotton, the son of a Methodist minister, returned to Canada and followed his father into the Ministry. In the Second World War he rejoined his country's armed forces and became a Chaplain in the Royal Canadian Air Force.

This catalogue of continuing successes gives the impression that Voss was unbeatable in the air and scored every time he went into action. But this is an illusion. Like all pilots of that bygone era he had his fair share of dud days, gun stoppages and mechanical failures that occasionally curtailed his activities in combat. Bad weather also played its part and all too often restricted flying. Moreover, now and then he met an opponent of like mettle who was prepared to put up a fight. Minutes after Selincourt and Cotton were rounded up by German troops on the ground, Voss and two companions, Könnecke and Schulmann, headed off in the direction of Lens. Here they came across a section of 60 Squadron Nieuport 17s. In their first attacking dive Schulmann shot down the Nieuport flown by a second lieutenant named Phalen. The German trio then gave their undivided attention to Captain Keith Caldwell, a New Zealander, who later wrote of their encounter: 'On May 28, 1917, I was near Lens at 7,000 feet. I had dived on two German two-seaters, but almost immediately I was attacked from behind by three hostile aircraft. One carried streamers and was hot stuff. I couldn't shake him off and he fought me down to 2,000 feet. My petrol tank, flying wires, aileron control, struts and main spar were shot through. I tried every conceivable stunt to shake off the enemy aircraft, but to no avail, and I lost height down to 1,000 feet. I allowed the aircraft to appear out of control, and the German pilot ceased shooting and followed me down to watch the crash. I pulled out just above the ground, reversed the attacking position, and chased the enemy aircraft east, firing 90 odd rounds, until it was obvious the range was too great. The enemy aircraft flew on, apparently in good order.' In a final comment on the encounter he added: 'Up until then I had never met a Hun that a Nieuport could not out-manoeuvre, but, of course, we were some 20 m.p.h. slower.' Keith Caldwell was quite a character. He was known to almost every man in the RFC as 'Grid', simply because he never referred to an aircraft as anything other than a grid. Eventually he went on to command 74 Squadron, but on an evening in late September, whilst still serving with 60 Squadron, he and the young Rhinelander would cross paths again.

Although Voss cared little for command and the responsibilities that came with it, being a Staffelführer did have its compensations. Pretty much given a free hand, he often flew lone sorties whenever the opportunity arose, and was seemingly here, there and everywhere. Even Edward Mannock noted an encounter with the inimitable Voss. His diary entry for 19 August 1917 reads: 'Ran into my old friend the "purple man" again a few weeks ago [this must have been some time in late June or early July]. No luck. He's a marvel. For ten minutes I was only three hundred feet over him, and he manoeuvred so cleverly that I was unable to get my gun on him once. He got away in the end.'

The 'purple man' may allude to a colour or colours on the machine flown by Voss at the time, although he never employed purple to any great degree. During the course of the war the Germans adopted several varied and colourful camouflage schemes, and unlike the Royal Flying Corps and Aviation Militaire, many German pilots decorated their aeroplanes with personalised colours and intricate patterns, which accounted for several Allied aviators being able to identify opponents they had met previously. Voss was no exception. The Albatros D III he flew with Jasta 5 was gaily painted. While the fuselage was left with the natural plywood finish, simply varnished for protection against the elements, it was encircled by a narrow purple band just forward of the all white tail plane. Not content with this, Voss set about having a large red heart with a white border painted on the sides of the fuselage just aft of the cockpit. When this had been done he and his mechanics, Rüser and Timm, stepped back and admired their handiwork, but the overall design was thought to lack balance. Given some thought, it was decided to add a white swastika between the red heart and the national insignia black crosses, and Voss was photographed painting this himself. When it was finished, Karl Timm suggested the swastika looked bare so it was encompassed by a green laurel wreath knotted at the base with a purple ribbon – the badge of a champion. Some time later, an additional red heart was added to the top of the fuselage decking aft of the cockpit to provide identification from above. The swastika, an ancient Buddhist good luck symbol, with no connotations to National Socialism at the time, was not painted on the top of the fuselage decking since there was little room to squeeze it in.

The exact colour scheme or pattern on the upper wing surfaces of Voss' D III has never been established, but it has been suggested that it may have been of the intricate staggered lozenge type, a factory printed fabric pattern first used by the Germans in 1917. Predominantly coloured in alternating purple, violet, green and dark brown, seen at a distance and in the right light, the depth of the cellulose matt finish on the fabric could have given the wings an overall purple hue, and this may have been what Mannock noticed; as despite all the stories of him suffering from limited vision he was in fact blessed with a keen eye.

On the morning of 4 June the Sopwith Pups of 54 Squadron ran into their old adversaries yet again. Elements of the squadron were escorting a flight of FEs over Douai when they were engaged by a Jasta 5 formation led by Voss. Leaving the FEs to continue the dangerous business of intelligence gathering, and to defend themselves as best they could, the Pups mixed in with the attacking Albatros Scouts. Among the whirling mass of aircraft turning and tumbling all over the sky, twenty-four-year-old Captain Reginald George Pixley was seen to be engaged by an enemy machine, but was then lost to view. A British anti-aircraft battery in the vicinity later reported seeing a Pup 'force-land' and provided 54 Squadron with the map co-ordinates: south-southeast of Douai. Pixley's squadron mates were heartened by the news from the battery, believing their captain had been taken prisoner and not killed in the fight. The Pup had indeed crashed at the location given by the gunners, but when German troops arrived on the scene they found Pixley slumped over the controls dead. Voss claimed the Pup downed at 07.10 hours German time, near to

Aubenscheul-aux-Bois, not too far from Douai.

The next morning a lone FE2b of 22 Squadron was patrolling in the area of Vaucelles when Voss attacked it from astern. The machine was badly shot about and both crewmen were wounded. The pilot, Captain Francis Percival Don, sustained a shattered left arm during the vicious attack and his observer, Second Lieutenant Herbert Harris, had the index finger of his left hand shot off. The FE was crippled and Don could only manage to spiral down to land some 2,000 yards southwest of Lesdaines behind the German lines. As the two RFC men tried to get out of the wreck Voss swooped down and raked the helpless FE with a murderous fire. Fortunately neither man was hit again and they were eventually carted off to hospital and captivity. This is the second incidence of Voss inflicting unquestionable savagery on a helpless victim when it was patently unnecessary. Like Thorne and van Baerle of 13 Squadron, Don and Harris were down in enemy territory and there was no need to shoot at them once on the ground; all and any secrets they had gathered would have fallen into German hands as a matter of course. There can be no defence for such an act, unless Voss was unsure of his topography on both occasions.

Francis Don spent many painful weeks nursing his wound, but despite the efforts of a kindly German doctor, who tended him throughout, his lower left arm was eventually amputated in a Berlin hospital. Due to the severity of his disablement he was repatriated in January 1918 but continued his career in the service. After the war he rose to the rank of air vice-marshal of the Royal Air Force and between 1934 and 1937 was Air Attaché to the British Embassy in Berlin. At one of the many receptions given there a female relative of Voss asked if she could be introduced to Don, as she knew of their wartime connection. [This may have been Werner's sister Margrit Rose who after the Great War is thought to have moved to Berlin where she found employment as a secretary.] Don, having good cause to remember the events of 5 June 1917 flatly refused to see her, and remained bitter about the strafing incident to the end of his days. Harris, one of the 10,000 Canadian volunteers who joined the RFC, was repatriated from Karlsruhe prison camp on 17 December 1918 sans index finger, but otherwise in good shape. He returned to his home in St. Catherines, Ontario in early 1919 then, restless, moved to Oakland, California in 1921. After yet another move he secured a good job with the Jensen Radio Manufacturing Company of Oak Park, Illinois, put down roots and died there peacefully in 1947.

On 6 June five Nieuports 17s of 6 Squadron (RNAS) were

involved in a big dogfight that took place over Bourlon Wood. Some thirty-forty hostile aircraft, that included Albatros D IIs and D IIIs, as well as the odd Halberstadt Scout, engaged more than thirty British machines from several squadrons. The fight lasted almost thirty minutes. As foe met foe in a whirling mass of machines tumbling about the skies, Jasta 5, led by Staffelführer Voss, appeared above the scene. Having the advantage of height, the Germans singled out the Navy Nieuports and swooped down to attack. Flight Lieutenant Fabian Pember Reeves soon found himself being chased by a most tenacious German who stuck to his tail like glue. He threw the little Nieuport all over the sky in an effort to shake off his adversary but it was to no avail. As Reeves slammed his aircraft into a particularly tight turn the wings suddenly folded back and ripped away from the fuselage. As noted earlier, parachutes were available throughout the war, and readily used by balloon observers, but controversially, they were never issued to Allied pilots: the powers-that-be considered the comfort of having a too handy means of escape at hand would readily encourage nervous pilots to abandon their aircraft long before putting up a determined fight. Without a parachute the Englishman was doomed. What remained of his machine fell behind the German lines, but on this day Voss claimed a Nieuport downed into the British lines and never mentioned any obvious shedding of wings, so it is unlikely that Pember Reeves was his victim.

The answer to Voss' claim may lie elsewhere. Seconds after Reeves' Nieuport broke up the German ace tangled with Flight Commander Christopher Draper, who far from being a novice put up a stiff fight. The encounter was short but violent. Both pilots claimed to have peppered the other whilst tail-chasing, and Draper later reported a number of hits on the Albatros D III flown by Voss – who is said to have collected a slight graze on the arm during this fight. With so many machines in the air, missing each other by inches and all firing as their guns came to bear, things were getting a little too hot for the two well-matched airmen. Choosing their moment carefully, they broke off the fight, dived for the lines, and flew home safely. Once on the ground Draper claimed one Scout destroyed and one down out of control. The 'out of control' undoubtedly referred to Voss, and the Nieuport claimed on this occasion by Voss 'downed into the British lines' was undoubtedly that flown by Draper. This was to be Voss' last claim whilst serving with Jasta 5.

A few days after this encounter with 6 Squadron Voss and

Richthofen shared at least part of a leave together, visiting Werner's family home in Krefeld, where papa Voss extended a standing invitation to Richthofen to use his hunting lodge in the Black Forest. There exists a series of photographs of the two German aces in the company of the Voss family taken during this leave. The photographs belie the myth that the pair never got on, and among other scenes, show them at Eglesberg field giving a flying display to the family in Werner's richly decorated aircraft. No doubt it was during this leave that, among other matters, the two aces discussed the prowess of the Sopwith Triplane that was giving the Germans so much trouble. Richthofen had previously written an uncompromising report to Kogenluft on the British machine after a RNAS pilot, Flight Sub-Lieutenant R.A. Little of Naval 8, made a single-handed attack on eleven Albatros Scouts of Jasta 11 over Lens, shot one down, and got clean away with it. Richthofen firmly believed the Sopwith was the best Allied fighter of the day, and now more than anything he wanted triplanes for JG1.

On 28 June Voss replaced Kurt Wolff as Staffelführer of Jasta 29, but this appointment proved all too brief. He hardly had time to settle in when, after only five days, he was nominated by Richthofen to succeed Oberleutnant Ernst Freiherr von Althaus as temporary leader of Jasta 14. Althaus, a Saxon aristocrat, who had just been given command of Jasta 10, entered the air service in April 1915 and was one of the original Eindecker pilots to fly with KEK-Vaux during the period known to the RFC as the 'Fokker Scourge.' He was credited with eight victories during those heady days of the war and became one of the earliest air service recipients of the Pour le Mérite, but he had not added to his score since July 1916, and this worried Richthofen, who given a free hand to organise JG1, expected his commanders to lead by example. What Richthofen was not aware of was the fact that Althaus was steadily going blind. Known to the Air Service as 'Hussar Althaus', he had been given command of Jasta 10 in the hope that its record of success would inspire him to greater effort. Unfortunately Richthofen was disappointed, Althaus was unable to rise to the occasion and could only manage a single Sopwith Camel of 70 Squadron downed on 24 July. Although this brought his official score to nine, it was followed four days later by a final Air Service posting to the Einsitzerschule at Valenciennes as chief instructor. But even here Althaus found life difficult; eventually, his worsening eyesight led to a return to his old cavalry unit where he finished the war as a company commander. Once again a rent appeared in the fabric of command and Voss was moved up another step on the ladder when on 30 July he was appointed to the permanent command of Jasta 10.

In the meantime the enforced moves and the home leave kept Voss out of the fighting for what remained of June and early July. At some point during the leave it had been arranged for him to visit the Fokker factory at Schwerin to test Fokker's V4 prototype triplane. Anthony Fokker has been called many things, ranging from genius to charlatan, but if nothing else he was an egotist who craved attention and praise at every turn. He had not produced a winner since the days of his famous E-type monoplanes that earned their keep during the long winter of 1915-16, and by now he was decidedly downhearted. Although significant numbers of his later D-type biplanes were in service towards the end of 1916 and early 1917, they were unable to match the performance of the Albatros and Halberstadt variants introduced about the same time, moreover there was something of a question mark on their reliability, consequently orders for Fokker aircraft had dropped off dramatically. The Flying Dutchman, as he liked to be known, was bitterly disappointed and was now most anxious to please the Inspektion der Fliegertruppen (the Inspectorate of Military Aviation, commonly abbreviated to Idflieg), charged with evaluating his new design. He knew his company's future in aircraft production was in the balance – one more failure could end his days as a manufacturer. Even so, Fokker was quietly confident his tri-winged fighter would impress, and felt sure having a pilot of Voss' fame and calibre to test fly it was a good omen. He was not wrong, Werner Voss was most impressed with the little V4 – he knew it was a thoroughbred from the moment he laid eyes on it.

Some fourteen German and Austrian aircraft manufacturers had been charged to produce triplane designs by the Flugzeugmeisterei (the Directorate of Aircraft Production), but only Fokker's baby and the Pfalz Dr I actually went into production. Richthofen flew one of the Pfalz prototypes in mid-December 1917, and even though he found it lacked the performance of the Fokker, he recommended it for service. One hundred were ordered but in the event it was never employed extensively and only ten went into front line service. Voss never got the chance to test fly the Pfalz, but he never needed to – he had fallen in love with the Fokker V4. Like earlier Fokker productions, the triplane had a light steel airframe that provided great strength; this was coupled with a revolutionary cantilever wing assembly, which increased weight-to-performance ratios dramatically. The V4 had an astonishing rate of climb and could reach over 3,000 feet in just under three minutes. Though temperamental at times, its controls were fairly easy to handle and delightfully sensitive, and its extraordinary manoeuvrability could not be matched, not even by the Sopwith Camel in a right-hand turn. In short, it was a fighter pilot's dream and Voss had no hesitation in recommending it to both Richthofen and Idflieg.

Although RFC pilots considered them wonder machines when they first appeared in the skies over western Flanders, Anthony Fokker's triplanes suffered from two significant shortcomings. Unlike its Sopwith counterpart, which could crash dive like a meteor, the Fokker was unable to sustain steep power dives, and its relatively slow maximum speed of just under 90 m.p.h. made it vulnerable to the faster SE5 and Sopwith Camel. However, German pilots who flew triplanes in combat soon learned to counter these failings; by mastering the magical zoom they could extricate themselves from almost all and any fight whenever expedient. This was a tactical manoeuvre employed by Voss on several occasions.

On 30 July, after completing his evaluation of the triplane, Leutnant der Reserve Werner Voss returned to the Front as Staffelführer of Jasta 10. He showed willing, but he was temperamentally unsuited for command at this level. This fighting Jasta was among the elite, a unit of the prestigious JG1, and as its leader he was expected to conform to the battle plans and dictates of Richthofen. This did not appeal to Voss at all; he was first and foremost a loner. Moreover, he realised that he had neither the inclination nor ability that his new responsibilities demanded of him, he soon found the administrative work tedious, and so, while he got on with the business of air fighting, he was content to leave the day-to-day running of the unit in the capable hands of Oberleutnant Ernst Weigand – who some say he looked upon as a father figure. Although a good pilot, Weigand never became an ace, but he and Voss got on well. Their partnership worked, and Weigand remained faithful to the end. He was to be shot down over Houthulst Forest just two days after his young commander. Above all, by now Voss was beginning to show signs of strain; chinks in the armour began to appear that he could no longer hide. The daily routine of alerts, aerial combats and his recent enforced moves had all taken their toll; his closest friends and comrades noticed a marked ageing in his appearance that could not be attributed to reaching maturity. Bodenschatz, who referred to Voss as 'a Daredevil First Class' also noticed this change, recalling that he continually slid around on his chair like a lively schoolboy at many wing briefings.

One of Voss' first tasks as commander of Jasta 10 was to prepare an assessment for the office of Kogenluft on the capabilities of Allied aircraft and the tactics they employed. In order to formulate his plans for what remained of 1917, General von Hoeppner needed to know not only what the Staffelführers of JG1 thought of the current situation, but also how they were coping with a resurgence in the fortunes of the RFC, for by now the new British fighters were proving extremely troublesome. The report submitted by Voss was based solely on his own experiences; seemingly he had little idea of the big picture, and doubtless found working with a large combat wing daunting. Though, in fairness, the three other commanders of JG1, Oskar Boenigk, acting leader of Jasta 4; Hans Adam, leader of Jasta 6; and Gisbert-Wilhelm Groos, acting leader of Jasta 11 fared little better. They offered no immediate solutions to the problems but made observations and suggestions on tactics employed to deal with specific Allied aircraft types. Voss' report reveals his ideas were simplistic, and that he possessed little more than a basic knowledge of how to present an assessment. More importantly, his report was written purely from a fighter pilot's viewpoint, and not that of a Staffelführer about to deploy his forces. It also suggests he had more than a healthy respect for his opponents, though notably, he made no reference to machines of the Aviation Militaire whatsoever.

The report is fairly brief. Voss wrote: 'All English single-seaters are superior to the German fighter aircraft in climb, handling and dive capabilities, and most of them are also superior in speed. Only the Sopwith Pup is slower.

'You should not, under any circumstances, attack formations of Sopwiths, which fly higher on the other side of the enemy lines, for you must then start the fight under unfavourable circumstances from the outset.

'Of the two-seaters, the FEs can be particularly dangerous in air combat; they band together in a circle.

'Vickers and FE squadrons respectively must be attacked together as a unit. Only then does the possibility of successfully dealing with them present itself.

'Most fighter pilots do not like attacking the FE directly from the front, but this very method of attack is the most advantageous for us against the FE since the enemy has the least protection in front, while our fighter pilots have good protection because of the engine [being in front of the pilot]. With this last type of attack, it is absolutely essential for the fighter pilot to keep himself below the enemy aircraft and not fly over the latter, under any circumstances.'

At the beginning of July Richthofen and JG1 had been moved up to airfields in the suburbs of Courtrai. Here they were closer to the more active Flanders Front, where the 'First Act' in the third battle of Ypres, known to the British as Passchendaele, had just commenced. The battle lasted until the end of November and was yet another unholy slaughter; on this occasion the butcher's bill amounted to over 350,000 British troops killed, wounded or missing, with similar losses to the Germans. The savage struggle that went on around the ancient cloth-weaving town attracted the best of both British and German front line fighter units, and air fighting over the Salient proved to be the hottest of the year. And yet, even though it had suffered fewer casualties during 1917 than the RFC, the Aviation Militaire was still getting over the trauma of Bloody April and was pitifully slow in licking its wounds. In consequence, many French Escadrilles de Chasse temporarily abandoned the offensive spirit and adopted an unauthorised policy something akin to laissez-faire, avoiding all combats on the enemy's side of the lines, thus allowing the Germans respite during what proved to be a crucial chapter of the war. This non-aggressive stance allowed Richthofen and the pilots of JG1 to concentrate all their efforts on the hard-pressed RFC. While Jastas 4 and 11 were comfortably accommodated on the estate of Baron Jean de Béthune at Marckebeke, where they had readily appropriated the Baron's magnificent chateau for Geschwader Headquarters, Jasta 6 settled in at neighbouring Bissenghem, whilst Jasta 10 made do with the airfield a short distance away at Heule. Here Voss prepared to do battle, but as the first few days of August were wet and windy, all combat flying was cancelled. Instead he and his pilots familiarised themselves with their new Pfalz D IIIs, with which the Jasta had been re-equipped towards the end of July. Pfalz and Albatros Scouts were fairly well matched for speed and performance, if anything the Pfalz was more manoeuvrable, and could dive faster and harder than any Albatros, yet many German pilots never favoured the type, and this included Voss. Although he scored four victories whilst flying a Pfalz he thought it less responsive and soon reverted to using an Albatros D V for patrol work.

On the afternoon of 10 August at least one French Escadrille was prepared to support its over-worked British Allies. Seven Spad XIIIs of Spa-31 were patrolling the Ypres Salient on this day when Voss, accompanied by Unteroffizier Hermann Brettel, surprised them south of Dixmude. The two Germans each singled out an opponent and dived to attack. The Spads put up a spirited fight but their pilots were no match for the courageous duo. Within minutes Voss had shot down Captain Henri Rousseau, and Brettel, who was slightly wounded in the engagement, smartly finished off the machine flown by Maréchal-des-Logis Camus. Both Frenchmen fell to their deaths near Klerken, southwest of Dixmude on the British side of the lines. Bodenschatz recorded both 'kills' at 16.25 hours German time.

It was another five days before Voss scored again. On the afternoon of the 15th a patrol of FE2bs from 20 Squadron was circling over Ypres when they ran into elements of Jasta 10. In the dogfight that followed Voss latched on to the FE of Second Lieutenant Charles Cameron, a twenty-one-year-old Canadian volunteer from Ottawa. He first disabled the engine with a telling burst of fire from his twin Spandau machine guns, and on his second pass killed Private Stanley Pilbrow, Cameron's observer/gunner. Pilbrow had been in the RFC for less than a month but was already credited with shooting down four enemy machines – three of these in one day. For this action he had been awarded the Military Medal, but after encountering Voss he never lived to receive it. As it fell away from the scene of the fight Cameron put the FE into a shallow glide heading west. Fortunately Voss, preoccupied with the fight above, never gave chase. Cameron finally managed to cross the lines at 18.00 hours British time and made a forced landing near Dickebusch Lake. The unlucky Brettel, Voss' trusty wingman, received a second minor wound to the arm in this fight and two days later a third that would put him out of action for the rest of the war.

The next day, 16 August, Captain Noel William Ward Webb, a fourteen-victory ace, led the Sopwith Camels of 70 Squadron on an offensive patrol in the area between Poelkapelle and Becelaere. The Camels first climbed to 14,000 feet without seeing any sign of the enemy. Webb, who had the distinction of being the first pilot to bring down an enemy machine whilst flying a Camel, then decided to see what was happening lower down and the patrol descended through thick cloud to 4,000 feet, but drew another blank. During the descent the formation split up and Webb was left with only one companion, Captain F.H. Laurence. The two

Camels then climbed once again, this time to 15,000 feet where they met up with a group of FE2s over Polygon Wood. The FE crews alerted the newcomers to about twenty enemy Scouts that were diving on them from above. Webb and Laurence were about to climb to meet their attackers when they spotted two enemy machines passing below them. Webb must have thought the opportunity too good to miss and dived his Camel at the leading German aircraft. Laurence followed his leader down, firing at the second German as he flashed past. After finally levelling out Laurence looked about for Webb, but he was gone – the sky was completely empty. Noel William Ward Webb had simply disappeared and neither his body nor his machine was ever located.

Interestingly, Douglass Whetton stated that the only Sopwith lost in the area on this day was a Pup flown by Second Lieutenant W.R. Fish of 32 Squadron; this came down close to St. Julien at 21.00 hours German time. This seemingly puts the identity of Voss' victim in dispute, but 32 Squadron were actually equipped with DH5s at this date, and no pilot named Fish is recorded as lost, so Whetton was mistaken. The RFC Communiqué for the period reports only successes and, in accordance with the decision taken in March, no details of losses are revealed. It states that fifty-four enemy aircraft were brought down between 11-16 August, and that, although the 16th was a day of considerable air activity, 70 and 32 Squadrons were employed solely on ground attack work, strafing German trenches and supply columns. There is no mention of aerial combats by either squadron. However, Voss claimed a Camel over Polygon Wood, some four miles south-southwest of St. Julien at 19.45 hours German time, and this corresponds with the disappearance of Webb. Bodenschatz also records a Sopwith downed by Voss on the German side of the lines in the area of St. Julien at 21.00 hours. Given a degree of latitude on the times, this also indicates it was the machine flown by Webb.

It was to be another week before Voss brought down his thirty-eighth victim, his last whilst flying the Albatros Scout. On the morning of 23 August Captain Arthur Gordon-Kidd of 19 Squadron took off at 07.47 hours British time on a lone patrol east of Ypres. Almost two hours later he tangled with Voss in the area between Noordschoote and Neuvekapelle. Kidd was flying an older type Spad VII, which although a good match for the Albatros was no match for Voss. After some pretence of tail chasing the German ace poured a withering fire into the RFC machine that sent it down spinning towards the British lines southwest of Dixmude. Kidd suffered a horrendous wound to his thigh during the short engagement, caused by either an explosive or fiery tracer bullet. Fighting pain, nausea and loss of blood, he managed to get out of the spin and landed at 23 Squadron's base at La Louvie, close by Poperinghe. Unfortunately he died of his wound four days later. Bodenschatz recorded this Spad in the JG1 War Diary as downed southwest of Dixmude, a short distance from Poperinghe.

Bad weather and routine work concerned with the long-awaited delivery of the new triplanes then kept Voss out of the air until 28 August, when in spite of rain and high winds, he made an evening flight in the machine earmarked for his evaluation. It was in fact one of the V4 prototypes he had seen at Schwerin. Its manoeuvrability and flying characteristics exactly matched his own temperament and flying abilities, and he flew the triplane almost exclusively until his death in late September. The machine allocated to Voss at Heule was designated model No. Fokker FI 103/17, the other, 102/17, was to be evaluated by Richthofen and pilots of Jasta 11 at Marckebeke. (The modified V4 triplane, test flown by Voss at Schwerin, had previously been sent to Budapest for evaluation by the Austro-Hungarian Air Service, and 101/17 became the test model, which was assessed at Adlershof and, according to the historian Peter Grosz, was subsequently brought up to Dr I specifications and finally ended its days at Jagdstaffelschule II in May 1918.) Later production models were given the Fokker factory designation V5, though after acceptance for service they were given the now famous military designation Dr I (Driedecker I). Shortly after the two triplanes were delivered in August a jubilant Anthony Fokker recorded several early flights Richthofen made in 102/17 on a hand-cranked cine-camera. Over the years, this unique footage has been used in a number of documentaries on the first air war.

Aerial activity on the first two days of September had been seriously hampered by low cloud, strong winds and driving rain, but the morning of the 3rd dawned bright, with a promise of sun and clear skies later on. Twenty-one-year-old Lieutenant Aubrey Heywood of 45 Squadron thought it was a good day to be aloft, and was last seen at something like 4,000 feet heading his Sopwith Camel out over the lines towards Comines; he was to be Voss' thirty-ninth victim and his first whilst flying the triplane. Heywood had just arrived over Zandvoorde, north of Houthem, when Voss caught up with him. As ever, there was no real fight to speak of as the German ace quickly shot the Camel down into the German lines, recorded by Bodenschatz at 09.52 hours. Later that day a German pilot dropped a message on the British side confirming Heywood, their courageous opponent, had been killed in aerial combat.

Two days later Voss scored another double. The first 'kill' of the day came in the mid-afternoon. This was a Sopwith Pup of 46 Squadron, flown by Second Lieutenant Charles Walter Odell. Voss, leading a mixed bag of Jasta 10 Pfalz D IIIs and Albatros Scouts, pounced on Odell and his comrades over St. Julien. In the ensuing mêlée he singled out Odell and shot his Pup to pieces. The Pup staggered and then fell away from the fight streaming blue smoke. Thankfully the German ace never followed it down and Odell, himself no novice, having served in the RFC since December 1916, skilfully managed to get his damaged machine down behind the British lines without injury. He survived the war with seven confirmed victories, and as an officer of the Volunteer Reserve, rejoined the army in 1939 and rose to the rank of major.

Voss' second victory was thought to be a French Caudron two-seater of Escadrille C-53, flown by Maréchal-des-Logis Thabaud-Deshoulières, accompanied on this day by an artillery lieutenant named Mulard. The young Staffelführer stated that he shot the French machine down into the Allied lines near Bixschoote at 16.30 hours German time, though records of the Aviation Militaire reveal only one Caudron loss on 5 September. This was brought down near Remoncourt on the German side and credited to a pilot of Jasta 3.

Again low cloud and light rain marred the next day, 6 September, and there was little aerial work over the Front, though it didn't prevent 56 Squadron mounting an early morning offensive patrol in the area of Houthulst Forest. Captain James McCudden, who had joined the squadron on 15 August, led the five-man patrol composed of himself, Lieutenants M.H. Coote and C.H. Jeffs, and Second Lieutenants R.H. Sloley and H.A. Johnston. Shortly after crossing the lines they ran into a formation of ten machines from JG1 that included two new type German Scouts – at least one Pfalz D III and two Fokker Triplanes. This was 56 Squadron's first encounter with either type and, despite the unfavourable position of being lower down and having the watery sun in his eyes, Sloley of A Flight attacked the Pfalz which he later described as a Fokker-type biplane. The Pfalz immediately turned away and flew east, as it did so one of the triplanes turned on Sloley and began shooting at him from extreme range, though its pilot showed little determination to develop the attack. McCudden took little part in the encounter; a defect in his C.C. interrupter gear put his Vickers gun out of action after only one shot. Luckily the SE5s were able to disengage and all returned safely to their airfield at 07.40 hours British time. Ordinarily, being shot at from long range was the mark of a novice, but this may not have been the case in this instance. It is also unlikely that the triplane pilot was Werner Voss – he would never have wasted so much ammunition, and would undoubtedly have pressed home the attack.

Later that day, FE2ds of 20 Squadron mounted an offensive patrol east of Ypres. Lieutenant John Oscar Pilkington, who hailed from the Isle of Man, and his twenty-two-year-old gunner, Air Mechanic Herbert Matthews, must have questioned the mission given the poor weather conditions: there were few enemy machines about and most that were, were circling well behind the German Front, but not all. Voss and his Jasta pilots were up on the British side. They were hovering high above Boesdinghe looking for customers when 20 Squadron strayed into their killing-ground. The nightmare of fire in the air was about to be visited on Voss' forty-second 'kill'. As the FEs passed below them, the fighter ace gave the signal and Jasta 10 swooped down on the British formation, which up till then had been flying straight and level. Voss got in close, lined up Pilkington in his gun sight, and pulled the triggers on his twin Spandaus. A long stream of orange tracer bullets curved into the British machine, danced along the fuselage nacelle and ruptured the fuel tank. Within seconds the FE burst into flames and fell like a fiery dart within the British lines near St. Julien, recorded at 16.35 hours German time. Pilkington and Matthews were both killed.

The weather over the next three days was abysmal, though by the 10th it had cleared a little. This day saw the second hat-trick of Voss' career. At 15.45 hours British time the Sopwith Camels of 70 Squadron took off on an offensive patrol that was to take them on a beat from Houthulst Forest via Roulers to Ledeghem and Gheluvelt. On the way they spotted eight enemy Scouts passing below and dived on them. Lieutenant L.F. Wheeler fired on one machine and later claimed it as downed out of control. He then ran into a triplane but it eluded him by climbing away at great speed. In his combat report Wheeler reported seeing a German machine falling in flames. In fact there were no Jasta 10 losses on this day. What he actually saw tumbling out of the sky was a Camel flown by his own squadron mate, Second Lieutenant

Arthur Smith Sisley, a Toronto Canadian who had been at the Front for just over three weeks. Second Lieutenant F.H. Bickerton was being kept busy lower down and almost collided with the burning Camel as it fell past him. He reported the flaming machine as being hotly pursued by a lone triplane. Smith Sisley's Camel dived into a heavily shell cratered area close to the village of Langemarck, but although it crashed on the British side, his body was never recovered.

Five minutes later Voss attacked another 70 Squadron Camel, piloted by Second Lieutenant Oliver Charles Pearson, to be confirmed as his forty-fourth victim. There was no elaborate ceremony about this 'kill' either. He quickly dispatched the Sopwith and Pearson was reported crashed southwest of Poelkapelle, again on the British side, but like Smith Sisley, Pearson also fell into the zone of heavy craters. Pearson, who had been slightly wounded on 20 August, and the wreck of the aircraft, were never found.

The RFC Communiqué for the 10th reveals an enigmatic and unconfirmed claim that arose out of 70 Squadron's encounter with hostile aircraft between Roulers and Staden on this day. It reports the squadron engaged eight Albatros Scouts, a two-seater, and two triplanes. Second Lieutenant F.H. Bickerton, who narrowly avoided collision with Smith Sisley, claimed he opened fire on one of the triplanes, which burst into flames and fell out of control. Did Bickerton actually see two triplanes during this engagement, and could he possibly have shot one of them down in flames? On the face of it it seems unlikely, historians and historical evidence indicate the only two triplanes at the Front during September were those of Richthofen and Voss. There were no Pfalz triplanes in service at the time, and Fokker factory records show no other triplanes were delivered to the Front until mid-October, although there is considerable eyewitness evidence to refute this. Richthofen, who was still recovering from a head wound, was on convalescent leave at the time, and as Jastas 10 and 11 reported no losses on the 10th, neither he, Voss nor any other pilot flying Richthofen's triplane could have been shot down during the engagement; on the face of it Bickerton's claim must therefore be considered spurious.

However, Voss was not finished for the day and the identity of his forty-fifth victim has given rise to yet another enigma. According to Franks and Giblin, twenty-five minutes after shooting down the two Sopwith Camels he came across a French Spad VII, which he also disposed of in double-quick time.

Aviation Militaire records for this day confirm one of their Spads, flown by Adjudant Pierre Tiberghien of Escadrille Spa 37 was lost over Langemarck, recorded in the War Diary of JG1 as falling at 18.15 hours German time. However, Revell and Whetton offer the theory that Voss' third victim of the day may have been either an SE or an FE. They were undecided because the Abschusse records it as an SE while the War Dairy of JG1 gives it as an FE. [RFC records reveal there were no SE or FE losses reported on this day.]

Bodenschatz notes Voss claimed his forty-sixth victory as a 'new type', brought down on the German side at 10.30 hours on the 11th. The War Diary of JG1 records no Spad 'kills' on this day, and while Franks and Giblin admit Voss' first victim of the 11th remains something of a mystery, they offer that it could have been either a Camel of 45 Squadron or a BF2b of 22 Squadron. But Voss was familiar with both types. He had shot down two Camels the previous day, and by this stage he must have been familiar with the BF2a, which was strikingly similar in configuration to the newer BF2b that came into service in early August. On the other hand, Voss was also familiar with the Spad. The mystery gives rise to an interesting possibility touched on by the author Peter Kilduff, that the forty-sixth victim of Werner Voss, shot down two miles east of Langemarck at 10.30 hours German time on 11 August, could have been the leading French ace of the day, and one of France's most famous sons, Capitaine Georges Marie Ludovic Guynemer of Escadrille Spa 3. The timing of the fight and the crash site fit almost perfectly into the necessary scenario, and a fight to the death between two titans of the first great war in the air would make very good copy. Unfortunately, Leutnant der Reserve Kurt Wissemann of Jasta 3 is credited with shooting Guynemer down, and it is so recorded in the Abschusse. However, it is known that the French ace was flying an older type Spad VII when he was killed which Voss would never have described as a new type. So the odds are seemingly against it being a Voss victory. Guynemer's own machine, a Spad XIII which he had christened Vieux Charles, was in the sheds undergoing repairs, and it is said that as he could not wait to get into the air, he 'borrowed' the older Spad. Guynemer was simply reported as missing in action. No details of his fate came to light during the war, and for many years the circum-stances of his death were known to but a few dedicated air enthusiasts who took the trouble to research the mystery. After the war, French authorities, deeply engrossed in rebuilding their battle-scarred country, failed to consult German archives until much later, and even when the mystery was eventually solved it was not widely publicised.

There was no doubt about Voss' second victory of the day; this was a Sopwith Camel of 45 Squadron. Captain Norman Macmillan, Commander of A Flight, led his seven Camels on an offensive patrol over their sector of the Front that covered an area east of Langemarck. It was a misty afternoon, but Macmillan had a keen eye and soon spotted a concentration of enemy aircraft flying below them. The formation, some twenty-one machines strong, was composed mainly of Albatros Scouts, but according to Macmillan included three Fokker triplanes. Despite some misgivings, Macmillan decided to attack, waggled his wings and dived on the enemy. As his Flight followed him down he closed in and got one of the triplanes in his sights. As his first burst of tracer went home he saw the triplane fall away before he pulled out of the dive. One of his younger pilots, Lieutenant Oscar Lennox McMaking, was so engrossed in chasing an Albatros he failed to see his leader pull out, continued in the dive, and passed right through the level of German machines. Werner Voss, never known to look a gift horse in the mouth, flipped his triplane over smartly, dived on McMaking, and commenced firing.

In 1929 Macmillan recounted the incident in his wartime memoirs *Into the Blue*, a book now regarded as an aviation classic. His brilliant description of the chase that ensued, and the cool calculating tenacity of Voss, is quoted here in full. He wrote: 'A burst of bullets caused the Camel pilot to look round and swerve away from the Albatros he followed. I saw a triplane close in upon the Camel's tail and I dived instantly upon it. As I dived I fired a short burst, before my sights were centred, because I knew that most Huns answered to the warning of bullets flying near. This fellow, however, was of a different breed. He looked round at me and, as I saw his begoggled face above his shoulder, he swerved slightly to one side, then followed on the Camel's tail.

'I think the Camel pilot [McMaking] was wounded by the triplane's very first burst, because he did not use the Camel to manoeuvre as he might.

'I increased speed and pulled closer to the triplane. Then I heard the splatter of Hun bullets rattling round my own ears. Glancing upward I saw two Albatros Scouts coming down upon me, but above them was another little Camel treating them the same.

'I was almost dead upon the triplane's tail when the pilot looked around again. The range was so close that I could almost read the man's expression. I gave him another burst and saw a stream of tracer miss his head by inches as he swerved outward from my line of sight. The Camel was below him falling steeply in a gentle curve. When my burst ceased the German pilot looked again ahead.

'Damn him! I thought. I'll get him next time. Each time I had fired a trifle earlier than I might have done, in the desire to shake him off the Camel's tail. And all the time we fell downward, losing height, fighting earthward from 14,000 feet along a pathway inclined at sixty degrees, rushing through the misty air towards the ground behind the German lines. From behind me came another burst of flying bullets.

'Out of the corner of my eye I saw a solitary RE8 heading towards us. I followed the swerving triplane and got squarely on his tail. Before I could fire he got out of my sights once more. Again I registered on him, dead. I pressed the triggers and saw my bullets flying home. His head didn't look round this time. His angle of dive suddenly steepened. I increased my own vertical, barely twenty feet behind him. Suddenly the RE8 flashed in front of me between the German and my bus. I saw the wide-open mouth of the horror-struck observer. The wings passed across my vision as the pilot vainly strove to turn away. . . .

'I yanked the Camel's stick hard into my stomach and flashed between the two-seater's wings and tail plane as my gallant little Camel answered to the pull. By a miracle we missed collision, by a miracle my Camel held together. I flat spun upside down on top of a loop and fell out sideways. I had lost height so rapidly in my downward rush from 14,000 feet that the pressure in my fuel tank had no time to stabilise to meet the higher atmospheric pressure, and my engine ceased to run. . . . The triplane and the Camel both had vanished.'

As recorded in RFC Communiqué No. 105, Macmillan claimed a triplane 'shot down out of control' but Voss had not been shot down, he simply disengaged and smartly headed back to Heule. However, the encounter with the Englishman must have shaken him considerably: Macmillan got within twenty feet of the triplane and put a stream of fiery bullets uncomfortably close to his head, a feat no other Allied pilot had achieved thus far. Leutnant der Reserve Alois Heldmann, credited with Jasta 10's final victory of the war on 6 November 1918, recalled: 'He [Voss] was on edge; he had the nervous instability of a cat. I think it would be fair to say that he was flying on his nerves. And such a situation could have but one end.' That very evening Staffelführer Voss wrote out and signed his own Ausweis (leave warrant). This authorised him to travel to Krefeld, Düsseldorf, Berlin and Schwerin.

His actual movements during this leave are not clear, but he undoubtedly dealt with whatever business there was to be conducted at home and across the Rhine in Düsseldorf. He then visited the Fokker Flugzeugwerkes at Schwerin where he flight-tested a production model V5 triplane. Then comes an unsubstantiated story. The night before his leave expired Voss is said to have attended a reception in Berlin, given by Anthony Fokker at the Bristol Hotel on Unter-den-Linden. This was said to be a gathering of eagles, supposedly held in honour of Bruno Loerzer who was to be awarded his Pour le Mérite there. [In fact Loerzer, who rose to command Jagdgeschwader Nr. III, did not receive the award until January 1918.] As well as the medal recipient, the story goes that Manfred and Lothar von Richthofen, Werner Voss, the diminutive Ernest Udet, and the infamous Hermann Göring were all in attendance, as was Luftstreitkräfte Commanding General Ernst von Hoeppner, who supposedly made the presentation. After the ceremony the General left the gathering and a gay party ensued that stretched into the small hours. Champagne, wine and spirits flowed freely, young ladies arrived and it is said no one was gayer than Voss, who led the singing around the piano. After much carousing, Werner Voss finally proposed a toast to Anthony Fokker and his magnificent triplanes and then, announcing that his leave was up, left the party and returned to the Front.

This story has to be a fanciful fabrication, dreamed up by the fertile imagination of a sensationalist historian, as there is no hard evidence to support it whatsoever. Even so, there may well have been a gathering of eagles at some time, as Fokker was renowned for throwing lavish parties during the trials of new aircraft types held at Adlershof, so perhaps there was a reception in honour of someone, and perhaps Voss did attend but if so who was holding the fort while the cream of the Imperial German Air Service was living it up in Berlin?

One star turn that was definitely not on the fictitious Bristol Hotel guest list was recently promoted Oberleutnant Kurt Wolff, Staffelführer of Jasta 11, whose pilots were yet mourning the death of Allmenröder. Wolff, who had become engaged on his last leave, had the use of Richthofen's triplane in his absence and on the afternoon of 15 September he led elements of Jasta 11 on a patrol over Wervicq. At some point he lost his companions and found himself alone in the empty blue. But he wasn't alone for long; suddenly he was pounced upon by seven Sopwith Camels from Naval 10. At that very moment his comrades re-sighted their leader and dived to the rescue. Too late! Flight Sub-Lieutenant N.M. MacGregor got on to Wolff's tail and closed to within twenty-five yards before firing one long burst into the weaving triplane from both Vickers guns; FI 102/17 staggered from the onslaught then span down out of control to crash close to the little hamlet of Nachtigall, just north of Wervicq. Contrary to popular belief, the triplane did not burst into flames or explode before hitting the ground, as photographs of the crashed machine on the ground clearly reveal there was no fire damage whatsoever. Richthofen was devastated, he had suffered yet another crushing blow: first Allmenröder and now Wolff. In an obituary that appeared in newspapers published in Wolff's home town of Memel (then in East Prussia, now in Lithuania), Richthofen bemoaned the loss of his young friend and comrade: 'In the history of the Geschwader he will live for all times as a model of soldier-like virtue and as an example that could be equalled only by the great.' But this was not to be the end of Richthofen's torment. In just over a week he was destined to lose three of his most promising stars. On the 21st the twenty-six-victory ace and commander of Jasta 6, Oberleutnant Eduard Dostler, was shot down and crashed to his death between the lines near Frezenberg; and if this was not enough, two days later a 'Daredevil First Class' was to follow him on the long road to Valhalla.

CHAPTER THREE

SEPTEMBER EVENING

Voss returned to Heule and was back in action on 23 September. The weather over the previous three days had been wet and windy and although low clouds had seriously hampered air activity in the mornings, a good deal of air fighting had taken place in the afternoons. The morning of Sunday 23rd was much the same. The grass at Heule field was covered in autumn dew and a low mist shrouded the field, but shortly after dawn it began to lift and Voss prepared for his first patrol of the day. If there had ever been any heavy drinking and gay carousing at the Bristol Hotel a day or so before it had little or no effect on Voss, he was on top form and his forty-eighth and final accredited victory came on this patrol. Up in the triplane, not too far from the airfield, and just before 09.30 hours German time, Voss sighted a 57 Squadron Airco DH4 bomber. The crew, Second Lieutenants Samuel Leslie Bramley and John Matthew DeLacy, were busily lining up targets over Hooglede when Voss surprised them. The engagement was over in moments and the bomber was seen to crash in flames south of Roulers, killing both crewmen. The German ace then returned to Heule to greet his brothers, Otto and Max, who had arrived at the airfield sometime during the morning. They had a leisurely lunch together, undoubtedly discussed family matters, and while Rüser and Timm inspected, refuelled and rearmed the triplane, the brothers posed for photographs by the sheds. These proved to be the last ever taken of Werner Voss.

Around 17.00 hours British time the celebrated German ace dragged on his flying gear for his final patrol of the day. While his brothers watched from the edge of the field, he settled himself into the cockpit of Fokker Triplane Fl 103/17, ran through the final checks, then taxied on to the grass and gunned the engine. He left Heule field at 17.05 British time accompanied by Leutnants der

Reserve Gustav Bellen and Friedrich Rüdenberg, both flying Pfalz D IIIs. Bellen was in good spirits, in a daring attack he had shot down a British kite balloon two days previously and was now looking to repeat the performance. At the time he had no way of knowing, but the balloon was to be his one and only victory of the war as Bellen was wounded in action on 11 October and invalided out of the service. Rüdenberg, one of the few German-Jewish airmen of the Great War, had joined the Fliegertruppe in 1914, qualified as a pilot in 1916 and had clocked up more than 200 sorties in two-seaters before being seconded to Jasta 10. Assigned straight from Jastaschule at Valenciennes less than two weeks earlier, he later recalled that he had been officially notified of his promotion to Leutnant der Reserve just one day before this historic flight took place. But despite being very able, Rüdenberg never scored a single victory as a fighter pilot – he claimed he was granted leave of absence in November to continue his studies as an electrical engineer in Berlin, thus putting him out of the fighting for what remained of the war. Many years afterwards he settled in Israel and made some attempt to write his memoirs, but these were never finished or ever published in full.

A few minutes later Voss and his two wingmen were followed by a second Ketten, which was led by Jasta 10's adjutant Oberleutnant Ernst Weigand, flying an Albatros DV. He was accompanied by Leutnants der Reserve Julius Bender and Rudolf Kuhn, both at the controls of Pfalz D IIIs. Last to take off as a pair were Leutnant Eric Löwenhardt, who went on to become Germany's third highest scoring ace, and Leutnant Alois Heldmann, who survived the war with fifteen confirmed victories. As soon as they lifted off the two more experienced pilots climbed hard to catch up with their comrades who were unerringly making for the Front. The Jasta mechanics, their work finished for now, stood in a little group by the sheds and watched as the nine machines bumped and swayed into the humid air of that September evening. The Staffel slowly drifted off into the haze and passed from sight. Heading southwest, they climbed steadily for the Zonnebeke sector. But while his companions were still struggling for height, Voss adjusted his throttle settings and the triplane easily out-climbed them all. Within minutes he had disappeared into the blue – never to return.

Unbeknown to the German pilots, about the same time of day, but on the other side of the lines and some thirty-odd miles southwest of Heule, eleven SE5s of 56 Squadron took off from their field at Estrée Blanche. The covey of British fighters made a circuit of the field, formed on their two flight commanders and turned in the direction of Houthulst Forest. Climbing to 8,000 feet, B Flight crossed the lines over Bixschoote then passed through several layers of wispy cloud before levelling out just below the main cloud bank, which on this day hung grey and foreboding at 9,000 feet. Almost every pilot was an experienced hand. Captain James T.B. McCudden, the RFC's ace of aces at the time, led the six SEs of B Flight; comfortably slotting into formation behind him were Lieutenants K.K. Muspratt, V.P. Cronyn – a likeable, but not so successful Canadian from London, Ontario, R.W. Young, C.H. Jeffs and Arthur Percival Foley Rhys Davids, a nineteen-year-old classics scholar who had joined the Royal Flying Corps straight from his studies at Eton College. The five machines of C Flight were led by the redoubtable Captain Geoffrey H. Bowman, who stood no nonsense from any one, especially Huns. He in turn was accompanied by Lieutenants R.A. Maybery, E.A. Taylor, S.J. Gardiner and another Canadian, R.T.C. Hoidge, who hailed from Ottawa. As they reached the edge of the forest the two Flights split up. Visibility towards the ground was poor due to the bank of thick cloud, so McCudden's Flight dropped below it and immediately attracted considerable anti-aircraft fire. According to Cronyn this proved far too accurate for his liking: German flak batteries had their height to a tee. Chased by an ever-lengthening stream of ominous detonations from exploding shells, McCudden turned his machines south and made towards Gheluvelt. Bowman's Flight had climbed above the cloud layer, levelled out at 10,000 feet, continued circling for some minutes, then came down again before turning in a direction that would take them from Westroosebeke to Houthem; they were also a target for the eagle-eyed German gunners. Bowman reported their fire as 'heavy and accurate'.

An epic encounter that ended in one of the most extraordinary aerial combats of the Great War was about to take place. It has been told, re-told, expanded upon and embellished by many historians since the enactment. Various conflicting renditions, summations and dramatisations of what exactly happened in a little under half an hour on that humid Sunday evening have appeared in print over the last eighty odd years. Moreover, there are contradictory British and German combat reports on the final outcome of the fight and the circumstances of Werner Voss' death. These reports, made about the same time, though naturally without knowledge of each other, present something of an enigma that may never be resolved, although the British version of events is decidedly easier to accept as it is based on several well-documented eyewitness accounts. For the most part, these are found in letters home to friends and relatives, diary entries, personal memoirs, and the combat reports of those actually involved. There is also a more recent record of the Voss action provided by Geoffrey Bowman, who was interviewed at length by Alex Revell in 1968; his recollections of that September engagement are of significance to the Voss saga and its final analysis. Then there is the curious statement made by a German pilot who claimed to have witnessed the final combat of Voss. His account was supposedly corroborated by the young ace's wingmen, Bellen and Rüdenberg, who are said to have concurred on the time of the crash and its location.

One notable rendition of events is found in the memoirs of James McCudden, *Five Years in the Royal Flying Corps*, written shortly before his death in 1918. This provides a narrative of the action, the events leading up to it and its conclusion. Another equally revealing account is derived from the letters home of Arthur Rhys Davids, who was eventually credited with shooting Voss down. The substance of his letters concerning the Voss fight cover a period of three days, during which time some confusion reigned as to the actual identity of the triplane pilot. Initially, only sketchy information came in from British ground forces who witnessed the crash; this was due to the fact that even identifying the aircraft type was difficult as the machine had been smashed to pieces. When subsequently told that the German pilot was in fact Werner Voss, Rhys Davids at first thought Lieutenant Hoidge had brought him down, simply because no one involved was aware the triplane was being flown by the German ace. Statements by Captain Bowman and Lieutenant Cronyn provide other pieces of the jigsaw, while Rüdenberg's papers, and a scattering of recently rediscovered correspondence between the historian Douglass Whetton and Karl Bodenschatz, helps put the German account into perspective.

McCudden set the scene perfectly when he wrote: 'As soon as we crossed over Hunland I noted abnormal enemy activity, and indeed there seemed to be a great many machines of both sides about. . . . We went north, climbing to about 6,000 feet. A heavy layer of grey clouds hung at about 9,000 feet, and although the visibility was poor for observation, the atmosphere was fairly clear in a horizontal direction. Away to the east one could see clusters of little black specks, all moving swiftly, first in one direction and then another. Farther north we could see formations of our own machines, Camels, Pups, SEs, Spads and Bristols, and lower down RE-8s.'

This clearly indicates it was a day of intensive air activity over the Front, and that the sky was full of German and Allied machines all going about their business amid the haze, which was greatest nearer the ground. En route, and after turning south, B Flight encountered a two-seater DFW over Gheluvelt, flown by Leutnant Gustav Rudolph and Unteroffizier Rudolphe Frake of Flieger Abteilung 6. McCudden attacked the DFW and made short work of the German reconnaissance machine. After getting in close, he put in a well-aimed burst from both guns and the German machine went into a vertical dive, and 'crashed to nothing' northeast of Houthem. For good measure, Rhys Davids also fired a long burst into it as it went down. The SE5s then turned back north, climbing once again to around 6,000 feet. As they came in over Poelkapelle, McCudden was about to give the signal to attack six Albatros Scouts that had just put in an appearance off to his right, when just ahead and slightly below, he saw an SE5 half spinning down pursued by a 'silvery-blue German triplane at very close range'.

At about 18.25 hours British time two flights of SE5s of 60 Squadron, led by Captain Keith 'Grid' Caldwell, who had experienced the hairy encounter with Voss back in May, were returning from an offensive patrol. A Flight, bringing up the rear, had been reduced to two SEs flown by Captain R.L. Chidlaw-Roberts and Lieutenant H.A. Hamersley. Chidlaw-Roberts, credited with a respectable ten victories by the end of the war, and Hamersley, who finished with thirteen, spotted an Albatros Scout diving on what they thought was a Nieuport. Hamersley dived to the rescue, only to be taken completely by surprise when the Nieuport turned out to be one of the new German triplanes that quickly changed direction and attacked him. The two machines approached each other almost head on and began blazing away. At the last moment Hamersley zoomed and banked to avoid a collision, only to find the triplane was already above him and coming in from the flank.

Hamersley recalled: 'I was keeping a very close watch on a large formation of enemy aircraft, about twenty to twenty-five Albatros DVs. I suddenly saw what I thought was an Albatros diving on a Nieuport Scout. I swung across to attack the DV and what I thought was the Nieuport turned towards me and I realised it was a "Tripe" as we spoke of them. It was a little below me and I put my nose down and opened fire. The "Tripe" passed under me and as I zoomed and turned the Hun was above me and heading straight at me, firing from about 30 degrees off the bow. There was a puff of smoke from my engine and holes appeared along the engine cowling in front of me and in the wings. Realising I could do nothing further in the matter, I threw my machine into a spin. The Hun followed me down, diving at me while I was spinning and I had to do an inverted dive to get away.'

Voss fired short accurate bursts that riddled the 60 Squadron SE5 from nose to tail, inflicting considerable damage. Realising he was in a hopeless position Hamersley threw his machine into the inverted dive in a desperate attempt to shake off his attacker, but the German stuck like glue. Effortlessly mirroring Hamersley's every manoeuvre, Voss shot several pieces off the stricken SE on its way down. Chidlaw-Roberts made a brave attempt to go to the aid of his comrade and fired several bursts at the triplane from short range, but without apparent effect. Pausing in his pursuit of Hamersley, the German ace flicked his machine around, got on Chidlaw-Roberts' tail, and in a flash shot his rudder bar to bits. The two 60 Squadron pilots knew they had met their match, disengaged and smartly limped west as fast as their badly damaged machines would take them.

Chidlaw-Roberts recalled: 'I turned to engage as soon as possible, but before I could fire a shot Hamersley was spinning away with smoke coming out of his engine. I fired a few rounds with both guns at the triplane at close range, but in seconds he was on my tail and had shot my rudder bar about. I retired from the fray and that is all I saw of it.' [In later life Chidlaw-Roberts wrote of his brief encounter with Werner Voss; unfortunately his account of the action did not concur with that of Geoffrey Bowman, who dismissed it out of hand.]

By now the uneven contest was practically underneath B Flight and McCudden gave the signal to attack by waggling his wings. His SEs dived at colossal speed to the rescue, and no doubt their unexpected appearance distracted Voss long enough for Chidlaw-Roberts and Hamersley to make good their escape. What happened in the next ten minutes has gone down in the annals of air fighting as one of the greatest aerial combats on record. As they came in above, McCudden banked and attacked Voss from the right, Rhys Davids attacked from the left. Muspratt and Cronyn followed them down in line. The SEs came in behind the triplane and began firing as they streaked past. It seems that Jeffs and Young took little or no part in the Voss encounter but remained above, possibly as top cover: higher up there were at least a dozen enemy machines milling about that needed careful watching. Luckily for 56 Squadron, they were already being engaged by an almost equal number of Sopwith Camels, Spads and Bristol Fighters. Cronyn believed at least one of his two comrades, Jeffs or Young, had sustained damage from anti-aircraft fire which he noted was pretty hot at the time, though after the fight both pilots accompanied B Flight on its return to Estrée Blanche and landed safely.

Caldwell, who by now was well ahead, missed the opening moments of the Hamersley tussle but recalled: 'The first thing I knew of anything happening was seeing an SE going down in a hurry towards Ypres with a blue-grey triplane in close attendance and thinking the SE had had it. We set off down to try and rescue the SE, but a flight of 56 Squadron's SEs (and a very good one too) had taken Voss off its tail and were busy with him in their midst. It was then really 56's affair and six to one was pretty good odds we felt. We were more or less spectators and in my opinion there was little room to join in.'

McCudden wrote: 'The German pilot saw us and turned in a most disconcertingly quick manner, not a climbing nor Immelmann turn, but a sort of flat half spin. By now the German triplane was in the middle of our formation, and its handling was wonderful to behold. The pilot seemed to be firing at all of us simultaneously, and although I got behind him a second time, I could hardly stay there for a second. His movements were so quick and uncertain that none of us could hold him in sight at all for any decisive time. . . . I now got a good opportunity as he was coming towards me nose on, and slightly underneath, and had apparently not seen me. I dropped my nose, got him well in my sight, and pressed both triggers [on the Vickers and the wing mounted Lewis]. As soon as I fired up came his nose at me, and I heard clack-clack-clack-clack, as his bullets passed close to me and through my wings. I distinctly noticed the red-yellow flashes from his parallel Spandau guns. As he flashed by me I caught a glimpse of a black head in the triplane with no hat on at all.'

Cronyn, who was bringing up the rear, was the last to dive on Voss. He put in what he thought was an accurate burst of fire, but as he pulled out of the dive he found his SE had lost considerable fuel pressure. The German rounded on him in seconds and began shooting as the Canadian desperately tried turning to shake him off. The indefatigable Voss flew like the devil, dazzling his opponents with expert zooms and lightening fast turns never before seen by any of the experienced British pilots, who for the most part were shooting at thin air whilst he was riddling them with murderous fire. To their utter frustration, every time they fired the German danced away in a series of spectacular sideslips and remarkable flat turns.

Cronyn returned to his native Canada after the war and somewhat belatedly published his memoirs in 1978. In his book, *'Shanachie' Other Days*, he wrote of the fuel pressure problem: 'In consequence my zoom was but a feeble climb. I take my hat off to that Hun as he was a most skilful pilot, but he did give me a rough passage. On seeing my feeble attempt, he whipped round in an extraordinary way, using no bank at all, but just throwing his tail behind him . . . He was at very close quarters and could hardly miss me. The bullets ripped all around me. I did not stick my machine down in an attempt to run, as I certainly would have done two months ago, but dived just enough to give me speed to turn under him and prevent him getting on my tail. The others were above, and I knew sooner or later they would drive him away, and the longer I stayed the better their opportunity to nail him. I don't know how many times I turned under him, I did not stop to count, but it seemed an eternity. He finally got too close for me, and I resorted in desperation to the old method of shaking a pursuing machine. On the completion of the second revolution of my spin, I flattened out, and to my intense relief the Hun was no longer following me. Nor had he escaped the others of the patrol, who were busily engaged scrapping him. I looked back once to see two more SE5s had joined in, and the Hun was making no attempt to escape; what is more he was holding his own against the very uneven odds.'

With his machine now *hors de combat*, Lieutenant Cronyn was forced to follow the hapless Hamersley and Chidlaw-Roberts. He quickly dived out of the fight and limped for home. Effectively Voss had now forced down three SE5as, all flown by experienced pilots.

Moments earlier Captain Bowman and what remained of C Flight had arrived above the scene: Taylor and Gardiner had got lost as they descended through the cloudbank and wandered off on their own. Bowman, Maybery and Hoidge soon became embroiled with a gaggle of German Scouts that had been milling around in the vicinity of Westroosebeke. Hoidge quickly shot down a green Pfalz D III that had been attacking Maybery and followed it down. [Rhys Davids at first thought this Pfalz, a new type, was the machine flown by Voss.] The enemy formation then scattered. By then the action with Voss had drifted slightly east, and seeing what was going on below Bowman and Maybery dived to the aid of their squadron mates. Hoidge arrested his pursuit of the stricken Pfalz, changed the empty drum on his Lewis gun, and climbed back up to the fight. Voss was now faced with the prospect of scrapping with a very salubrious array of British aces from the most famous RFC squadron on the Western Front. In the course of the war this little band of flying mayhem collectively accounted for close on 170 enemy aircraft: McCudden fifty-eight, Bowman thirty-two, Hoidge twenty-seven, Rhys Davids twenty-two, Maybery twenty-one and Muspratt a creditable eight.

The running fight had now descended to 2,000 feet. Undaunted by the formidable odds against him, Voss banked, rolled, zoomed and dived among the SEs time after time, firing at every machine as it came in line with his gun sights. Maybery zoomed to get above him then dived to attack, but just as he was about to fire a red-nosed Albatros, possibly the same machine Hamersley had seen 'attacking the Nieuport', got on his tail and he was forced to do a climbing turn to shake it off. The triplane and the Albatros both singled out Maybery for treatment, but were smartly attacked by McCudden and Rhys Davids. As Rhys Davids dived on the triplane the Albatros turned on him, got in behind, and started shooting. The others saw a stream of tracer bullets seemingly engulf the young pilot and his machine, but Maybery quickly recovered from his fright and shot the German off his friend's tail. The Albatros then dived out of sight and did not reappear. [The identity of the Albatros pilot has never been established beyond doubt, but it is important to note this particular event.]

Bowman, who experienced stoppages to both his Lewis and Vickers guns, recalled: 'We were then at about 2,000 feet and a mile behind the German front line. This left Voss alone and in the middle of seven of us which did not appear to deter him in the slightest. At that altitude he had a much better rate of climb, or rather zoom, than we had and frequently he was the highest machine of the seven and could have turned east and got away had he wished to, but he was not that type and always came down into us again.' Voss was not found wanting. Undaunted by the formidable odds he now turned on Muspratt and disabled his SE in a flash. Several bullets tore into the radiator and the sump, and an oil pipe was shot away. Realising he had but a few minutes before his engine seized, Muspratt dived smartly for the British lines trailing steam and oily black smoke. Voss had now accounted for four of his experienced antagonists, but he was now alone and surrounded by the remaining SEs of 56 Squadron, and all were intent on bringing him down.

McCudden wrote: 'The triplane was still circling round in the midst of six SEs, who were all firing at it as opportunity offered, and at one time I noted the triplane in the apex of a cone of tracer bullets from at least five machines simultaneously, and each machine had two guns.'

The SE pilots thought they had the German trapped but, according to Major Rothesay Stuart-Wortley, the pilot of a Bristol Fighter, who was watching the action from above, Voss suddenly shot his way out of the circle and climbed away. In his book, *Letters from a Flying Officer*, Stuart-Wortley, who went on to command 88 Squadron, recalled the moment: 'For eight minutes on end he fought the eight, while I sat 1,000 feet above, watching with profound admiration this display of skill and daring. The dexterity of his manoeuvring was quite amazing. He was in and out and round about our Scouts, zigzagging like forked lightning through the sky. None of our men could get at him. Then he broke off the fight and darted off to join a flight of Albatri [Rhys Davids thought there was between eleven to fourteen of them], which had appeared upon the scene – and were hanging about some distance away as if hesitating to take part. Placing himself at the head of this formation he again wheeled to the attack. But the Albatri proved themselves unworthy of their would be leader. They followed him to just within range of our machines and they turned away and fled.' It should be noted however, that although members of B and C Flights mentioned that Voss did climb above the fight several times when manoeuvring for position, none claimed he broke off the engagement to encourage the Albatri to join the action. As it was, the German pilots above had their hands full, they were all busy fighting off the wheeling Spads, Camels and Bristol Fighters. Whatever the truth of the matter Voss did not hesitate, he dived straight back into the fight – and a hail of tracer bullets.

Bowman continued: 'His machine was exceptionally manoeuvrable and he appeared to take flying liberties with impunity. I, myself, had only one crack at him: he was about to pass broadside on across my bows and slightly lower. I put my nose down to give him a burst and opened fire, perhaps too soon; to my amazement he kicked on full rudder, without bank, pulled his nose up slightly, gave me a burst while he was skidding sideways, and then kicked on opposite rudder before the effects of this amazing stunt appeared to have any effect on the controllability of his machine.' As Voss was flying nose on to

McCudden, Hoidge saw his chance and fired a long burst into the triplane from the starboard flank. Seemingly this had no result. Rhys Davids, who had flown off to the side of the fight to change the drum on his Lewis gun, now returned to the action. He closed on the German, approached from behind and slightly above, then fired off the entire contents of the fresh Lewis drum. No doubt being kept busy by the others, Voss had not seen Rhys Davids return, and for the first time was now flying in a straight line.

Rhys Davids was still closing, and was scant yards away before Voss turned to get out of the line of fire. Whether already hit in the last few minutes of the fight by one or more of the several hundred rounds that must have been fired at him, or if Rhys Davids had scored on this attack no one knows for certain, but for Voss to fly straight when up till then he had been throwing the triplane all over the sky and thwarting all and every attempt to catch him napping was out of character. Arthur Rhys Davids pulled up to avoid a collision and as he turned so did Voss – in the same direction. Leutnant der Reserve Werner Voss had now made two classic errors: flying in a straight line for far too long and turning in the same direction as his attacker. Rhys Davids thought they would collide and so pulled away to the left. He turned and next saw the triplane gliding west with its engine off, dived again, and got a single shot out of his Vickers gun. Remaining in the glide he reloaded and fired another twenty to thirty rounds into the falling machine before he overshot then zoomed away.

The triplane was now in its death dive. McCudden and Bowman were both watching as it neared the ground. McCudden was well above the fight and Bowman was somewhere below him, no doubt both still shaken by Voss' lightning fast reflexes of but a few moments before. McCudden reported that Voss crashed north-northwest of Zonnebeke, yet curiously he omitted this important detail in his memoirs. He wrote: 'I had temporarily lost sight of the triplane whilst changing a drum on my Lewis gun, and when I next saw him he was very low, still being engaged by an SE marked I, the pilot being Rhys Davids. I noticed that the triplane's movements were very erratic, and I then saw him go into a fairly steep dive and so I continued to watch, and then saw the triplane hit the ground and disappear into a thousand fragments, for it seemed to me that it literally went to powder.' Bowman contradicted this statement, recalling that: 'When near the ground the triplane turned over on its back and hit the ground in this position just our side of the Lines. At no time was the angle of descent greater than an ordinary glide-in to land.' Sometime later Bowman was told the pilot fell out of his cockpit when the triplane inverted, though he said he did not see this happen, nor has any authority ever substantiated this detail.

That Voss gave a good account of himself is evidenced by the damage he inflicted on his adversaries. McCudden noted that he had 'put some bullets through all of our machines'. This was a classic understatement: Hamersley and Chidlaw-Roberts of 60 Squadron had both effectively been forced down and Muspratt had been forced to land at 1 Squadron's field near Bailleul with a seized engine, so was also effectively forced down. Cronyn only just managed to reach his home base at Estrée Blanche; his SE was so badly shot about that it was refusing to respond to the controls and was dangerously close to stalling as he made his approach to the field. After dinner that night he left the squadron mess to look at his gravely wounded machine, which was being inspected for battle damage in the sheds. His mechanics reported the left lower longeron was almost severed, and that another on the right had a bullet hole clean through it. Several internal bracing wires and aileron controls were cut. A tailplane rib was fractured, the two main spars were shot through and there was a neat bullet hole through the propeller. It was subsequently declared a write-off. In all Cronyn counted forty-two holes in his SE and it was only by some quirk of fate that it had not broken up in mid-air. He later wrote to his father, cataloguing his battle scars, and finished by penning a dry witticism: 'Besides these few details, the machine was all OK!' Although he later confessed: 'I went to bed as soon as I had a good look at my machine, but could hardly sleep a wink. I just lay in bed perspiring quarts of liquid, though it was a cold night.'

Before and during the fight Bowman had engine problems and could only manage to limp back to base at a snail's pace. Maybery's machine sustained a broken longeron that necessitated a return to the depot for major repairs. Hamersley had come off worse than anyone else and was lucky to get back at all. Damage to his SE was incredible: the left-hand lower engine bearer was shot clean through, both top planes and the centre section had been hit in many places, spars, wires, ribs, the rudder and a king post were also broken; bullets had gone through the radiator, the water jacket on the left-hand side of the engine, the CC gun interrupter gear, the generator, oil pipes and the propeller. The machine was un-repairable and eventually scrapped. All others involved had amassed numerous holes in various parts of the fabric and spars. Many wings had been riddled and several

bracing wires shot through, yet incredibly not one RFC pilot had
sustained even the slightest personal injury.

In the mess of 56 Squadron that night there was much speculation
about the identity of the triplane pilot. Although opinions varied
as to whether it could have been Wolff, Voss, or even the great
Richthofen himself, there was no doubt in anybody's mind that he
was one of the best, but no news had yet come through from Wing
Intelligence. Over at 60 Squadron's mess at Bailleul a similar
discussion was taking place, though 'Grid' Caldwell had little
doubt as to who the pilot was. Years later he recalled: 'I, for one,
felt it could only have been Voss as I had experienced him before.
He was a terrific chap, and rated easily No. 1, including
Richthofen.'

The celebrations held at 56 were decidedly muted; there was
none of the gay frivolity that usually followed such a hard fought
victory, although as to be expected, Arthur Rhys Davids came in
for a shower of congratulations from his squadron mates, all
accepted in his usual modest manner. Not surprisingly, the
applause came from those who had not been involved in the fight.
Those who had been were in a more sombre mood. After the war
Cronyn wrote: 'During the discussion at dinner, we somewhat
theatrically stood and toasted a very courageous and tenacious
fighter, who could have disengaged himself from the combat at
any time. To detract from the tribute or credit deservedly received
by Rhys Davids is the last thing I would wish to do. I had a great
admiration for him as a brave young man of high moral courage.
On the other hand, it is inconceivable that no one else who took
part in the fight with Voss contributed by gun fire to his defeat. In
truth, such horrible glory must be shared between Rhys Davids
and 56 Squadron.'

Bowman recalled: 'Our elation was not nearly as great as you
might have imagined. It was an amazing show on the part of Voss.
I remember at the time feeling rather sorry it had to end the way
it did. Rhys Davids, I think, was genuinely upset.' This is
evidenced by the comment he made during dinner. Turning to
McCudden, Rhys Davids mumbled: 'Oh, if only I could have
brought him down alive.' An emotion surely felt by all who took
part in the action. In stark contrast to these noble sentiments,
when news of Richthofen's death reached the mess of 74
Squadron in April 1918, a junior officer rose from his seat at table
to propose a similar toast to their gallant foe. Edward Mannock, a
flight commander at the time, was less charitable and refused to

join in. Remaining seated, he coldly expressed the hope that 'the bastard sizzled all the way down'.

At Heule airfield there was also speculation, but of a different kind. Ernst Weigand and the pilots of Jasta 10 milled about on the grass watching as the sun slowly dipped to the horizon. Voss had not returned and the hour was getting late – too late to hope that he was still in the air somewhere over the lines. Bellen and Rüdenberg had returned alone; as usual Voss had left them early on during the sortie and gone off looking for customers on his own. Rüser and Timm were deeply concerned: Leutnant Heldmann said he had last seen their leader heading in the direction of the British lines hotly pursued by an SE5 spitting bullets. Could Voss be down on the other side? Or could the telephone possibly ring at any moment to say he'd landed nearer the Front low on fuel? Ernst Weigand had already telephoned across to Bodenschatz at Marcke to report his Staffelführer missing, and even now JG1's Adjutant was calling other fields hoping for news – but there was none to be had.

Later that night a front line infantry unit reported seeing six Englishmen shoot down a lone German machine that fell on the other side of the lines.

Werner Voss, 'Daredevil First Class', crashed close by an entrenched position known to the British as Plum Farm, three-quarters of a mile northwest of Frezenberg village. The wreckage of his machine was so badly pulverised no one on the ground could positively identify it as a triplane, nor who the pilot was. It was not till the mangled remains were seen by RFC officers on the 24th that the picture became clear. A report was then sent back to 56 Squadron, simply stating the downed machine was a triplane, that the pilot had been wearing the Boelcke collar (the Pour le Mérite cross), and that from papers found on the body, he was identified as the German fighter ace Werner Voss. A number of aviation historians have romanticised that Voss was accorded full military honours and buried with due dignity by British soldiers on the scene. Unfortunately this is not true. His body was recovered from the wreckage and unceremoniously slipped into the nearest shell hole by gunners of 174 Brigade, RFA, 58th Division, under the command of a Lieutenant Keegan. Such was the method of interment for all who died in the front lines, friend and foe alike.

According to Rolf Italiaander, papers found on an unnamed English prisoner of war included a report on the demise of Voss dated 6 June 1918. This was supposedly written by Major C.F.

Gordon, 5th Brigade Headquarters the RFC. The report names Keegan and notes that he was later promoted to captain but then posted to Egypt, which of course is of no consequence to the saga. However, it does note that Keegan buried Voss where he fell, without a coffin and without ceremony, the grid reference of the grave and crash site being given as Sheet 28. map ref: C.24. C.8.3.

There is also an unsubstantiated German claim that Voss survived the crash only to be killed by ground troops, but being shot to death by bloodthirsty Tommies is pure fabrication. During his correspondence with Alex Revell, Douglass Whetton mentioned that he was in possession of a report submitted by a British Divisional doctor who claimed to have made a cursory examination of the body before burial. This revealed Voss had been hit by three bullets. One through the right hand side of the chest, exiting behind the top of the left shoulder, a wound consistent with being shot from low on the starboard flank, and two through the lower part of the back, exiting through the stomach, consistent with being shot from almost directly behind. This suggests Voss was probably already dead or fatally wounded before Rhys Davids fired his last twenty to thirty rounds into the triplane. Hoidge had attacked from the flank and fired some 150 rounds at the German machine, any one of which may have produced the chest wound. This would neatly account for remarks made by Rhys Davids in a letter home. He wrote: 'The aircraft made a slow right hand turn, wing down, I couldn't see the pilot's head, as it seemed to be low in the cockpit.' This clearly indicates Voss had slumped forward and was probably already unconsciousness before the final attack unleashed by the young Eton scholar. By coincidence, some seven months later, Manfred von Richthofen was killed by an almost identical through and through wound to the chest: modern medics are of the opinion that damage and the trauma caused by an injury of this nature invariably results in death within less than a minute. This is of course purely academic; for killed in the air or not, Voss could not possibly have survived the impact of the catastrophic crash that occurred at Plum Farm shortly thereafter.

The triplane's engine, one of the few pieces of identifiable wreckage recovered, was found to be a captured 110 h.p. Le Rhône unit bearing the serial number T6247J. Ironically, this engine had been salvaged by the Germans from a Nieuport 17 lost by 60 Squadron on 5 April 1917. The distinctive comma-shaped rudder, emblazoned with its black crosses, was sent to Arthur Rhys Davids along with the machine's compass as souvenirs. The rudder was something of an eye-opener; contemporary sources noted it had eleven bullet holes in it, though nine of these had been repaired, indicating they had been collected in an earlier engagement. There is also an unsubstantiated story that the bent and buckled engine cowling was among the items sent to Estrée Blanche, and as the spoils of war these trophies were kept in the mess of 56 Squadron whilst it remained on active service in France. The rudder, at least, was returned to England in July 1918 and given to a member of the Rhys Davids family. Sometime in the 1920s it was donated to the Imperial War Museum in London, where it remains to this day, locked in some dusty vault and long forgotten. Whatever became of Voss' most prized possession, his Pour le Mérite, has never been determined. RFC intelligence officers noted he was wearing the award, and one of them may have appropriated it as a souvenir; but it is equally possible that members of the burial party relieved him of his personal effects before anything could be placed in safe keeping. This may seem a heartless act, but making good use of pickings from the field of battle is an age-old tradition in almost any army, and a Pour le Mérite, sold to the right buyer, would undoubtedly have bought Tommy Atkins several tins of cigarettes and a good few beers.

CHAPTER FOUR

AFTERMATH

As on the previous day, Monday 24 September saw yet another misty morning at Estrée Blanche that prevented flying until early afternoon. Twelve miles away at St. Omer, Major General Hugh Trenchard, GOC of the RFC, was having lunch when the news came in: Werner Voss, the star German pilot had been brought down on the British side of the lines by 56 Squadron. This was a major coup for the RFC. German newspapers and magazines had been following the exploits of aces like Voss, Richthofen, Wolff and other celebrities for many months throughout 1917, as had Trenchard, and he lost no time sending his ADC, Maurice Baring, over to 56 to get full details of the Voss action. In his memoirs: *Flying Corps Headquarters 1914-1918*, Baring recorded the following statements made by Rhys Davids, Maybery, Hoidge and James McCudden. From their recollections it is clear they encountered two triplanes during the engagement with Voss. And although their matter of fact comments raised few eyebrows at the time, they have caused consternation among historians and aviation researchers ever since.

Rhys Davids told Baring: 'I saw three Huns attacking one SE; one triplane, light grey and brown, with slight extensions, one red-nosed V-Strutter, one green-nosed Scout. I never saw the green Scout again after the first dive. I then saw four SEs fighting the triplane and the red-nosed V-Strutter. The triplane's top-plane was larger than the middle-plane. The engine was not a Mercedes, but I thought it was stationary. I wasn't sure. It had four guns. I thought the pilot was wearing a black leather flying-cap. Fired six or seven times and then went off to change my drum. The Hun either had armoured plates or else he was very lucky.

'Last dive but one, I went for him. He came from the east. Not quite straight behind, fired from a hundred yards to 70 and emptied a whole drum. The triplane only turned when 20 yards away. I turned to the right, so did he. Thought situation impossible, and that there would be a collision. I turned left and avoided him. I next saw the triplane at 1,500 feet below gliding west. Dived again, opened fire at about 100. Got one good shot out of my Vickers (my Lewis drum was empty) without taking sights off. Reloaded my Vickers. Fired another twenty or thirty rounds. He overshot and zoomed away. Changed drum, then made for the red-nosed V-Strutter and started firing at about 100 yards. The V-Strutter was flying at an angle of about 45 degrees across the front, and I came at him slightly above. We both fired at each other. He stopped firing. I dived underneath him and zoomed up the other side. I saw the V-Strutter about 600 feet below spiralling northwest. I then lost sight of him. During the whole scrap there were 11 to 14 E.A. higher east who made no attempt to fight.' [These were undoubtedly the enemy Scouts noted by Rothesay Stuart-Wortley, the Bristol Fighter pilot.]

From this statement it would certainly appear that Rhys Davids was still somewhat bewildered. Although he had recovered from the trauma of the previous day, he thought that the triplane he had engaged was equipped with four guns and a stationary engine. He also neglected to mention that in his combat report he said the fight lasted some twenty minutes, nor did he corroborate Maybery's sighting of a second triplane. More importantly, Baring seems to have got the impression that it was Voss who performed the magical zoom.

Another example of confusion experienced during the fight was outlined in a letter Second Lieutenant V.P. Cronyn wrote to the author Evan Hadingham in April 1967. He noted: 'The possible uncertainty that appears to exist respecting the Voss scrap, and just where his machine crashed, is probably due to the difficulty of determining exactness of lines or area of no man's land during a fight. This is of course understandable when the engagement takes place at a considerable height. But even when following a plane till it crashed, self-preservation dictated that the pilot kept looking above and behind his machine to avoid being surprised by enemy attack. One gained impressions rather than clearly recording a factual sequence of events. At times, movements were purely instinctive, and made on such split second action that no impression was recorded. For example, Muspratt asked me at dinner. "Why did you fly on your back so much when you were engaged with Voss?" Neither at the time of the fight, nor when Muspratt asked me the question, was I aware of flying upside-down. On the other hand, I did recall passing under Voss and missing the opportunity to pull down my Vickers (*sic*) and fire upwards through the underside of his plane. Here again, though the incident was evident at the time, it did not grow to be a picture in my mind's eye until it came to the surface out of the impression of an opportunity missed.'

Clearly, Rhys Davids was not alone in fighting to gather his wits whilst engaged in combat, yet in a letter to his mother dated the 25th, the old Etonian was less ambiguous. He wrote:

'Dearest Mums,

Just a hurried line before going to the war to thank you ever so much for the book and birthday letter, both of which turned up yesterday! Never mind, two days early c'est rien n'est ce pas. [Arthur celebrated his twentieth birthday on September 26th.] I enclose a telegram I got last night from the dear old general – all for little me, after I had got my nineteenth Hun – a two seater who burnt furiously all the way down. Three nights ago we had the most wonderful fight. After the leader [McCudden] had got one two seater crashed, six of us took on four Huns – two triplanes, their new machines; one of another new type [the Pfalz D III] and one ordinary Albatros. Maybery drove one triplane off, the other was the bravest man I have ever seen and shot two of us about badly – Muspratt and another, before I slew him. He is down in No Man's Land, and we do not know who was in it yet. My hat! He was equally a brave man and brilliant pilot and had the devils luck in not being killed three times instead of once. Meanwhile Voss, the great German star after Richthofen, is down this side in the new type machine and was one of the other two machines – we got all the other three besides the second triplane. I got the great triplane and one other – I thought an ordinary Albatros – and Hoidge – our PM a Canadian who has now got 20 – or rather claimed 20 – got the other. So Voss and the triplane are both to our credit, perhaps both to me, but probably Hoidge's Hun was Voss. Still that will be known soon.

                                        Must fly. Best love A.'

McCudden's statement was brief and to the point, he simply told Baring he saw a triplane crash N.N.W. of Zonnebeke, which is interesting in the light of Rhys Davids' comment about No-Man's-Land. However, given the confusion of the previous day's epic fight, this may mean little or nothing.

Maybery said: 'I saw the triplane and went down after it. It was grey with slight extensions as far as I can remember. It was followed by a green Scout. Someone came and shunted the green Scout. After that I saw Rhys Davids dive on the triplane, followed by a red-nosed Scout. I attacked the red-nosed Scout. I zoomed up over him and couldn't see anything of them. I saw a triplane going east, [Voss was gliding west when Rhys Davids lost sight of him] but this one seemed to be different and green.' This second triplane was almost certainly the machine referred to by Bodenschatz in a letter to Douglass Whetton, and probably the same triplane encountered by McCudden, Sloley and Jeffs on 6 September.

Hoidge said: 'I saw a bright green Hun going down on Maybery's tail at about 3,000 feet, and I fired with Vickers and Lewis at about 100 yards in order to frighten him. When about 30 yards away, the Hun turned south, and was flying directly in the line of fire. I finished a full drum of Lewis gun at about 10 yards from him. He turned right over and went down in a short dive and turned over again. The last I saw of him was going straight down in a dive at about 800-1,000 feet. I stopped following him because the triplane was right above him and I had an empty drum. I flew to the line climbing, and put on a full drum and came back and attacked the triplane from the side as it was flying nose on to McCudden. I attacked him four or five times, but I didn't see what happened after this. I never saw the red-nosed Scout at all. The green man didn't get a chance to scrap.' In his combat report Hoidge stated he fired some 150 rounds from his Vickers and half a drum of Lewis gun ammunition during the fight with Voss, which like Rhys Davids he estimated as lasting twenty minutes.

Hoidge then added to the confusion by affirming only Rhys Davids, Maybery and himself were present when Bowman was close enough to observe Voss fall. Bowman stated that at the moment of the crash: 'The only other machine I saw was that of Rhys Davids. I don't know where McCudden was. He reported Voss down in the German lines which suggests he was somewhere else and perhaps saw the red-nosed Albatros crash.' In fact James McCudden was also nearby, but higher up than the remnants of the patrol. It is of course possible that he may have mistaken the crash of the red-nosed Albatros, which occurred soon after, for that of the triplane, though this is very unlikely as the Albatros made a forced landing, it did not crash to pieces. McCudden is generally accepted as being very accurate in matters of detail. Over the years, several former RFC pilots that served with him commented on his amazing ability to recall times, dates, people and places, months or even years after the event. Moreover, he was one of the most experienced pilots in the RFC, having served since 1913, and had encountered dozens of Albatros Scouts in his time. More than that, he knew the difference between a triplane and a biplane.

Even though the fight took place over one of the most devastated areas of the Front, where intense fighting was taking place on the ground, and where few landmarks were visible among the mass of shell craters and shimmering ground haze, McCudden made no generalisations, in fact he was most specific: he told Baring he saw a triplane crash 'N.N.W. of Zonnebeke' and meant it. This would put the site at little over a mile northeast of the ruined village on the German side of the lines, and just over a mile from where Voss actually fell. However, it should be noted that the area under consideration here is comparatively small: the two Flemish villages are less than two miles apart, and practically on the same line of latitude. Therefore, in the light of Cronyn's statement, a topographical error made in the heat of battle would be perfectly understandable. But there is evidence, albeit unsubstantiated, that adds substance to the keen observations of McCudden: Douglass Whetton noted that a patrol from 57 Squadron reported a crashed triplane seen on the ground close to Zonnebeke on the 24th. This sighting possibly occurred whilst Baring was still at Estrée Blanche making his inquiries; although to be fair he made no mention of it in his book. But if it is true, it could only have been the machine McCudden said 'crashed to pieces, about 6.35 p.m.'

An RFC Intelligence Summary covering the action of the 23rd, and recorded at St. Omer, gives credence to the possibility that a crashed triplane was seen by pilots of 57 Squadron. The text has suffered from several corrections. A number of lines have been crossed through and additional information has been added by hand at a later date. The summary, PRO document A 455, commences with part of the combat report submitted by Rhys Davids, which remains unaltered. There is then a short second paragraph that originally read: 'The triplane destroyed by this pilot has since been seen crashed on the ground east of the lines.' This indicates that a reconnaissance could have taken place, or at least there had been a sighting of a downed machine on the German side. The words: 'has since been seen crashed on the ground east of the lines', were then crossed out in ink and substituted with: 'was flown by Werner Voss who was killed on our side.' This last correction could only have been made after

The famous Sanke postcard portrait of Voss wearing his Pour le Mérite cross. *(Alex Imrie)*

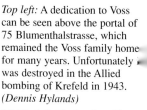

Top left: A dedication to Voss can be seen above the portal of 75 Blumenthalstrasse, which remained the Voss family home for many years. Unfortunately it was destroyed in the Allied bombing of Krefeld in 1943. *(Dennis Hylands)*

Middle left: The brothers Voss. Otto, Max and Werner pose for an early photo taken shortly after the turn of the century. *(Alex Imrie)*

Bottom left: Voss, in an off-duty moment, poses with the motorcycle given to him by his parents on his eighteenth birthday. *(Dennis Hylands)*

Bottom right: Hauptmann Oswald Boelcke, Staffelführer of Jasta 2. *(Alex Imrie)*

Top left: Oberleutnant Stephan Kirmaier, who took command of Jasta 2 on the death of Boelcke. *(Alex Imrie)*

Top right: Manfred Freiherr von Richthofen greets Generalleutnant Ernst von Hoeppner, Kommandierenden General der Luftstreitkräfte (Kogenluft). *(Dennis Hylands)*

Bottom left: Hauptmann Franz Joseph Walz, who succeeded Kirmaier on 29 November 1916. By mid-1918 he had been christened 'The Eagle of Jericho' by those under his command, and had completed more than 500 combat sorties by the war's end. In recognition of this he was awarded the Pour le Mérite, and remained one of the few two-seater pilots to receive the honour. *(Alex Imrie)*

Bottom right: Oberleutnant Karl Bodenschatz, seen here at Avesnes-le Sec in December 1917. He eventually rose to the rank of Generalmajor der Flieger in Adolf Hitler's Luftwaffe. *(Alex Imrie)*

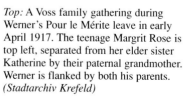

Top: A Voss family gathering during Werner's Pour le Mérite leave in early April 1917. The teenage Margrit Rose is top left, separated from her elder sister Katherine by their paternal grandmother. Werner is flanked by both his parents. *(Stadtarchiv Krefeld)*

Bottom left: Voss concentrates on painting the white border around the red heart that has just been added to the fuselage on his Jasta 2 Albatros D III. Karl Timm

completed the job by encompassing the Swastika motif within a purple laurel wreath. Later still, for the purpose of identification from above, another red heart was added to the fuselage decking aft of the cockpit. *(Alex Imrie)*

Bottom right: The final day of his Pour le Mérite leave. Voss with his parents and younger brother Max beside his gaily-painted Albatros D III at Eglesberg. Note, the red heart has still to be added to the decking aft of the cockpit. *(Stadtarchiv Krefeld)*

Top left: Voss adjusts the strap on his flying helmet before climbing into his machine. *(Stadtarchiv Krefeld)*

Top right: Captain Albert Ball, 56 Squadron, was one of the most respected Allied pilots of the war, a measure of which was demonstrated by the large number of German officers who attended his funeral. *(Dennis Hylands)*

Bottom: Voss, middle row, third from left, with pilots of Jasta Boelcke at Pronville in early May 1917. Another famous German ace, Fritz Otto Bernert, sits to his right. Bernert, who was awarded his Pour le Mérite on 23 April, celebrated the very next day by shooting down no less than five Allied machines in approximately twenty minutes. *(Alex Imrie)*

Top left: Two recipients of the Pour le Mérite stand arm in arm - Voss and his comrade Bernert. Bernert was credited with twenty-seven victories before finally succumbing to the virulent influenza outbreak in October 1918. *(Alex Imrie)*

Top right: Captain Keith 'Grid' Caldwell, 60 Squadron. *(Dennis Hylands)*

Bottom: A line up of Jasta 5 pilots and personnel at Boistrancourt-Suererie in June 1917. Staffelführer Voss is second from the right. *(Dennis Hylands)*

Top: An unusual photo: Voss is seen here mixing with the mechanics and riggers under his command at Boistrancourt.
(Stadtarchiv Krefeld)

Middle: Manfred von Richthofen as a guest in the Voss family home. This photo was taken in June 1917, when Voss and Richthofen shared at least part of a leave together.
(Stadtarchiv Krefeld)

Bottom: Voss and Richthofen on the day the two aces left Krefeld, with Richthofen already dressed to go aloft.
(Stadtarchiv Krefeld)

Top left: A fond farewell before departure. This photograph clearly shows the red heart has now been added to the fuselage decking of the D III, which dates this to sometime between 7 and 26 June 1917. *(Stadtarchiv Krefeld)*

Top right: Voss in the cockpit of the prototype V4 Triplane designed by Anthony Fokker. This photograph was taken at Schwerin, probably in late June or early July 1917, when Voss was charged with evaluating the new fighter. *(Alex Imrie)*

Bottom: Oberleutnant Ernst Wiegand, Adjutant of Jasta 10, (fourth from right), was looked on as a father-figure by Voss but survived him by only two days. Taken in July 1917, when 'Hussar' Ernst von Althaus, (fifth from left), was still in command of the unit. On the extreme right are Leutnants Alois Heldmann and Eric Löwenhardt, two of the unit's most successful aces. *(HAC - University of Texas at Dallas)*

Top left: Pilots of Jagdstaffel 11 photographed at Roucourt airfield near Douai in April 1917. From left to right: (standing) Ltn. Allmenröder, Ltn. Hintsch, Vzfw. Festner, Ltn. Schäfer, (in cockpit) Manfred von Richthofen, Ltn. Wolff, Ltn. Simon, Ltn. Brauneck; (sitting) Ltn. Esser, Ltn. Lothar von Richthofen, Ltn. Kreft. *(Alex Imrie)*

Top right: Captain Edward 'Mick' Mannock, 40 Squadron, KIA 26 July 1918. *(Dennis Hylands)*

Bottom: In July 1917, and before Voss took command of the unit, Jasta 10 were re-equipped with the new Pfalz D III. Here, Ernst Eversbusch , director of the Pfalz Fluzeug-Werkes, chats to Jasta 10's personnel beneath the propeller of a brand-new D III. Alois Heldmann and Eric Löwenhardt are again at the extreme right of the picture. *(HAC -University of Texas at Dallas)*

Top: Another well known, though rarely published, view of Voss standing in front of FI 103/17 at Heule in early September 1917. The moustachioed face painted on the engine cowl was based on the stylistic designs found on Japanese kites. *(Alex Imrie)*

Middle: Anthony Fokker, in the cockpit of FI 102/17, talks with Generalmajor von Lossberg, Chief of the General Staff, IV Armee, while von Richthofen and Hans von Adam, Staffelführer of Jasta 6, look on. This photograph was taken soon after 102/17 and 103/17 were delivered to Marckebeke in late August. *(Alex Imrie)*

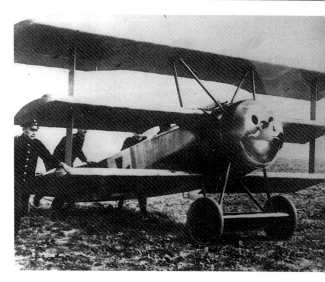

Bottom: Rüser, on the lower starboard wing, and Timm on the tailplane, steady 103/17 seconds before take-off. *(Alex Revell)*

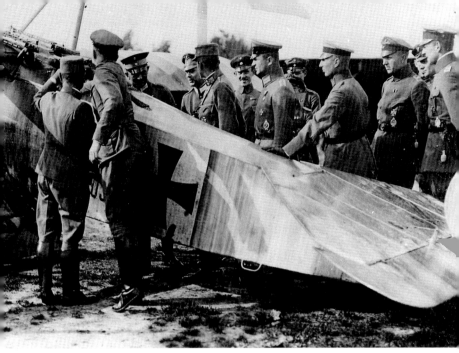

Top: Voss, back to camera, explains the cockpit layout of his triplane to Archduke Karl-Albrecht (heir to the Austro-Hungarian throne) as senior officers and dignitaries look on. Photo taken in September 1917 on the occasion of the Imperial visit to the Western Front. *(Alex Imrie)*

Bottom left: After the demonstration Voss and Karl-Albrecht stroll through a street in the northern suburbs of Courtrai on their way

back to the mess of Jasta 10. Notice the closed curtains and black ribbon on the door handle of No. 66, denoting a death in the family. *(Stadtarchiv Krefeld)*

Bottom right: Kurt Wolff, Staffelführer of Jasta 11. KIA 15 September 1917. Wolff had just become engaged to be married and was promoted to Oberleutnant only three days before being killed in combat whilst flying Richthofen's FI 102/17. *(Alex Revell)*

Unser erfolgreiche Kampfflieger
Oberleutnant Freiherr von Boenigk
673

Top left: The wreckage of FI 102/17 being inspected by German ground troops in a field near the hamlet of Nachtigall, Belgium. Note, there is no evidence of fire damage, which belies the myth that the triplane exploded in mid-air. Wolff's remains were returned to his hometown of Memel, East Prussia, for burial. *(Alex Imrie)*

Top right: Leutnant der Reserve Alois Heldmann, seen relaxing beside his Pfalz D III, joined Jasta 10 on 24 June 1917 and by the end of the war was credited with fifteen victories. *(HAC -University of Texas at Dallas)*

Bottom left: Anthony Fokker with Voss by his side. This Fokker company photograph proves beyond doubt that Voss visited Schwerin sometime between 11 and 22 September 1917. *(Alex Imrie)*

Bottom right: Oberleutnant Oskar Freiherr von Boenigk, Staffelführer of Jasta 4. *(HAC -University of Texas at Dallas)*

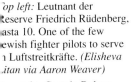

Top left: Leutnant der Reserve Friedrich Rüdenberg, Jasta 10. One of the few Jewish fighter pilots to serve in Luftstreitkräfte. *(Elisheva Litan via Aaron Weaver)*

Top right: Captain Robert L. Chidlaw-Roberts, 60 Squadron. *(Alex Revell)*

Bottom left: This indistinct image is the only known photograph of Lieutenant Harold A. Hamersley taken on the Western Front. The 60 Squadron pilot was the first to be attacked by Voss on the evening of 23 September 1917 and was lucky to survive. *(Norman Franks)*

Bottom right: The last image of Werner Voss captured on camera: standing in front of the sheds at Heule with brothers Max and Otto. Taken on the morning of 23 September. *(Alex Imrie)*

Top: Second Lieutenant Arthur P.F. Rhys Davids, B Flight, 56 Squadron. KIA 27 October 1917 *(Alex Revell)*

Bottom left: McCudden seated in the cockpit of SE 5a, B4863, the machine in which he led B Flight into action on 23 September 1917. *(Alex Revell)*

Bottom right: Second Lieutenant Verschoyle P. Cronyn, B Flight, 56 Squadron. *(Alex Revell)*

Top left: Second Lieutenant Keith N. Muspratt, B Flight, 56 Squadron. Killed in a flying accident in March 1918. Shortly after tangling with Cronyn, Voss put several shots into Muspratt's SE5; fearing his engine would seize at any moment, he was forced to land at 1 Squadron's field near Bailleul. *(Alex Revell)*

Top right: Captain Geoffrey H. Bowman, C Flight, 56 Squadron. *(Alex Revell)*

Bottom: Lieutenant Reginald T.C. Hoidge, C Flight, 56 Squadron. *(Alex Revell)*

Top left: Lieutenant (later Captain) Richard A. Maybery, C Flight, 56 Squadron, KIA 19 December 1917. *(Alex Revell)*

Top right: Squadron commander, later Air Vice-Marshal, Raymond Collishaw, 10 Squadron RNAS, in the cockpit of a Sopwith Camel in the autumn of 1917. *(Terry Treadwell)*

Bottom left: Leutnant Rudolf Wendelmuth, Jasta 8, killed in an aerial collision on 30 November 1917. He told officers at Heule he witnessed Voss being shot down by two 'Sopwiths'. *(Alex Imrie)*

Bottom right: Leutnant Werner Junck, Wendelmuth's Jasta 8 comrade, who apprised Raymond Collishaw of the alternative account concerning the death of Voss. *(Norman Franks)*

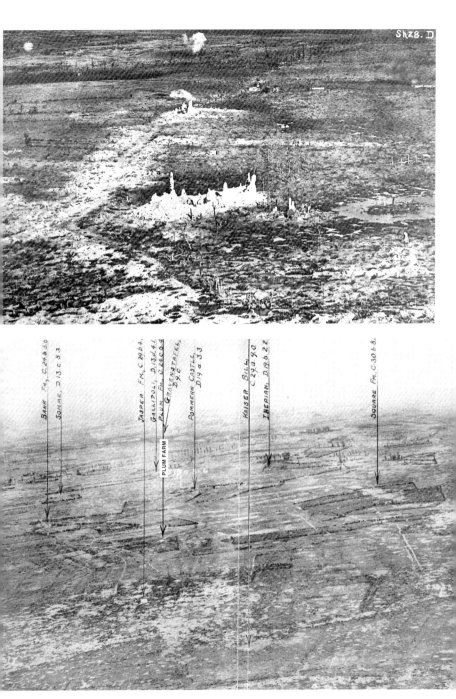

Top: An emotive image: an aerial photograph of the devastation caused by intense artillery fire on and around Zonnebeke shortly after its capture in October 1917. *(Dennis Hylands)*

Bottom: The only known photograph showing the position of Plum Farm, arrowed left of

centre. Voss fell approximately 120 yards slightly north of the farm. The heavily cratered area in the foreground is the German front line. The outskirts of Frezenberg village can just be seen on the upper right hand edge of the picture. *(Author)*

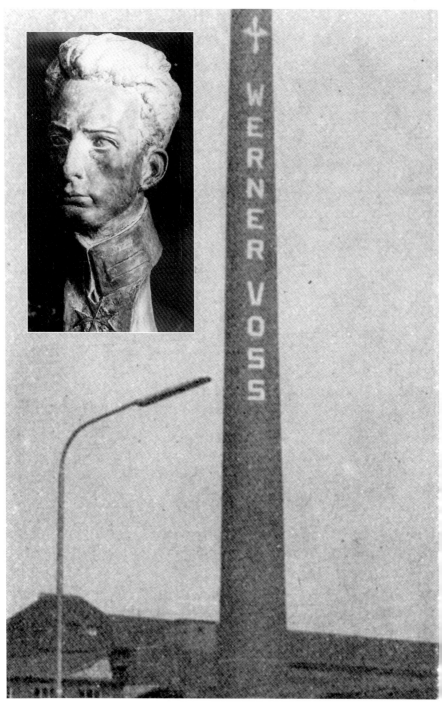

Inset: The bronze bust of Leutnant der Reserve Werner Voss, commissioned by the family after his death, now in the Stadtarchiv Krefeld.

Main photograph: After the war Werner's father Max had this impressive chimney erected at his factory on Geburstsstrasse as a memorial to his son. *(Alex Imrie)*

The Aircraft

Left: The success of the Sopwith Triplane surpassed all expectations. Its outstanding agility and phenomenal rate of climb electrified the German High Command into charging aircraft manufacturers to come up with home-grown triplane designs of their own. *(Terry Treadwell)*

Right: Voss' Fokker Triplane FI 103/17 photographed at Heule field in late August or early September 1917. In this side-on view the streaky camouflage scheme looks decidedly washed out compared to the Dr Is that arrived at the Front in October. *(Alex Imrie)*

Left: Eindecker! Introduced in mid-1915, the Fokker M5K monoplane, given the military designation E.1, was the first true fighting Scout to be equipped with a synchronised forward-firing machine gun. *(Alex Imrie)*

Top: Halberstadt Scouts replaced the ageing Fokker E-type monoplanes in late 1916. Introduced about the same time as the Albatros D II, their slender lines and frail looking tail units belied the fact that they were in fact very robust machines that could withstand long, steep dives and tight manoeuvring. Voss is said to have gained his first four victories whilst flying a Halberstadt. *(Terry Treadwell)*

Middle: The DH2 pusher-type fighting Scout together with the French Nieuport and the FE2b were more than a match for the Fokker and Pfalz E-type monoplanes of 1915-1916. *(Terry Treadwell)*

Bottom: Like the DH2, the lattice tail FE2b was more than capable of dealing with the early German monoplanes, and could hold its own against the new enemy fighters introduced in the autumn of 1916. *(Terry Treadwell)*

Top: The BE2c and later variants formed the bulwark of RFC two-seater reconnaissance squadrons throughout most of the war. Though its inherent stability made it the perfect observation and photographic platform, at speeds that rarely exceeded 75 m.p.h. it was an easy target, and extremely vulnerable to faster German fighters: incredibly, in all models the observer/gunner was placed in the front seat surrounded by a latticework of bracing wires and struts that seriously restricted his field of fire in almost all directions. *(Dennis Hylands)*

Bottom: The two-seater reconnaissance RE 8, introduced in late November 1916, was designed to replace the ageing BE; but even though it was better armed, and some 10 m.p.h. faster, its design and performance was little removed from its progenitor. It had a preponderance to spin at low altitudes and almost always caught fire in a crash. On the plus side, its new configuration allowed for the observer/gunner to occupy the rear seat, from where he enjoyed a greater field of fire. *(Terry Treadwell)*

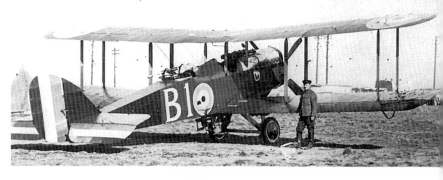

Top: The DH4, designed by Geoffrey de Havilland as a two-seater day bomber and reconnaissance-fighter, was one of the great success stories of British aircraft manufacturing during the war. Well able to defend itself, it became a firm favourite with crews. *(Terry Treadwell)*

Middle: Despite grave concerns about the number of structural failures experienced by Allied airmen whilst flying the little Nieuport 17, it was possibly the best loved of all the Nieuport variants. Armed with a single upper-wing-mounted Lewis gun it could easily outmanoeuvre the heavier German Albatros. The machine shown here was flown by Flt/Lt. Fabian Pember Reeves of 6 Squadron RNAS. Whilst

executing a tight turn in an attempt to shake off an opponent on 6 June 1917 it suffered a catastrophic wing failure, and Reeves was killed in the resulting crash. *(Terry Treadwell)*

Bottom: Compared to the Nieuport Scouts, the SPAD VII lacked manoeuvrability but this was more than compensated for by its greater strength and turn of speed: 120 m.p.h. at ground level. The type is associated with several legendary French aces: René Fonck, Charles Nungesser and Georges Guynemer. *(Terry Treadwell)*

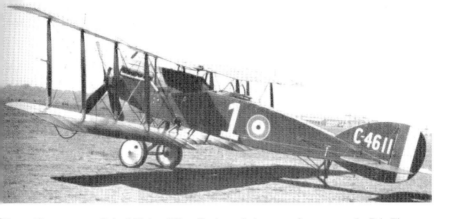

Above: The two-seater Bristol Fighter F2b, affectionately known to its crews as the Bris-Fit, definitely proved its worth in combat, and was considered by many the best fighter reconnaissance aircraft produced during the war by either side. German pilots had a healthy respect for the Bristol and tended not to attack the type unless they had overwhelming numerical superiority. *(Terry Treadwell)*

Middle left: The Sopwith 1¹/₂ Strutter was the first British aircraft to go into action with a forward-firing Vickers machine gun. Coupled with the additional firepower provided by the observer's Lewis gun, the 1¹/₂ Strutter was no easy prey for German fighting Scouts. Many later examples were converted to single-seat bombers; on occasions it was even used as a night fighter. *(Terry Treadwell)*

Bottom left: The SE5 A/4563, seen here, was the third prototype and the first to have the 200 h.p. Hispano-Suiza engine fitted, and as such it embodied all the major features of the first SE5a. This machine was flown by Lieutenant V.P. Cronyn on the evening of 23 September and was badly shot about by Voss. Undoubtedly the best fighting Scout to come out of the Royal Aircraft Factory, the SE5a ranks alongside the F1 Sopwith Camel as one of the two most successful British fighters of the war. Its fine flying qualities, physical strength and performance exceeded all expectations. Both were a match for the Albatros variants that formed the backbone of the German Air Service in 1917. *(Terry Treadwell)*

Top: The Sopwith Pup was the forerunner of the Camel, and a dream to fly. Entered into service with the RNAS in September 1916, its ease of handling and almost unique ability to maintain height in a dogfight made it a firm favourite with pilots who flew the type, though its single synchronised forward-firing Vickers gun was its main shortcoming. *(Terry Treadwell)*

Middle: The Sopwith F1 Camel succeeded the Pup and the Triplane, but had none of their docile handling qualities; it had to be mastered before it could be flown successfully. Yet by the end of the war the Camel had accounted for more enemy aircraft than any other Allied type. *(Terry Treadwell)*

Bottom: A line up of Jasta 10 Pfalz D IIIs at Heule in the autumn of 1917. All appear to be sporting black engine cowlings, when in fact the cowls were painted in the unit colour of chrome yellow. *(Alex Imrie)*

RFC officers had established the crash site was close to Plum Farm on the British side.

Below this, in pencil, was a third paragraph originally crediting Hoidge with the destruction of the triplane – even though the plucky Canadian never claimed a triplane at any time. The first lines referring to Voss, and ending with 'brought down by' were crossed out, but initially read: 'On the 23rd, Werner Voss was shot down in our lines. This pilot is reputed to have shot down forty-six Allied machines, and is believed to have been brought down by 2nd Lieut. R.T. Hoidge: 56 Sqn. This pilot observed an E.A. attacking Lieut. Maybery from behind, so dived at it, and the enemy machine immediately changed its course, flying directly into Lieut. Hoidge's line of fire, who put a full drum of Lewis into it, after which it fell over and over out of control.' No doubt this paragraph owed its origins to the report submitted by the gunners of 174 Brigade who, being unable to identify the badly smashed machine as a triplane, believed an ordinary biplane had been downed near their position. Staff at RFC Headquarters then assumed Rhys Davids had simply confused the biplane with a triplane and associated it with the gunner's sketchy report. It was not until after the wreck was inspected by RFC staff officers that a second report arrived at Estrée Blanche confirming Voss had actually crashed in a triplane. And although Rhys Davids had already been awarded the victory, seemingly RFC Headquarters chose to ignore any other discrepancies and filed the summary as was.

As evidenced in the letter to his mother, Rhys Davids believed the triplane he and his comrades had been fighting fell between the lines. McCudden said the machine he observed crash fell north of Zonnebeke on the German side; though Voss, as correctly reported by Bowman, actually came down on the British side. McCudden said the triplane went into a steep dive before it hit the ground, whereas Bowman stated that at no time was the angle of descent steeper than an ordinary glide-in to land. The two experienced flight commanders were the only 56 Squadron pilots to witness a crash – but did they see the same crash? Judging by their comments it seems there is a very real possibility they did not, but the odds on two triplanes falling within minutes of each other and just over a mile apart, must be pretty long. Even so, the possibility gives credence to the author's theory that the Germans had several of their wonder machines in service at the time – and that they were steadily being shot down. If this is accepted, it brings us to a very interesting question: although the RFC only ever claimed one triplane downed on the 23rd, is it possible that two were actually brought down on the same day?

The only narrative of 56 Squadron's return to Estrée Blanche on the evening of 23 September is to be found in the book written by Lieutenant V.P. Cronyn, whose SE5 had a crocked engine. He recalled that there was little headwind on the way back, and that after a convoluted and hair-raising flight, he arrived at 18.40 hours. Once on the ground, and very shaken by his near death experience, he practically collapsed with relief and was led to a bench by 56's commander, Major Blomfield, where he was given a good swig of brandy. But before Cronyn had pulled himself together he noted the other SE5s had begun to arrive back – led in by McCudden. Rhys Davids was so excited after climbing from his machine he hyperventilated and stammered uncontrollably for several minutes before he could blurt out his story. Blomfield, with two wrecks on his hands could only continue administering the brandy before seeing to the other pilots. Everyone realised they had taken part in and witnessed an epic encounter. They also knew that the confusion experienced in what was in effect a one-sided dogfight, during which they had all sustained some battle damage, was not going to be easy to commit to paper. In consequence minor contradictions appear in their combat reports, though in the main these centre on timings, the numbers of enemy aircraft and types involved and who actually got whom.

The first air war was an education for pilots on all sides, combat in the air was new, and there was no like experience to draw upon, no manual to read and no rules to play by. The lessons of air fighting were learnt by men like Voss and McCudden the hardest possible way – in actual life and death contacts with the enemy. Nerves were strained to the limit every time they went into action, and perception of events during encounters thousands of feet above the tortured front lines were, understandably, and all too often, the product of youthful over-excited minds rather than incontestable fact. As a result, many questions surrounding the death of Voss may never be resolved, but whatever the truth, a young man of unparalleled courage and tenacity died after what was in reality a reckless attack on the experienced pilots of 56. According to Bowman and Cronyn he could have extricated himself from the fight at any time – but Werner Voss chose to fight to the death.

News of the epic fight was finally released to the Associated Press a week after the event, when the following statement was issued: 'British Headquarters in France and Belgium, 1 October

1917. The body of the famous German airman, Lieut. Vosse (*sic*), who was recently reported in a German official communication as missing, has been found within the British lines, and British airmen have already dropped messages behind the German front, giving notification of his death.

Vosse was killed on 23 September while engaged in a spectacular combat with a British airman. He died fighting determinedly and magnificently.'

This was the first official Allied communication noting the death of Voss, although a short item had appeared in *The Times* (London) on 26 September. German intelligence would certainly have picked this up immediately and informed JG1 of the revelation, and yet, if we are to believe the narratives of Bodenschatz and Rüdenberg it took ten days for news to filter through to them at the Front, and this is said to have been provided by the Swiss Red Cross. According to the Associated Press, British airmen had already dropped messages behind the German lines, a common practice to both sides, especially when relating to a pilot of Voss' notoriety, and this would have been affected within days not weeks; yet neither Bodenschatz nor Rüdenberg confirmed this had happened at any juncture. In fact news of the epic fight and the demise of Voss actually reached Krefeld in double quick time: the *Niederrheinische Volkszeitung* ran a notice of his death on 25 September, and the *Krefelder Zeitung* of 7 October included an obituary and a full page of tributes from, among others, Crown Prince Wilhelm, Generalleutnant von Hoeppner, Oswald Boelcke's ageing father, Anthony Fokker and the Kommandeur des Krefelder Husaren Regiments, Oberst Bruno von Gillhaussen, Werner's first commanding officer in the field. It will come as no great surprise to some that any tribute from von Richthofen was conspicuous by its absence.

CHAPTER FIVE

RUMOURS OF AN UGLY DEATH

It is widely believed that Werner Voss had a sweetheart, some say
a fiancée, but she has never been positively identified, and we are
only told that her name was Doris. During the course of his
military career, and like most heroes of the hour, Voss was often
surrounded by admiring young ladies, many of whom had their
photograph taken with him – but was Doris ever among them?
This is a tantalising question which we will now examine in
detail. Despite the destruction of their home at 75
Blumenthalstrasse in 1943 many precious photographs of the
Voss family, their relatives and friends, survived and a goodly
number have been published here and there over the last eighty
odd years. Companies such as Leica and Goerz had developed
small 35mm cameras shortly before the war began, and even
though they were considered expensive toys by the masses, they
were in popular use by 1917. Werner is thought to have acquired
a keen interest in photography and it is quite probable that he or
perhaps a member of the family either owned or had access to one
of these soon to be termed 'pocket cameras'. There is of course no
mistaking his sisters Margrit and Katherine in surviving
photographs – the family resemblance is all too striking. The two
girls and their talented brother appear in several shots together, as
does Richthofen on his visits to Krefeld. Yet, it is almost
inconceivable that Werner and Doris, two young people who by
all accounts were extremely fond of each other, never
demonstrated their affection by posing arm in arm for at least one
family snapshot. So who was she, and did she really exist?

According to Douglass Whetton, Doris wrote to Max Voss in
1918 asking if it were true that Werner had been killed by British
troops on the ground. Just how she got wind of the story is
unclear, but Mathilde Voss was greatly distressed by the

revelation. In the 1970s Whetton contacted a first cousin of Werner, identified only as a Frau Müller. He maintained she still had the original letter to papa Max in her possession as well as other official documents relating to Werner's service career. Unfortunately, if Whetton ever had a copy of the original Doris letter it was lost along with his other papers shortly after his death in 1979.

There is of course no way of knowing if the rumour of Voss being shot to death on the ground really did the rounds, but there is a very good chance that it did, and it probably filtered through from the Front shortly after he was brought down. The rumour almost certainly originated with Alois Heldmann, who was in action above Voss on the evening of 23 September. Heldmann, who also corresponded with Whetton in the 1950s, was adamant Voss survived the crash of Fokker triplane FI 103/17 only to be killed as he extricated himself from the wreckage. In truth, this was not an uncommon occurrence. There are several recorded incidences of downed airmen being shot out of hand by incensed, bloodthirsty ground troops, notably when the pilot had just been strafing their trenches and had perhaps killed a comrade or two. Stories of this nature were rife within the RFC, the Aviation Militaire, and of course Luftstreitkräfte during the war; inevitably, and for propaganda purposes dramatised versions of such murders occasionally appeared in the press at home. So what led Heldmann to this grizzly conclusion? It is entirely possible that in between fighting for his own life he caught sight of the triplane going down in what Geoffrey Bowman described as an ordinary glide into land, and assumed Voss suffered little more than a survivable forced landing, rather than the catastrophic crash that actually occurred. When news eventually filtered through to Jasta 10 that Voss had been killed in the crash Heldmann refused to believe it, and came to the far reaching assumption that the young ace must have been shot to death on the ground – and no doubt made it known to all and sundry. Whatever the truth, Heldmann stuck to this story until his own death in the 1980s.

Seemingly, when Doris realised she had opened a can of worms she wrote directly to Frau Voss on 2 July 1918 refuting the rumour. This single page letter has survived, and although its authenticity has never been challenged, it is considered genuine and is now in the Charles Donald collection. The letter was reproduced photographically in the 1962 booklet by Walter Musciano: *Werner Voss, Germany's Greatest Teenage Ace.*

Doris wrote in a very neat hand:

'Dear Muttchen, [endearment of Mother, but can also mean courageous one], I forgot to write you something about Werner's death. Bellen wrote: "I and Lt. Reudenberg can swear, that Werner hopelessly crashed, having already received the death blow in the air! That Voss was alive on the ground is not true. Please tell me the name of the officer, who made that ugly statement." I believe them both and I think it's mean of this man, to say such a thing. We already worry much about that point and the thought he could still have been alive, opens the wounds again. But I don't believe it and I don't want to believe it. Tell me, how can a human being be so mean and say such a thing and – how can Uncle Max tell you that. No, Werner died in honourable air action and wasn't murdered insidiously. Don't worry any more about that and believe the two eyewitnesses. How is Otto? The boy will be famous – he will avenge Werner and will maintain his promise. Now tell me please, who told you such a thing about Werner, he is --- a rascal!

Kind regards to Uncle Max
for you a kiss.
from your true Doriskind

Here, Doris twice refers to Max Voss as 'uncle', which begs the question is this simply a term of endearment or does it indicate that they were in fact related? If they were, then Doris and Werner would have been cousins and not linked romantically at all, but in fact were simply very close through ties of blood. Perhaps the present author was looking in all the wrong places, but his own research failed to establish any romantic link between Werner and someone named Doris, or indeed any positive bond of kinship: it is simply another perplexing question that requires investigation by a more competent authority. But if one is allowed to speculate, there is the distinct possibility that as a first cousin Doris may have acquired the Voss family papers, and in later life became the mysterious Frau Müller contacted by Whetton in the mid-1970s.

If Mathilde Voss ever sent a reply to the Doris letter it has been lost. However, Alois Heldmann is unquestionably the rascal she referred to, and his statement concerning the whereabouts of other members of Jasta 10 during the Voss fight does suggest that Bellen and Rüdenberg could actually have been close enough to see their Staffelführer shot down. If this is so they may have written to Doris or the Voss family about the incident. On the other hand, in his unpublished memoirs Rüdenberg clearly states that Voss left them almost as soon as they took off from Heule airfield – never to return. Whetton's evidence of a cursory medical examination of the body points to the distinct probability that Voss was fatally wounded during the engagement in the air, though he may have controlled the falling triplane until nearing the ground when, as reported by Bowman, it turned over onto its back. In fact, Voss was almost certainly unconscious or dead before FI 103/17 ploughed into the ground; and it is important to note that at the time, and throughout the remaining months of the war, the precise details of the young ace's death would not have been known to any of the German pilots involved in the fight.

So who was telling the truth? Whetton stated that among the Bodenschatz papers there was a letter from Richthofen that touched on the loss of his protégé Wolff and his friend Werner Voss. Richthofen was clearly incensed about this double blow to JG1, and was particularly angry about the death of Werner. He blamed two pilots, who he said ran out on Voss at a critical moment during the action. He did not name Bellen or Boenigk but he did name Rüdenberg who is said to have been packed off forthwith. Gustav Bellen was wounded in action and invalided out of JG1 on 11 October 1917, Boenigk was given command of Jasta 21 in late October which, depending on the viewpoint, could be seen as a promotion, and in his unpublished memoirs Rüdenberg claimed he was given leave of absence to continue his studies. However, the most likely scenario is that the newly promoted Leutnant der Reserve, who had very little experience of flying fighters, was indeed made the scapegoat, and that his leave of absence was tantamount to dismissal. But if this be so, why would Richthofen privately single out only this very junior pilot for criticism and not the more experienced flyers like Löwenhardt and Boenigk, or of course Heldmann himself; all of whom were circling above and should have gone to the aid of their leader? There was undoubtedly an inquiry into the death of Werner Voss, but at what level, and whether or not punishment was meted out in consequence is another matter. In all probability they were all criticised, but it is unlikely Heldmann would have admitted any admonition to Whetton, or indeed that Rüdenberg would have disclosed the shame of an ignominious dismissal in his memoirs.

CHAPTER SIX

ALTERNATIVE ACCOUNTS
AND CONCLUSION

With the ending of the conflict and the passing of the years, the story of that incredible fight in the war-weary skies over western Flanders became the stuff of legend, a heroic battle against overwhelming odds and a fight to the death worthy of any Wagnerian epic. In consequence the final combat of Werner Voss was the subject of much study by historians and aviation buffs during the early 1960s; many made useful contributions to the ongoing debate, whilst others published their findings as articles that sadly owed more to artistic flair than to actual authenticated fact. As a result baulked out pieces that appeared in aviation journals and magazines revealed little, compounded errors, and served only to shroud the whole Voss saga in mystique. And yet, there is no real mystery to speak of: there can be no question that Voss was shot down and killed on 23 September 1917. It is also a fact that he was engaged by elements of 56 Squadron RFC and subsequently crashed nearby the ruined village of Frezenberg on the British side of the lines. However, and notwithstanding the widely accepted British reports of the action, there is another astonishing account of his final combat derived from the statement of a German pilot who claimed to have witnessed the death of Voss on that fateful September evening. The story came to light during what was termed 'extensive' research carried out by Air Vice-Marshal Raymond Collishaw when preparing his memoirs for publication in the 1960s. At odds with accepted British accounts, Collishaw's version of events came in for considerable criticism and it has subsequently been rejected by many aviation historians as spurious. Needless to say it was never widely publicised, but it would be unjust to dismiss it here without re-examination and analytical comment. More importantly, any study of Voss would be incomplete without its inclusion.

As chief administration officer of Jagdgeschwader Nr. 1, Karl Bodenschatz kept the Combat Wing's War Diary. He was also close to Richthofen and good at his job: the two met in 1916 when both served with Jasta 2. On being given command of Jasta 11, the Red Baron requested the twenty-six-year-old former Bavarian cavalryman for adjutant, and when Germany's most famous war hero was killed in April 1918 Bodenschatz was devastated. In 1935 he published his history of the Richthofen Squadrons, *Jagd in Flanderns Himmel*, a work dedicated to the glorious memory of his former leader and fallen comrades. It is in parts fanciful, and altogether idealistic, but it notes the statement of Leutnant der Reserve Rudolf Wendelmuth of Jasta 8, who claimed to have witnessed Voss being shot down by two 'Sopwiths'. There can be little doubt that the brief statement of this pilot forms the basis of the alternative account, which may well have been disseminated throughout Luftstreitkräfte during the war, but was forgotten thereafter. The story was then resurrected and embellished by Collishaw, a Canadian volunteer, who flew Sopwith Triplanes with the RNAS in 1917 and finished the war as Britain's third highest scoring ace with sixty accredited victories. In 1968 the story appeared in *The Fighting Triplanes*, a scholarly work written by Evan Hadingham, a young but very bright fifth-form schoolboy. Hadingham enlisted the help of Collishaw on his project, and the Canadian not only provided the budding author with a mine of information on the British triplane, both technical and operational, but also wrote the foreword to his book.

Over a period of several weeks there was a regular exchange of correspondence between Collishaw and Hadingham, and the alternative account was frequently mentioned. Collishaw's letters reveal he was obsessed with the idea that Voss had been shot down, not by Arthur Rhys Davids, but by a Sopwith pilot at 18.55 hours British time, some twenty minutes after 56 Squadron had left the scene of the fight. Hadingham, no doubt in awe of the famous ace, had no reason to question his findings, and although he had already prepared a well researched piece covering the Voss saga, he was persuaded to incorporate the alternative account. Collishaw made it quite clear he gave the story much credence, claimed he had unearthed new evidence to support it, and further maintained it had appeared in a number of German newspapers both during and after the war, though he never named any of them.

The account assumes that after the engagement with McCudden and 56 Squadron, Werner Voss, miraculously unscathed, restarted his engine and evaded Rhys Davids by slipping through the lower cloud level that, according to Collishaw, hung at approximately 300 feet on that fateful day. He then flew west towards Frezenberg, a short distance over the lines from Zonnebeke. On the way he met and joined up with two pilots of Jasta 8, Wendelmuth and his Staffelführer, Oberleutnant Konrad Mettlich. Wendelmuth, a fourteen-victory ace who went on to command Jasta 20 but was killed in an aerial collision in November 1917, is said to have subsequently informed officers at Heule, that although he knew the only triplane left in Flanders was attached to Jasta 10, he did not realise at the time it was being flown by Voss. This seems unlikely, as towards the end of September it was fairly well known that Fokker FI 103/17 had been placed at the sole disposal of Voss. However, there are two possible reasons why Wendelmuth may not have known who the pilot was: (1) According to one of Collishaw's letters, Wendelmuth noted the triplane that he and Mettlich accompanied over to Frezenberg did not sport the famous moustachioed face painted on the engine cowl. This implies he knew such a device was used by Voss and would have recognised it immediately had he seen it. [As noted previously, on the day Voss was shot down the cowl on his machine was thought to be a replacement, and was probably not the one usually seen in contemporary photographs.] (2) Wendelmuth was well aware that more than two Fokker triplanes were at the Front during September, as evidenced by a covey of RFC pilots who engaged them in combat.

The story goes on to tell how Voss and his new found companions came in over Frezenberg, where they spotted an SE5 at 18.50 hours. The three Germans lined up to attack, but as Wendelmuth jockeyed for position on the lone SE, two 'Sopwiths' suddenly intervened. As Voss began to tail-chase the first Sopwith, the second closed unseen behind his tail and shot the triplane down at 18.55 hours. [Collishaw probably extrapolated the times given from the incident report returned by Lieutenant Keegan to 174 Brigade headquarters on the evening of 23 September, as they have not been found elsewhere and no times were reported by Wendelmuth or by Bodenschatz.] Wendelmuth is then said to have chased and shot down both Sopwiths behind the German lines: the first over Frezenberg, the second near Ypres. The pilots were claimed to be two Frenchmen named Sellier and Janet, though their units were not given. One was supposedly killed and the other taken prisoner, but never returned to his native France. Then for some unexplained reason, Wendelmuth force-landed his undamaged Albatros in a field east of St. Julien. In later years this part of the tale is thought to have been corroborated by Werner Junck, an ex-member of Jasta 8. He recalled his comrade returned by motorcar late on the 23rd and told him the whole story. Bellen and Rüdenberg, Voss' companions from the outset, who did not figure in the fight with the Sopwiths, and took no part in the fight with 56 Squadron either, are said to have witnessed the action, landed back at Heule airfield and confirmed Wendelmuth's version of events.

Could there possibly be any substance to this alternative account? JG1's War Diary throws little light on the matter. The brief entry for 23 September reads: 'Casualties: Lt. Voss (Jasta 10) took off with his Staffel at 6.05 p.m., [German time] did not return from this flight. Probably crashed fatally on the other side of the enemy lines following air combat. Aircraft: Fokker Triplane.' While the entry for 24 September, also tantalisingly short, does note the involvement of two 'Sopwiths' it reads: 'Jasta 10 reports that, according to statements by Lt. Wendelmuth (Jasta 8), while in air combat with a Sopwith, Lt. Voss was shot down from behind by a second Sopwith. He is said to have crashed just north of Frezenberg (other side).' No time of crash or other details are given, nor does Bodenschatz mention the incident again save for a curious entry in the War Diary for 3 November. This short note is sandwiched between reports on the funerals of three pilots killed in action, and reads: 'No special occurrences. Vfw. Lautenschlar's funeral, 3.00 p.m. Information concerning the downing of Lt. Voss (Jasta 10). Lt. Müller and Lt. Pastor conveyed from St. Joseph's Church in Courtrai, 11a.m. Very hazy.'

As far as can be determined, the alternative account has never appeared in print in any publication other than that offered by Hadingham. Although Wendelmuth was credited with two victories for 23 September, both recorded in the Abschusse as Sopwiths, the authors Franks, Bailey and Guest have identified these 'kills' as a Nieuport Scout [of 29 Squadron] shot down north of Ypres at 12.30 hours and an Airco DH5 [of 32 Squadron] that crash-landed west of Frezenberg at 18.30 hours. The times given are German, and there is no mention of two unlucky Frenchmen. Moreover, there is no proof that Wendelmuth ever claimed to have downed the victors over Voss; this notion has its origins in more recent times and is again linked with Collishaw's twisted theories. Wendelmuth and Mettlich were both killed before the war's end, so on the face of things, this left Bellen, Rüdenberg, and Junck of Jasta 8 to perpetuate the story. It seems Bellen and Junck never wrote of their wartime experiences, but Friedrich Rüdenberg at least made some attempt to do so. Autobiographical notes, letters to his brother and other papers have recently come to light in Israel, where he ended his days, and where the documents have long been preserved by his daughter Elisheva Litan. Rüdenberg's notes, published as an article in the aviation journal *Over the Front*, make no mention of the fight with 56 Squadron, or two Sopwiths, and this is simply because he and Bellen were probably nowhere near Voss when he was shot down; as usual the young ace left his men to their own devices shortly after taking off from Heule. Rüdenberg, who described Voss as totally fearless, rapidly comprehending, and in his conduct a very simple man, wrote: 'Militarily he had the weakness of being an absolute loner. Often he separated from his Staffel over the Front, and did not train us very systematically.' Rüdenberg also recalled: 'In the morning of 23 September, Voss returned from the Front with a looping over the field indicating a victory, [the DH4 shot down in flames over Roulers]. In the evening we flew again to the Front with Voss; again he left us – never to return.'

Rüdenberg went on to state: 'At night we received news from the front line about an aerial combat between one German and six Englishmen, the German crashed. The next morning we all flew over the Front and dropped a letter with a long black-white-red banner requesting notification about the fate of Voss. About ten days later the Geneva Red Cross reported that Werner Voss was found dead after the aerial fight and was buried by the RFC.'

If Rüdenberg is to be believed, his notes make nonsense of the assertion that he and Bellen confirmed Wendelmuth's story on the evening of the 23rd: it is inconceivable that anyone would not have mentioned the death of his unit commander if he had actually witnessed the event. But can we be sure Rüdenberg was correct about the date of the Red Cross report on Voss? He puts receipt of this information at around 3 October; it is an unimportant detail, but did he make a mistake about the month? He was obviously writing from memory and not diary entries. This is borne out by his report on the death of Ernst Weigand, who immediately took command of Jasta 10 on the death of Voss, and who in error Rüdenberg named Weiler. He wrote: 'And so happened just one week after Voss' death another disaster.' In fact Weigand was killed only two days after Voss, which brings into question Rüdenberg's powers of recall. If the Red Cross report was received much later than ten days it could account for Bodenschatz's curiously short note in the JG1 War Diary for 3 November.

Raymond Collishaw probably never knew or ever heard of

Rüdenberg, who died aged eighty-one in Israel on 4 May 1977. Even so, there can be little doubt that during the period he was researching for his own memoirs, *Air Command, A Fighter Pilot's Story*, Collishaw did make contact with someone who knew about the events of 23 September 1917. But who this was, and whatever 'new evidence' he uncovered concerning this alternative version of the Voss engagement, he never personally recorded it for posterity, which is somewhat surprising considering the enormity of the subject. If the Canadian knew the story in the 1960s there would have been more than ample time for him to have included it, if only in passing, in his memoirs which were published in 1973 – but he never so much as touched on the matter. Instead, he left it to a young and impressionable schoolboy to do the honours.

So who provided Collishaw with his new evidence? Almost certainly Werner Junck, who ended the First World War as a Leutnant but rose to the rank of General Leutnant in the Second World War, went on to command all German fighter squadrons in France from October till December 1943 then retired at the end of 1944. In later life he became Chairman of the German Fighter Pilot's Association, where Collishaw made his acquaintance, and from whom he got the story. Given the mountain of evidence provided by British sources, it would seem Junck's rendition of the final combat of Voss is based primarily on aviation gossip and little else. It can safely be assumed that a story of sorts did the rounds within Luftstreitkräfte shortly after Voss was brought down, and that Wendelmuth's brief statement, either by chance or design, was later embellished by Junck or others to explain the mysterious Sopwiths. It is also fair to assume that whatever the true facts of the matter, the story was mulled over in the mess of Jasta 8 many times on those cold winter nights of 1917, and no doubt helped along by the occasional warming cognac or fiery schnapps it grew with the telling, thus spawning the controversy. The account then passed into the realms of aviation fantasy, and has been perpetuated ever since by a generation who have all too readily accepted it as gospel.

Air Vice-Marshal Raymond Collishaw was one of a rare breed: an exceptional air fighter and a very brave man. So why would a pilot of his reputation give so much credence to a version of the Voss engagement that was at very best questionable? Throughout his correspondence with Hadingham it is clear the Canadian was at pains to refute the accepted British evidence. In fact his letters reveal he had something of a fixation about the prowess of 56 Squadron, and in particular that of James McCudden. It has often been said, though never written, that with the passing years Collishaw grew to resent the fact that of the top four RFC pilots of that first great war in the air he was the only one not to have been awarded the Victoria Cross, Britain's highest decoration for valour; yet he was credited with more victories than McCudden who bagged fifty-eight enemy machines and made fourth place. Towards the end of his life, and having stumbled upon an alternative version of events, Collishaw formulated the hypothesis that the pilots of 56 Squadron, unable to bring Voss down during their ten-minute engagement, only claimed they had in order to save face. This is of course a contentious theory, but if a different version of the story, and in particular the one postulated by Collishaw, had come only half way to being accepted it could have added considerable weight to what can only be described as a perverse hypothesis designed to vilify McCudden. To this end he went to a lot of trouble to convince Hadingham he was dealing with factual information based on thoroughly researched evidence, yet from his correspondence it is obvious very few verifiable facts were forthcoming. At times the Canadian offered several conflicting scenarios in which he suggested the Sopwith pilots could have been any two of several Allied flyers shot down on 23 September 1917: English, French, or even Belgians. However, despite the time spent sifting through casualty lists and other air service records, it became increasingly difficult to pin down who the Sopwith pilots could possibly have been. In the end young Hadingham was charged with the daunting task of sorting it all out, and by a process of elimination reasoned, that if the story was to be believed at all, they could only have been Frenchmen: simply because there were no British Sopwith losses reported in the Ypres Salient for 23 September that can be matched for type, time, or location.

After being badgered to come up with a solution, Hadingham finally offered the very plausible explanation that, even though he was an experienced air-fighter, Wendelmuth must have mistaken SE5s for Sopwith Camels. In the event he was not far wrong. At the time the Germans thought the SE5 was a product of the Sopwith Company, and the term Sopwith was widely used by pilots of Luftstreitkräfte to describe almost any British types they were unsure about. Hadingham was well aware of this, but despite making every effort to obtain complete details on Sellier and Janet, what they were actually flying on the day, or where and when they were shot down, he drew a complete blank. Recent research reveals that two Frenchmen of Escadrille C28, Adjudant

Sellier and Lieutenant Janet, were indeed shot down behind the German lines on 23 September, and yes they were flying a Sopwith, but this was a 1½ Strutter engaged on a reconnaissance mission: the only recorded French two-seater loss of the day. Neither were taken prisoner as both men were killed: Sellier was the pilot and Janet the observer. What is more, their Sopwith was not brought down within the Ypres Salient, it fell in the Nancy Sector, some 220 miles south-east of Paris.

By the autumn of 1917, nine RFC and four RNAS squadrons had been re-equipped with the F1 Sopwith Camel; McCudden noted there were a number of them milling around in the vicinity of the Voss fight. That evening of Sunday 23 September saw aerial activity over the Salient seldom matched for intensity, and in the skies above Frezenberg machines of all types were locked in individual, flight and squadron strength combats at altitudes ranging from little more than ground level right up to 8,000 feet or more. Therefore, it would have been quite remarkable if Voss and his companions did not run into Sopwiths at some point before being attacked by 56 Squadron.

In deference to an ageing air-fighter, Evan Hadingham published a story bereft of any hard evidence. Sadly, it sparked a controversy that tarnished an otherwise valuable work of reference. It would also appear that it dampened Hadingham's keen young spirit: to this day he has never written another word on that first great war in the air. But in the final analysis, the credibility of Collishaw's alternative account hinges on just one vitally important factor, the assertion that Werner Voss evaded Rhys Davids, only to be shot down twenty minutes later at 18.55 hours British time. Herein lies the flaw: Alex Imrie, acknowledged as one of the greatest living authorities on German First World War aviation, calculated that as Voss glided west after the final attack by Rhys Davids his engine was in all probability dead. Fokker triplanes had fuel tanks that held between seventy-two and eighty litres of petrol, depending on the model. The British intelligence report on FI 103/17 estimated the fuel tank capacity at a generous eighteen gallons [eighty-two litres]; given normal throttle settings this was just about enough for a sortie lasting approximately one and a half hours. As Voss fought the SE5s of 56 Squadron, he had already been in the air for all of that time, and by then the triplane must have been at the absolute limit of its endurance. Having taken off at 17.05 hours British time, patrolled the Zonnebeke sector for an hour and twenty-five minutes, fought an epic battle that lasted at least ten minutes –

during which time he would almost certainly have been flying at full throttle – Voss could not possibly have restarted his engine and remained in the air for an additional twenty minutes before crashing at 18.55 hours.

And what of the British account? Yes, the combat reports of British pilots who took part in the Voss action do raise a number of questions, but these can be explained. What can be determined with a high degree of certainty is that Geoffrey Bowman, nursing a crocked engine, saw everything from his vantage point 2,000 feet above Frezenberg, as evidenced by his interview with Alex Revell. If nothing else, and but for minor inconsistencies in his 1942 narrative, the pertinent images of that September evening of 1917 remained indelibly etched on the memory of Bowman for more than fifty years: he watched Rhys Davids dive on the triplane as it glided west with its engine apparently off; he saw his young squadron mate pour a murderous fire into the stricken German machine as it went through 1,000 feet, and in the last few seconds he saw it turn over on to its back then crash on the British side of the lines, the crash site later being identified as close to 174 Brigade's position near Plum Farm. No other triplane was brought down on the British side that day. And the identity of the pilot was later confirmed by 9th Wing Intelligence, so there can be no doubt whatsoever, Bowman saw and correctly reported the Voss crash.

Yet another controversial story, that is still doing the rounds, concerns Second Lieutenant G.R. Baynton of 32 Squadron, who was flying an Airco DH5 on 23 September 1917. Notwithstanding the lack of any concrete evidence, several historians give credence to the possibility that Baynton could have shot Voss down after he evaded Rhys Davids. Collishaw was of this opinion at one point, but there is no real proof that Baynton took part in any fight with Voss, either before or after the German ace tangled with elements of 56 Squadron. At some time during that fateful day Baynton, who had little experience of air fighting, was shot down behind the German lines and taken prisoner; though, despite an extensive search funded by Raymond Collishaw in the 1960s, no details of where, when and how he came to grief have ever surfaced. Alex Revell conducted the search on behalf of Collishaw, and was at pains to find the details he desperately needed to support this theory, but no information could be gleaned from air service records or the PRO, other than the fact that Baynton survived the rigours of a POW camp and returned to England after the war, only to be killed in an automobile accident in 1926. However, the question can now be resolved. Wendelmuth was credited with the shooting down of a DH5 at 18.30 hours German time (17.30 hours British time), and as there was only one DH5 lost in combat that day, there can be little doubt that his victim was Baynton. This indicates that the 32 Squadron pilot was on the ground and probably already in captivity an hour before 56 Squadron engaged Voss. Leaving this aside, if Baynton did have anything at all to do with downing one of Germany's most famous aces he had almost eight years of life ahead of him in which to say something about it, but he did not. Despite the lack of any substantive evidence, and by now clutching at straws, it is clear from Collishaw's letters he believed the Baynton story and tried to guide Evan Hadingham in that direction, but the young author was not of the same opinion and can be forgiven for finally opting for the two French airmen.

As demonstrated here, Collishaw's various theories and the so-called alternative account were primarily based on his vivid imagination and what can only be described as wishful thinking. As such they must be discounted.

A more credible scenario lies within the reports, letters, and memoirs of those that took part in the Voss fight. It is of course based on the more widely accepted British accounts, but by adding hitherto unpublished information to the equation it may be possible to get a little closer to the actual sequence of events. The unpublished information is found among letters exchanged between the historians Alex Revell and Douglass Whetton, who corresponded with Karl Bodenschatz in the 1960s and early 1970s. Tragically Whetton was killed in an automobile accident in 1979 and during the winding up of his estate almost all his private papers were lost; among them a priceless photograph album acquired from JG1's former adjutant. Despite extensive searches Whetton's private papers and Bodenschatz's album have never been found. (Their importance is inestimable to first air war research, and greater efforts ought now be made to locate them.) Fortunately, Alex Revell recently discovered a scattering of Whetton's letters among his own correspondence and made them available to the author. These provide snippets of relevant information obtained from Bodenschatz and other pilots who were connected with the events of 23 September 1917. From the evidence recorded by Whetton it is clear Bodenschatz made several astonishing revelations concerning the deployment of German triplanes and the circumstances surrounding the death of Voss; not least of which is the fact that a second triplane was in the vicinity of the fight and that it was being flown by

Oberleutnant Oskar Freiherr von Boenigk, acting Staffelführer of Jasta 4. Karl Bodenschatz described this machine as dirty grey, green-brown in colour and said it had been delivered to Marckebeke on 5 September. This was almost certainly the same triplane that fired on Sloley on 6 September, and the machine seen eighteen days later by Maybery and Rhys Davids.

True to form, on the evening of Sunday 23 September 1917, and shortly after lifting off from Heule field, Voss left his Staffel to their own devices. Although there is no conclusive proof, on this occasion it was almost certainly to keep a prearranged rendezvous with Boenigk; this would be in keeping with the author's long held theory that, whenever practical, the first German triplanes operated together as a matter of policy. The two Staffelführers then patrolled JG1's sector of the Front for perhaps an hour or more. What happened during that time may never be come to light, or whether the two German aces were involved in any engagements or not. Boenigk certainly made no victory claims for the evening of the 23rd and Voss was never to get the chance, but a little before 18:25 hours British time the young Rhinelander teamed up with at least one bright green Albatros Scout, sporting a red engine cowl. (In his 1942 narrative Bowman recalled there were two.) In statements to Maurice Baring, Maybery and Rhys Davids both confirmed Voss was accompanied by at least one red-nosed Scout, neither said there were two, but Rhys Davids did note 'a new type' in attendance. He did not describe it but it was most probably the green Pfalz DIII engaged by Lieutenant Hoidge.

The three Germans then began stalking a number of SE5s they had seen heading west. What Boenigk was doing at this juncture is uncertain, but he must have been close by, perhaps cautiously watching events unfold.

The SEs being stalked by the Huns were of course 60 Squadron machines led by Grid Caldwell, with Hamersley and Chidlaw-Roberts of A Flight bringing up the rear. The colour scheme of the red-nosed Albatros Scout suggests it could have been from Jasta 8; if this is correct then it is likely that Wendelmuth was at the controls. Unfortunately the identity of the pilot flying the 'new type' Scout remains a vexing question, if indeed a 'new type' was ever present. Douglass Whetton was convinced there was and believed the pilot was Hans Waldhausen of Jasta 37, but Waldhausen was flying an Albatros DV on the day he was shot down and, according to Franks, Bailey and Guest, this did not occur until 27 September 1917 – four days after the Voss fight.

The term 'new type' naturally brings the Pfalz DIII to mind, and Hoidge claimed a victory over what was later to be confirmed as a Pfalz, but the author can find no records of any Pfalz Scouts being brought down on the day, and Jasta 10 reported no losses other than Voss.

It is difficult to place Mettlich within this scenario unless he was actually flying the machine that disappeared. If he was then he and Wendelmuth must have joined up with Voss much earlier than stated by Collishaw or Junck, certainly earlier than 18.25 hours British time, and sometime before Voss was attacked by elements of 56 Squadron. The correspondence, memoirs and combat reports of those on the British side who took part in the action clearly note one of the escorts disappeared almost as soon as the fight began and did not return. This could have been Mettlich, but what became of Jasta 8's Staffelführer is uncertain; earlier in the day he and Wendelmuth had each shot down a Nieuport Scout of 29 Squadron. Wendelmuth's victim fell north of Ypres, and Mettlich's south of Kruistraat. Both 'kills' are recorded in the Abschusse as being downed at 12.30 hours German time, but what involvement Mettlich had in the Voss engagement has never been clearly established; Collishaw's correspondence throws no light on the matter, it makes only brief reference to him being with Wendelmuth on the day.

Boenigk must also be a candidate for the disappearing Scout, for if nothing else he never fully committed to the Voss fight: Rhys Davids noted that Maybery drove a triplane off, and this could only have been Boenigk, who by his own admission cleared east shortly after the action began and returned to his field unscathed. Bodenschatz noted his lacklustre performance and his excuse for returning to Marckbeke in a letter to Whetton, who translated the Jasta 4 pilot's unashamed comments as: 'Hell, the sky was full of damned English, so I stuffed my nose down and cleared off.' Some historians believe this cavalier attitude and blatant disregard for the fate of his more famous comrade accounts for why Boenigk was transferred out of JG1 in October 1917, despite the fact there is no corroborative evidence to support the theory. Although Richthofen had a reputation for dumping pilots at the drop of a hat, no matter what their rank, he made no great song and dance about having Jasta 4's Staffelführer removed. And yet, it is improbable that Boenigk would not have been censured in some form or other, unless of course a 'closing-of-the-ranks' crept in somewhere; Richthofen and Boenigk both hailed from Silesia and were practically neighbours. Added to the fact that they were of the 'genteel' class, it would have been extremely embarrassing to all concerned had any condemnation of his actions, or indeed his honour, been made public. Given the loss of one of Germany's finest air fighters, Boenigk's comments to Bodenschatz were at best insensitive, but it would be uncharitable to condemn an otherwise experienced pilot without consideration of the circumstances he faced on the evening of 23 September. His departure from the scene of the fight may well have been influenced by factors other than the sky being full of damned Englishmen: by this time his triplane must also have been very low on fuel and, more importantly, Voss had already acquired an escort of at least one red-nosed Albatros Scout, possibly two, and of course the 'new type' mentioned by Rhys Davids.

Rudolf Wendelmuth reported that Voss had been shot down by a Sopwith and, according to Junck, shortly thereafter Wendelmuth landed in a field near to St. Julien, just under two miles northeast of Frezenberg. Until now it was widely believed the red-nosed Albatros Scout involved in the Voss fight was being flown by Vizefeldwebel Karl Menckhoff of Jasta 3, a line of thought that has led to considerable deliberation among historians over the years; but Menckhoff's memoirs have recently been found in Germany and he makes no mention of the Voss fight or being anywhere near it on the day. In the light of this information there can be little doubt that the pilot of the Albatros attacked by Rhys Davids shortly after Voss fell was indeed Wendelmuth, and despite Junck's assertion that his comrade's machine was undamaged, it is unlikely a pilot of his experience would have put down on uncharted ground unless he was obliged to do so.

Interestingly, Alois Heldmann, whose statements are also mentioned in Whetton's letters to Revell, gave no credence to the Wendelmuth story whatsoever. Heldmann claimed to have been one of several Jasta 10 pilots milling around above the fight, others are said to have included Kühn, Löwenhardt, Bender and Bellen, all flying Pfalz D IIIs. By all accounts they were having a pretty rough time of it; the Camels and Spads above the Voss action were keeping them very busy indeed, and there was no possibility of going to the aid of their Staffelführer. Heldmann noted that Wendelmuth, Mettlich, Schwanz and Francke of Jasta 8 were also in the area, but were driven off by twelve Spads. He also recalled that shortly after the Voss engagement Wendelmuth, Franke and Schwanz were all shot down by SE5s, not Sopwiths. What is more, Heldmann firmly believed Voss was not killed in the air, but survived the crash only to be shot to death by ground troops, and, as noted earlier, his conclusions became the foundation of the rumour communicated to the Voss family in 1918.

In the final analysis, there can be no doubt that Voss was shot down by elements of 56 Squadron, and no one else. There were no mysterious Sopwiths involved in his final engagement and he was not killed by bloodthirsty troops on the ground. Instilled with the invulnerability of youth, his confidence in Fokker's marvellous little triplane and, up till then, his ability to out fly anything the Allies could put into the air, he had reckoned without running into pilots of like mettle and simply took on more than he could handle. At some point during the action he doubtless realised his mistake and, even though he had been flying on his nerves for more than a month, he had not lost that impetuous, headstrong streak that did so much to shape his military career; like the Teutonic warriors of legend he chose to fight to the end – and paid the ultimate price.

At the time of his death Werner Voss was just twenty years old, whilst Arthur Rhys Davids was a bubbly boy of nineteen who celebrated his own twentieth birthday three days after their epic encounter. Just over a month later, on the chilly morning of 27 October 1917, Arthur met his own nemesis. He was almost certainly, and perhaps fittingly, shot down by Leutnant Karl Gallwitz, acting Staffelführer of Jasta Boelcke. McCudden, who was on leave at the time, was deeply shocked by the news, and just as he was to pen a most fitting epitaph for Voss in his memoirs, he did the same for his young protégé. He wrote: 'If one was ever over the Salient in the autumn of 1917 and saw an SE fighting like Hell amidst a heap of Huns, one would find nine times out of ten that the SE was flown by Rhys Davids.' Arthur fell on the German side within five miles of where Voss lay buried, and like his worthy opponent has no known grave. It has recently been claimed that the Voss grave was found after the war, that his remains were removed to the Kameradengrab at Langemarck, (the war cemetery where over 45,000 German dead are interred), and that his name is commemorated on memorial panel number 63. It is true that the name of Pour le Mérite Flieger Werner Voss appears on the panel, but like the British memorial at Arras, which bears the name of Lieutenant Arthur Rhys Davids, these panels are dedicated to the fallen that have no known grave. In the weeks that followed the deaths of these two young men there was fierce fighting in the Ypres Salient, the battle for Passchendaele Ridge raged on well into November, and both their graves, like so many in that war to end all wars, were lost amid the mud and countless shell holes of what was then the Western Front.

56 SQUADRON COMBAT REPORTS

Discerning aviation enthusiasts question all official and unofficial documents relating to the first air war as a matter of course, and quite rightly so. Only by this means can the truth be ascertained; yet such documents occasionally reveal ambiguities that leave facts open to the interpretation of the individual. The combat reports of 56 Squadron pilots involved in the Voss fight of 23 September 1917 are a case in point. Minor inconsistencies are apparent, but in the main these concern times given for the offensive patrol, the identification of enemy machines engaged, and the location of the Voss crash site. These anomalies can now be rationalised, though it should be noted the analyses offered here are those promulgated by the author, and are by no means conclusive.

It is now widely accepted that the Voss engagement commenced somewhere between Poelkapelle and Westroosebeke on the German side of the lines, drifted in the direction of Zonnebeke, then ended with the fatally wounded (or already dead) German ace gliding across the lines to crash northwest of Frezenberg. Rhys Davids thought the triplane came down between the lines, though at the time the opposing armies were scant yards apart, and it would have been difficult for anyone to determine where the actual front line was. Whether McCudden saw FI 103/17 dive into the ground or not, he reported seeing a triplane crash to pieces north of Zonnebeke; only Bowman correctly reported the crash on the British side. To explain these contradictions it is important to picture the scene and consider the moment. Zonnebeke is almost due east of Frezenberg, and less than two miles distant. Both villages had been pulverised by artillery fire and were reduced to little more than heaps of rubble, the area between the villages was heavily pockmarked with shell craters and there was a ground haze that made observation lower down difficult. Bearing in mind that all pilots involved were fighting for their lives, it is not difficult to appreciate that they had neither the time nor opportunity to accurately record their positions and in all probability identifying the site of a crash whilst engaged in combat was down to an educated guess. Moreover, any one who has ever been aloft in a light aircraft will tell you that, given the perspective, it is difficult to recognise even well known landmarks from the air at relatively low altitudes, so the confusion over the location is perfectly understandable.

The inconsistencies concerning times given by pilots of 56 Squadron for the patrol can also be explained. At first glance timings appear to contradict each other. However, it should be noted that RFC pilots did not normally record the duration of a patrol, but noted the times when either combats in the air commenced and ended, or noted the actual time spent in enemy air space after crossing the lines. This of course differed for each pilot, which undoubtedly led to the variations. Bowman and McCudden's Flights both took off at the appointed hour of 5 p.m. (17.00 hours), and are so recorded in the Squadron Record Book. Both Flights were back on the ground and accounted for by 7 p.m. (19.00 hours).

The following narratives, with the exception of those dated 6 September, were all submitted within hours of the Voss fight. They not only provide details of the encounters and events of the day but also illustrate that perception was pretty much down to the individual and the particular circumstances in which they found themselves. The SE5s of B and C Flights took off separately, formed up and climbed for height on the British side before venturing into enemy territory. Rates of climb would have varied for each machine, and this accounts for the time spent reaching patrol height before crossing over: B Flight crossed the lines at 8,000 feet at around 5.40 p.m., while C Flight continued to climb, passed through the heavy cloud bank, and crossed at 10,000 feet between 5.45 to 6.00 p.m. Both Flights patrolled their sector of the Front separately, and it was to be close on forty-five minutes before they joined forces again for the Voss engagement.

For the sake of conformity the reports reproduced here have been tidied up, and where an occasional indecipherable word occurs in the original text the author has provided the probable word in parenthesis. The author's comments are also inserted in parenthesis, this without affecting the substance of the text. Annotations added by 9th Wing intelligence and cataloguing marks used by the Public Record Office in London have been omitted. Other than this, the original narratives and punctuations have not been altered in any way.

Report of Capt. J.B. McCudden M.C.

Combats in the Air
1
Sheet No.1. Capt. J.B. McCudden M.C.

Squadron: 56   Date: 23/9/17
Type and No. of Aeroplane:
  SE.5 No. B.4863   Time: 5.40 – 6.30pm
Armament: Vicker's and Lewis   Duty: Offensive patrol
Pilot: Capt. J.B. McCudden M.C.   Height: 8,000ft.-3,000ft.
Observer: none.
Locality: Houthem – Zonnebeke

Narrative

Crossed lines at 5.35pm. at 8,000ft. over Bixschoote, and was unable to go over any higher owing to thick layer of clouds. Patrolled Houthulst-Becelaere.

At 6.00pm. saw a two-seater E.A. coming N. just S. of Houthem at 3,000ft., I dived followed by SE.5 formation and attacked E.A. from above and behind him at 160 yards.

I closed to 20 yards and finished a short burst from both guns. I had to do a climbing turn to avoid running into E.A., and looked over my fuselage and saw E.A. dive vertically into the ground just N.E. of Houthem.

At 6.25 I saw an SE.5 being driven down W. of Poelkapelle by a hostile triplane.

An SE.5 and I then engaged this triplane who left the SE.5 and for the next 10 minutes E.A. triplane fought about 5 SE.5s with great skill and determination and owing to his skill and manoeuvring did not offer an easy target.

I saw this triplane after being engaged very low by an SE.5 (Lt. Rhys Davids) dive into the ground just N. of Zonnebeke, and crashed to pieces, about 6.35pm.

Second Page   23rd Sept.

LICHTERWELDE-LEDEGHEM-INGELMUNSTER

Heavy and accurate [Anti-aircraft fire].
Many formations seen and engaged.
1 E.A. 2-seater destroyed N.E. of Houthem by Capt. McCudden.
1 E.A. Triplane destroyed N.E. of Ypres Salient by Lt. Rhys

Davids.

1 E.A. Scout driven down out of control by Lt. Rhys Davids N.E. of Ypres Salient.

Capt. McCudden returned at 7pm
Lt. Rhys Davids   do.
Lt. Young   do.
Lt. Jeffs   do.
Lt. Cronyn   do.
Lt. Muspratt landed at No. 1 Squadron.

[McCudden gave his patrol heights as 8,000 feet (maximum) to 3,000 feet (minimum), which is consistent with his being slightly higher up when he witnessed Rhys David's final attack on Voss, after which he saw a triplane crash north of Zonnebeke.]

Report of Capt. G. H. Bowman M.C.

Combats in the Air
1

Squadron: 56   Date: 23/9/17
Type and No. of Aeroplane:
  SE.5 No. B.2.   Time: 6 – 6.30pm
Armament: V & L
  [Vicker's and Lewis]   Duty: Offensive patrol
Pilot: Capt. G. H. Bowman M.C.   Height: 10,000ft.-1,000ft
Observer: none.
Locality: Westroosebeke

Narrative

Crossed lines at 10,000ft. above clouds, dived down through clouds at Houthem. Saw 6 E.A. S. of Houthulst Forest, dived and attacked, fired about 50 rounds from both guns but without effect & E.A. cleared east.

Then saw 4 E.A. below us over Westroosebeke, dived on one E.A. and fired 40 rounds from Lewis and 10 rounds from Vickers, both Guns stopped. Six or seven E.A. came out of the clouds on top of us, I turned west with 5 E.A. on my tail. Lt. Maybery drove them off. Later saw an E.A. triplane and 1 E.A. V. Strutter S.W. of Westroosebeke, dived and attacked. Several SE.5s. attacked E.A. triplane, I fired about 10 rounds Vickers and 50 Lewis. Both guns stopped also engine. Engine picked up, and went in a series of jerks. I could not keep my height and crossed lines at 1,500ft. and at 500ft. at Ypres Canal, engine picked up & I returned to Aerodrome.

<u>Stoppages</u>

Vickers Gun. Chute blocked by empty cases.

Lewis Gun.   An ill fitting drum which caused bad loading.

<u>Second Page</u>   23rd Sept.

LICHTERWELDE-LEDEGHEM-INGELMUNSTER

Many formations seen and engaged.

1 E.A. Scout driven down out of control N.E. of Ypres Salient by Lt. R.T.C. Hoidge M.C.

1 E.A. 2-seater driven down out of control N.E. of Dixmude by 2/Lt. S.J. Gardiner.

Capt. Bowman returned at 7pm

Lt. Hoidge   do.

Lt. Maybery   do.

Lt. Gardiner   do.

Lt. Taylor   do.

[Bowman's report is consistent with him being lower down than McCudden. This indicates he was in a better position to note where the front lines were and where the Voss triplane actually fell, but see also the 1942 narratives of G.H. Bowman and R.L. Chidlaw-Roberts.]

<u>Report of 2/Lt. A.P.F. Rhys Davids M.C.</u>

Combats in the Air

2

Squadron: 56   Date: 23/9/17

Type and No. of Aeroplane:

   SE.5 No. B.525.   Time: 5.45 – 6.35pm

Armament: V and L (Vicker's

   and Lewis)   Duty: Offensive patrol

Pilot: 2/Lt. A.P.F. Rhys Davids. M.C. Height: 8,000ft.-1,000ft.

Observer: none.

Locality: W. of Westroosebeke-Houthem

Narrative

Crossed lines with formation and flew over clouds for some time, ground was not visible and we returned and came down west of Ypres. Then patrolled over lines at 8,000ft. under clouds under very heavy and accurate A.A. fire.

After some manoeuvring at 6pm. leader dived on an E.A. 2-Seater (D.F.W.) making N. from west of Comines.

Leader got very close and fired as E.A. turned N.E. Smoke came out of centre section and I dived very steeply and fired a short burst into E.A. which was diving N. into cloud. E.A. engine stopped and he turned west and dived slowly into the ground about 1,000 yards E.N.E. of Houthem.

Rejoined leader and climbed to 7,000ft. and patrolled area again. At 6.25pm. saw an SE.5 being attacked by an E.A. triplane and one red nosed Albatros Scout. Our second SE.5 formation now appeared and for 20 minutes, leader, myself, Lt. Hoidge and Lt. Maybery engaged the two and one other Scout west of Westroosebeke. About 11 other E.A. awaited us higher and further east, but did not come down as there were six Spads & four Camels protecting us very well.

The other E.A. Scout now vanished but the red nosed Albatros and the triplane fought magnificently. I got in several good bursts at the triplane without apparent effect and twice placed a new Lewis drum on my gun. Eventually I got past & slightly above the triplane and made for it & got in a whole Lewis drum and a corresponding number of Vickers into him.

He made no attempt to turn until I was so close to him I was certain we would collide. He passed my right hand wing by inches and went down. I zoomed. I saw him next with his engine apparently off, gliding west. I dived again and got one shot out of my Vickers. However I reloaded and kept in the dive, I got another good burst and the triplane did a slight right hand turn still going down. I had now overshot him (this was at 1,000ft) zoomed and never saw him again. Immediately afterwards I met the red nosed Scout who was a short way south east of me. I started firing at 100 yards, the E.A. turned and fired at me. At 50 yards range I finished a Lewis drum & my Vickers stopped so I dived underneath him and zoomed.

Sheet No. 2.

When I looked again I saw the E.A. spiralling down steeply out of control.

I am quite sure he did not clear east.

I then fired white light and returned. E.A. having all cleared far east.

[Rhys Davids noted the triplane gliding west, which would conform to Bowman's comment on the angle of descent being no more than an ordinary glide-in to land, but is inconsistent with McCudden's comments.]

<u>Report of Lt. R.S. Maybery M.C.</u>

Combats in the Air

3

Squadron: 56	Date: 23/9/17
Type and No. of Aeroplane:	Time: 5.40 – 6.30pm
SE.5 No. B-1	Duty: Offensive patrol
Armament: Vicker's and Lewis	Height: 10,000ft.-3,000ft.
Pilot: Lt. R.S. Maybery, M.C.	
Observer: none.	
Locality: Westroosebeke	

Narrative

Patrolled with SE.5 formation crossing lines at 10,000ft. above clouds. Dived down through clouds coming out over Houthem. Flew north and just S. of Houthulst Forest, dived to attack 6 E.A. I attacked and got a good burst with my Vickers gun but my Lewis stopped. Another E.A. dived at me & I turned and again opened fire with my Vickers but it stopped. I broke away and cleared my guns, E.A. cleared east.

Later dived to attack 4 E.A. over Westroosebeke but saw 3 E.A. come out of the clouds to attack Capt. Bowman, so turned and attacked firing a short burst with both guns into one E.A. which went down steeply east. The other 2 E.A. attacked me but Lt. Hoidge drove them off. Later saw E.A. triplane and red nosed Albatros V. Strutter north of Westroosebeke, so dived to attack and got a burst from both guns into the triplane.

Zoomed and found the V. Strutter on my tail so did a climbing turn and again dived at the triplane and again fired with both guns but Lewis stopped. Both E.A. turned at me but 2 SE.5s turned and attacked them and a general mêlée ensued during which I fired a separate burst at the triplane with Vickers gun but he seemed invulnerable. Saw Lt. Rhys Davids attack the triplane & the red nosed V. Strutter attacked Lt. Rhys Davids, so attacked the red nosed V. Strutter firing my Vickers. Overshot and could see nothing of the V. Strutter, the triplane or Lt. Rhys Davids, but E.A. Scouts appeared so turned west and climbed. Joined Lt. Hoidge but could see no E.A. in the sky so returned.

Stoppages

Lewis Gun. No. 4   Vickers Gun. No. 4

Lewis Gun. Handle just above safety catch stopped.

[Interestingly, Maybery made no mention here of two triplanes being in the vicinity, or that he saw one going east. His final patrol height of 2,500ft indicates he was a little lower down than McCudden when Voss fell, but he never witnessed the crash.]

Report of Lt. R.T.C. Hoidge M.C.

Combats in the Air

2

Squadron: 56   Date: 23/9/17

Type and No. of Aeroplane:

  SE.5 No. B.506   Time: 5.40 – 6.30pm

Armament: Vicker's and Lewis   Duty: Offensive patrol

Pilot: Lt. R.T.C. Hoidge, M.C.   Height: 10,000ft.-2,500ft.

Observer: none.

Locality: Westroosebeke

Narrative

Flew north and S. of Houthulst Forest, dived and attacked 6 E.A., fired about 10 rounds Vickers and it stopped (No. 4). Zoomed to correct it and when I turned E.A. were far east.

Later I dived with formation on 4 E.A. over Westroosebeke.

We were then attacked by 6 E.A. from the clouds.

Fired Vickers and Lewis at one E.A. on tail of Lt. Maybery. E.A. dived steeply east.

Later saw one bright green E.A. going down on tail of Lt. Maybery, E.A. was flying west, but when I fired, turned south and was then flying directly in my line of fire.

I put full drum of Lewis into E.A. and he went down absolutely out of control. E.A. rolled over, nose dived and turned on his back and then went vertically down. I was then at 2,500ft. and saw him till he was about 1,000ft., going down absolutely out of control. When I saw E.A. triplane above, there were 3 light green E.A. at first and after only 2, I went west and changed drum climbing. Returned and attacked triplane which was flying end on at Capt.

McCudden. I fired about 150 rounds Vickers and $1/2$ drum Lewis during the fight which lasted about 20 minutes.

[Hoidge's E.A. out of control was undoubtedly the green Pfalz D III he was later credited with. There is no conclusive proof, but in the light of comments made by Alois Heldmann the three light green E.A. above were probably all machines from Jasta 10.]

Report of 2/Lt. S.J. Gardiner

Combats in the Air

4

Squadron: 56   Date: 23/9/17
Type and No. of Aeroplane:
  SE.5 No. B. 508   Time: 5.40 – 6.30pm
Armament: Vicker's and Lewis   Duty: Offensive patrol
Pilot: 2/Lt. S.J. Gardiner.   Height: 10,000ft.-1,500ft.
Observer: none.
Locality: Houthulst Forest

Narrative

Crossed lines at 10,000ft. S. of Ypres, turning S.E. The SE.5 formation dived, during dive I lost formation & seeing a machine going E. in 2nd. film of clouds I put my nose down thinking it to be one of our machines but getting fairly close saw it to be a 2-seater E.A., I attacked it, E.A. turning N.E. and zig-zagging, Observer shooting at me. After my first burst Observer ceased firing and collapsed in his cockpit.

E.A. continued zig-zagging, side slipping, N.N.E., I followed shooting in bursts to 1,500ft where E.A. went completely out of control, turning on his back and then going into a slow spiral with nose down. As soon as I saw E.A. out of control I zoomed and climbed due west crossing line N. of Dixmude at about 5,000ft.

[Clearly, having lost the rest of C Flight in the dive, Gardiner's report has no bearing on the Voss engagement.]

The following three reports relate to 56 Squadron's first encounter with Fokker Triplanes on 6 September 1917. These reports clearly indicate that McCudden, Sloley and Jeffs all saw two triplanes operating together.

Report of Capt. J.B. McCudden

Combats in the Air

1

Squadron: 56   Date: Sept. 6th 1917
Type and No. of Aeroplane:
   SE.5 No. B.4863.   Time: 6.30 – 7.40 am
Armament: Vicker's and Lewis   Duty: Offensive patrol
Pilot: Capt. J.B. McCudden   Height: 11,000-3,000ft.
Observer: none.
Locality: Houthulst Forest, Zandvoorde.

DESCRIPTION OF NEW-TYPE E.A.
TRIPLANE:-
This machine has stagger single struts, middle plane larger than
top, and bottom plane shorter than the middle plane, and chord of
the planes decreases from top to bottom planes. The wings are
staggered outwards from the machine. 'Halberstadt' type rudder
with no fin. No dihedral. Stationary motor.

FOKKER:-
This has slight dihedral and stagger, very sharply turned Morane-
type wings, tail piece, and rudder. Bottom plane smaller than top.
Am uncertain whether it has 'V' struts or parallel. Am also
uncertain whether engine is stationary or rotary.

Narrative
Crossed lines at 11,000ft at Bixschoote, and saw numerous E.A.
Scouts over Houthulst Forest, including two enemy triplanes, and
a new type Fokker biplane.
   Indecisive fighting took place here, during which Vickers would
not fire a shot owing to defect in C.C. gear.
   I now observed two 'V' strutters going north over Poelkapelle
and dived followed by SE.5 formation. I secured favourable
position behind one E.A. and opened fire at 100 yards. My Lewis
fired a shot and stopped, due to hard extraction, and whilst putting
Lewis [right] E.A. spun and got away. Later I dived from 8,000 to
3,000ft. [over] Zandvoorde, and attacked one of four 2-seater E.A.
After finishing [last] drum of Lewis at E.A. he dived east into a
fringe of mist under [?].

[Unusually, McCudden was wrong about the triplane's engine

being stationary; yet this was an easy mistake to make considering its cowling, which unlike those found on many Allied machines almost enclosed the entire engine. The Fokker with the Morane-type wings was in fact later identified as the new Pfalz D III, which had recently been brought into service.]

Report of Second Lieutenant R.H. Sloley

Combats in the Air

3

Squadron: 56   Date: Sept. 6th 1917
Type and No. of Aeroplane:
   SE.5. A 4865   Time: 6.30 – 7.40am
Armament: Vicker's and Lewis   Duty: Offensive patrol
Pilot: 2/Lt. R.H. Sloley   Height: 11,000-4,000ft.
Observer: none.
Locality: Houthulst Forest

DESCRIPTION OF two new-type HOSTILE MACHINES INCLUDED IN NARRATIVE BELOW and UNDERLINED.

Narrative

We found E.A. Scouts (about ten) above us over Houthulst. Our lack of height and the position of the sun made it difficult to attack. I turned and engaged an E.A. Scout (a biplane of "Fokker" type, with Fokker tail and Albatross [sic] type planes, sharp and cut away at wing tips, and grey colour). I fired a drum at this machine, which turned east and flew under the remainder of E.A. formation, in which was at least one triplane (I thought I saw two), the remainder being ordinary "V" strut Albatrosses. The triplane had a long top plane, a shorter middle plane, and the bottom plane shortest. The chord of the planes appeared to decrease similarly. The fuselage was of large square section, and the rudder large, partly balanced, and without fin, and was coloured yellow and brown.

As I turned away from engaging the first E.A. Scout a triplane dived on me firing at long range, appearing from the large amount of tracer smoke to have two guns. It showed little determination in spite of a very favourable position.

We dived upon four E.A. 2-seaters at 7.40am. at 4,000ft. south of Houthulst Forest. I closed on one, as Capt. McCudden left it owing to gun trouble, and fired a drum from Lewis (Vickers failed with air lock in C.C. gear) at close range. This 2-seater went into a slow right hand spiral, as I zoomed away and did not try to fly further east or to flatten out. I watched it from 4,000 down to about 1,000 ft. and it had not straightened out.

The two-new-type E.A. described appeared quite equal to the Albatross Scout in performance at that height 11,000 ft.

Patrolled low over lines until 7.50, seeing no more 2-seaters, and re-crossed lines at 8,000 ft.

[The triplane that fired at Sloley from long range was almost certainly the machine delivered to Marckebeke on 5 September 1917. It was being flown by Oberleutnant Oskar Freiherr von Boenigk of Jasta 4 at the time, who, in all probability, was familiarising himself with the type, and dared not risk a full-blooded encounter with an SE5 at this juncture.]

Report of Lt. C.H. Jeffs

Combats in the Air
2

Squadron: 56	Date: Sept. 6th 1917
Type and No. of	
Aeroplane: SE.5 No. B.586.	Time: 7 – 7.30am
Armament: Vicker's and Lewis	Duty: Offensive patrol
Pilot: Lt. C.H. Jeffs	Height: 10,000ft.-1,000ft.
Observer: none.	
Locality: Poelkapelle	

Narrative

We crossed the line at 10,000ft north of Ypres and saw numerous E.A. Scouts, including triplanes. I saw the leader dive on two E.A Scouts at Poelkapelle. I dived on one and drove him down to 1,000 ft, and after putting a good burst into him with my Vickers gun saw him crash east of Poelkapelle Station. I turned back to the line, and had four more E.A. above me, but they did not attack. Later I picked up the SE.5 formation.

[Jeff's use of the plural clearly indicates he had seen more than one triplane.]

THE 1942 NARRATIVES OF
G.H. BOWMAN & R.L. CHIDLAW-ROBERTS

Geoffrey Bowman ended his service in the Royal Air Force in December
1941 with the rank of group captain. He made a lot of friends during his
career. Seemingly he kept in touch with many, and on the evening of
30 July 1942 he had a meeting with an old acquaintance, Squadron
Leader Hector Bolitho, who was then attached to the Air Ministry. For
some undisclosed reason Bolitho asked Bowman's permission to publish
an account of the Voss action based on his personal recollections.
Initially Bowman was not so keen and objected to the idea; however, he
must have had a change of heart as he wrote to Bolitho the very next day
enclosing his typewritten account of Voss' final combat.

By coincidence, prior to meeting Bolitho, Bowman had been
contacted by Group Captain Ira 'Taffy' Jones, who, whilst collecting
material for his memoirs, *An Air Fighter's Scrap Book*, had been sent an
account of the Voss fight penned by Captain Robert Chidlaw-Roberts,
the 60 Squadron pilot attacked by Voss moments before McCudden's B
Flight appeared on the scene. Jones, who served with 74 Squadron
during the Great War, had asked for criticism of this narrative, but
Bowman never sent a reply, instead he passed a typewritten copy of
Chidlaw-Roberts' rendition on to Bolitho together with a copy of his own
account. As with details gleaned from 56 Squadron combat reports, and
indeed other 'official' sources concerned with the epic engagement, the
narratives reveal a number of contradictions that over the years have led
to flawed interpretations of the circumstances surrounding the German
ace's final combat that do not conform to generally accepted British
versions of the event.

Bowman's typewritten covering letter to Bolitho:

Squadron Leader Hector Bolitho,   Heston Aircraft Coy.
Air Ministry,   Heston,
King Charles Street,   Middlesex,
London W.C.2.   31st July, 1942.

Dear Bolitho,
I was very pleased to see you again last night, if only for a short time.

I was not serious about my objection to you printing the episode of twenty odd years ago. I quite agree that some people read them with interest and that they do some good, in fact, a great deal of good.

I am enclosing an account of the death of Voss. I had better explain what the various documents are.

Taffy Jones sent me an account of Voss's death, which had been sent to him by Chidlaw-Roberts, and he asked for my criticisms. I wrote my account but never sent it to him.

The sentiment expressed is perhaps not a very wise one at the moment, as you will see we were all genuinely upset at having killed such a fine fighter. One point of interest is that Chidlaw's account which purported to be that of an eye witness is certainly not the account of an eye witness, as you will see that he thought Voss was in a bi-plane. Such a mistake could not be made.

Yours Sincerely,
Geoffrey Bowman.

[He then added a handwritten post-script.] If you can make any use of this in any form please do so. We preferred 'albatri' as the plural of Albatros to the verbal atrocity of 'albatroses.'

Bowman's typewritten reply to Ira Jones, which was never dated, completed or sent:

Dear Taffy,
I was very pleased to hear from you and also get news of Chidlaw. I will give you my recollections of the scrap with Voss before reading Chidlaw's because the incident was some considerable time ago and I do not wish my memory to be either contaminated or assisted by another account.

[It can only be assumed that at this point Bowman penned his own narrative.]

I will now read Chidlaw's account and see how it compares with mine.

I have done so. The comparison is not favourable; when we arrived on the scene what we saw was undoubtedly a rout. We had never seen the blue triplane before but we had heard that 60 Squadron had and were definitely scared of it, perhaps for a very good reason.

I have now read the account in the official history. I see that Voss is referred to as being 'dazzlingly elusive'. It sickens me to see what was an epic fight garnished with such journalistic garbage. The use of the word 'elusive' gives the impression that Voss was trying to escape from danger (*see* Oxford Concise); nothing is further from the truth.'

Chidlaw-Roberts' account of the Voss action originally sent to Ira Jones:

About Voss' last scrap. We, that is 60 Squadron, were returning from an evening O.P., I think all three flights were out, anyway I was leading the rear one, as we were getting near the lines I saw a dozen or so huns up above us to the east with a biplane* a little below them, soon the latter started to dive on my tail man Hammersley [*sic*]. My flight at once turned to engage him, Hammersley I believe getting off a few rounds at Voss before he had to spin away with his engine and machine pretty well shot up. This happened in about three seconds by which time I was having a crack at the biplane, he was on my tail in no time and put a good few holes in my machine before the rest of the squadron arrived and took him on, it was about this moment I believe that 56 Squadron arrived and administered the coup de grace. I did not see the actual end nor as far as I can remember did anyone else in either squadron, anyway that evening Rhys Davids, Barlow and I think Bowman came over and wanted to know if we could confirm anything. I believe that they knew they had got an Albatros and thought they had got Voss. I seem to remember hearing that Voss' body fell the other side of the lines and his machine this (our side**) also that the Le Rhône engine was one of a 60 Squadron machine that had been shot down.

I rather think Grid*** was leading 60 Squadron and probably Soden and Pope amongst others were in the show. Hammersley is an Australian and I don't know his whereabouts, anyway any one of the survivors of the squadron of that time will know about it.

It was a very fine effort on Voss' part, I imagine that he was relying on help from the rest of his formation which however with the exception of the one did nothing.

[On the copy sent to Bolitho Bowman was added the following hand-written comments to the starred notations in the text.]

* Voss was in a Triplane. G.H.B.

** Voss' body fell our side and was buried our side. It was from papers in his pocket that we found out that it was Voss. G.H.B.

*** I am certain that it was not Grid Caldwell who was leading 60 Sqdn. on that particular occasion. They would not have been chased out of the sky had he been leading. G.H.B.

You will note Chidlaw makes no mention of a triplane. He cannot therefore have seen Voss. G.H.B.

Clearly, Bowman was not impressed with Chidlaw-Roberts' narrative, and was less than charitable about his use of the term 'biplane.' In an age when the vast majority of aircraft were of the biplane configuration it seems somewhat absurd to condemn a comrade for using the term in error, when it is patently obvious he actually meant to use the word triplane. At this point readers can be forgiven for questioning the uncompromising stance adopted by Bowman, who was possibly attempting to establish his authority on the subject of the Voss fight. Ironically, and as incredulous as it may seem, even after 20 years had passed Bowman had yet to discover that it was in fact 'Grid' Caldwell leading 60 Squadron 'on that particular occasion.'

Bowman's account of the Voss action as sent to Hector Bolitho. The narrative is dated 31 July 1942, the day after the two met, but it was almost certainly written earlier for the benefit of Group Captain Ira Jones. It is not signed, and it was never sent to Jones:

On the afternoon of 23rd September 1917, I and two members of my flight, Hoidge and one other, went out on offensive patrol. According to my Log Book we had two scraps which appear to have been indecisive, before joining up with McCudden, Rhys Davids and Barlow. We joined forces as the air was pretty thick with Huns. I then saw about six SE5s being chased back to our lines by three Huns; two green Albatri with red noses and a sky-blue triplane. We were quite low down and near the lines. The SE5s passed under us and we attacked the three Huns. A dogfight ensued and my recollections from then on are almost entirely personal. One of the Albatri almost at once disappeared. I don't think he was shot down; I think he went east. The second Albatros was shot down about a mile on the other side of the lines after having put up a very good show. We were then about 2,000 feet and a mile behind the

German front line. This left Voss alone in the middle of six of us which did not appear to deter him in the slightest. At that altitude he had a much better rate of climb or rather zoom than we had and frequently he was the highest machine of the seven and could have turned East and got away had he wished to, but he was not that type and always came down into us again. His machine was exceptionally manoeuvrable and he appeared to be able to take flying liberties with impunity. I, myself, only had one crack at him; he was about to pass broadside-on across my bows and slightly lower. I put my nose down to give him a burst and opened fire, perhaps too soon; to my amazement he kicked on full rudder without bank, pulled his nose up slightly, gave me a burst while he was skidding sideways, and then kicked on opposite rudder, before the results of this amazing stunt appeared to have any affect on the controllability of his machine. Rhys Davids was then on his tail. Whether or not, to have a crack at me, this flat turn of Voss's enabled Rhys Davids to get there I cannot say, but I should like to think so, as I doubt if any SE5 could have got onto the tail of the triplane had Voss not had his attention distracted, but Rhys Davids was there with his prop boss almost on Voss's rudder; at that particular moment Voss and Rhys Davids were flying west; Rhys Davids was firing and Voss was flying nose-down and straight for the first time in the whole scrap. Rhys Davids remained on his tail and then turned away. When near the ground the triplane turned on its back and hit the ground in this position just our side of the lines. At no time was the angle of descent steeper than an ordinary glide-in to land. Later we heard that Voss had fallen out when the machine was upside down; I did not see this. I do not think the whole thing can have lasted more than five minutes; although, as you know, one's impression of time on these occasions is very unreliable. It was an amazing show on the part of Voss. I remember at the time feeling rather sorry that it had ended in the way it did. During the whole of this fight a formation of 6 or 8 Albatri were above us; they made no attempt to come down. Had they done so, the result might have been very different. On my return I found that we were all fairly well riddled, but whether, in the case of myself and my two other machines this was by Voss, or as a result of the two previous scraps we had been in, I cannot say. It was not until later that night that we heard that it actually was Voss in the triplane. Our elation was not nearly as great as you might have imagined. Rhys Davids, I think, was genuinely upset.

Over the years Bowman's account has appeared in several publications, though for reasons best known to the authors concerned the first paragraph, and other lines of the text, are rarely included. The first paragraph clearly indicates that C Flight had arrived on the scene whilst Voss and his two companions were still stalking the 60 Squadron machines, and this must have been shortly before B Flight had engaged the German ace. If this is correct then C Flight also arrived in the vicinity a little before 18.25 hours British time.

The longer, and final paragraph details the fight and conforms to much of what has been said previously; yet several glaring errors are apparent. One is immediately struck by Bowman's failure to identify Richard Maybery as the 'other' member of his flight. Maybery was an exceptional pilot who had been in France since June and was well known to Bowman; he not only played a key role in the Voss engagement but went on to become a twenty-one-victory ace before being killed in action in December 1917. But the anomalies do not end here, Bowman also failed to mention two other members of his own Flight, Taylor and Gardiner, both of whom took off with their commander but became separated early on.

Bowman then goes on to mention another famous 56 Squadron pilot, Leonard Barlow, who did not in fact accompany either flight on that fateful day. Nor was 56 Squadron informed of the triplane pilot's identity that same night; it was not until the 24th that a signal arrived confirming that, from papers found on the body, the pilot had been identified as Voss. Ordinarily one could forgive these seemingly innocuous errors; after all, Bowman was writing about events that had taken place twenty-five years previously, but in the light of his dismissal of Chidlaw-Roberts' account, which was also written many years after the Voss engagement, readers have every right to be judicious. These errors clearly indicate that Bowman's own powers of recall in 1942 were not so good as he liked to think.

In essence the two narratives are not too dissimilar. They do diverge here and there and they do leave questions unanswered, but both clearly indicate that Voss was shot down by elements of 56 Squadron. The fact that there are a number of anomalies in the accounts simply demonstrates yet again that memory is based on perception of the individual, governed by the circumstances they found themselves in at the time, and does not always reveal the truth. There is nothing unusual about this: it is an established fact that out of a dozen witnesses to a road traffic accident 50% are likely to give conflicting statements as to 'exactly' what happened, even when questioned immediately after the incident. In summation, if nothing else, these two accounts of the Voss engagement make interesting contributions to the saga. In their own minds the authors undoubtedly aimed at the truth, but when considered in tandem their apparent contradictions serve only to add fuel to the on-going debate concerning the circumstances surrounding the death of Werner Voss, and of course indicate the distinct probability that certain details of long-accepted British accounts of the action are not so iron-clad as some of us would like to believe.

WERNER VOSS – SERVICE RECORD

Translated from the original German document of 20 May 1917, the date Voss took command of Jagdstaffel 5. Later postings have been gleaned from established historical sources. Words in parenthesis are those of the author.

First & Family Name:	Werner Voss.
Religion:	Evangelical Lutheran (Protestant).
Place & Date of Birth:	Crefeld, Prussia, April 13, 1897.
Occupation/Residence:	Businessman, Merchant or Accountant, Crefeld.
Marital Status:	Single
Parents' Occupation/Residence:	Father, Max Voss, Manufacturer. Mother, Mathilde Voss, née Pastor. Crefeld, Blumenthalstrasse 75.
Date on entering service:	November 16, 1914. Enlisted Hussar Regiment No. 11.
Service 1914-15 [Eastern Front]:	November 30, 1914 – July 26, 1915. To active Regiment. January 27, 1915. Promoted to PFC [Russia]. May 18, 1915. Promoted to Corporal [Russia].
Service 1915-17 [Western Front]:	May 20, 1915. Returned to Replacement Squadron [Hussars Paderborn]. July 15, 1915. Declared unfit for further Infantry & Cavalry Duty.

July 1915. To Crefeld [on leave].
August 1, 1915. To FEA 7,
Cologne.
September 1, 1915. To Pilot
Training School, Crefeld.
February 12, 1916. To FEA 7,
Cologne, 1st Company.
March 2, 1915. Promoted to
Sergeant Major.
March 10, 1915. To
Kampfstaffel 20.
Kampfgeschwader IV.
March 30 – May 11, 1916. Battle
of Verdun.
May 31 – July 5, 1916. Reserve
Officers Course, Lochstadt
Camp, East Prussia.
July, 1916. Battle of Somme.
October, 1916. Balkans
[Bulgaria].
September 9, 1916. Promoted
Lieutenant of Reserve.
November 2, 1916. Somme.
[Seconded to Jagdstaffel 2?].
November 21, 1916.
Permanently ordered to
Jagdstaffel 2, shot down 28
enemy aircraft. (Acknowledged
by Kogenluft.)
May 20, 1917. Ordered to
command Jagdstaffel 5. Shot
down his 29th enemy aircraft on
May 24. Kogenluft
acknowledged. Furthermore 5
additional victories for which the
reports have been partly
submitted.

Additional postings: June 28, 1917. Temporary
command of Jagdstaffel 29.
July 3, 1917. Temporary
command of Jagdstaffel 14.
July 10, 1917. Permanent

command of Jagdstaffel 10.
September 23, 1917. Shot down
his forty-eighth enemy aircraft.
Killed in action, buried map ref:
Sheet 28: C.24. C.8.3,
Frezenberg, Belgium.

Decorations: May 18, 1915. Iron Cross 2nd
Class.
May 28, 1916. Pilot's Badge, by
order of May 21.
December 19, 1916. Iron Cross
1st Class.
March 27, 1917. Knights Cross
with Swords of the Royal House
of Hohenzollern Order.
April 8, 1917. Pour le Mérite.

THE VOSS VICTORY LIST

Sources differ as to the strict chronological order of Voss victories, especially those claimed for the same day. Moreover, occasionally confirmations of a victory would be awarded days later, causing it to be recorded later than actually achieved. Opinions also differ among historians as to the identity of certain victims and the aircraft they flew, these are noted in the comments at the end of the list. Taking this into consideration the list should not be considered definitive. In two-seater losses the pilot's name is given first. All times given are German.

Notations:
W.B.L. crashed or landed within the British Lines.
W.G.L. crashed or landed within the German Lines.
R.T.B. returned to base or friendly field.
P.O.W. prisoner of war.
W.I.A. wounded in action.
K.I.A. killed in action.
D.O.W. died of wounds.

POSTED TO JAGDSTAFFEL 2: 21 NOVEMBER 1916

Victory No.	Date	Claimed	Location/Time	Pilot/Crew/Aircraft Flown
1	27/11/16	Nieuport	Miraumont 09:40	Capt. G.A. Parker. K.I.A. No. 60 Sqn. RFC. Nieuport – A281, W.G.L.
2	27/11/16	'Vickers'	S. of Baupame 14:15	Lt. F.A. George. W.I.A. A/M. O.F. Watts. K.I.A. No. 18 Sqn. RFC. FE2b – 4915, W.B.L. (See Comments.)
3	21/12/16	BE2	Miraumont 11:00	Lt. D.W. Davis. W.I.A., P.O.W. 2 Lt. M.V. Cotton. K.I.A. No. 7 Sqn RFC. BE2d – 5782, W.G.L.
4	01/02/17	DH2	Essarts 17:30	Capt. A.P.V. Daly. W.I.A., P.O.W. No. 29 Sqn. RFC. DH2 – A2614, W.G.L.
5	04/02/17	BE2	Givenchy 15:40	2 Lt. H.M. Massey. W.I.A. 2 Lt. N. M. Vernon. K.I.A. No. 16 Sqn. RFC. BE2d – 5927, W.B.L.
6	10/02/17	DH2	SW. of Serre 12:25	Capt. L.P. Aizlewood. R.T.B. No. 32 Sqn. RFC. DH2 – A2548. (See Comments.)
7	25/02/17	DH2	Arras 14:55	Lt. R.J.S. Lund. W.I.A. No. 29 Sqn. RFC. DH2 – A2557, W.B.L.
8	25/02/17	DH2	Arras 15:00	Capt. H.J. Payn. R.T.B. No. 29 Sqn. RFC. DH2 – 7849. (See Comments.)

Victory No.	Date	Claimed	Location/Time	Pilot/Crew/Aircraft Flown
9	26/02/17	BE2	N. of Arras 16:50	Lt. H.E. Bagot W.I.A. 2 Lt. R.L.M. Jack. K.I.A. No. 16 Sqn. RFC. BE2c – 2535, W.B.L.
10	27/02/17	BE2	Blairville 10:45	2 Lt. E.A. Pope. K.I.A. 2 Lt. H.A. Johnson. K.I.A. No. 8 Sqn. RFC. BE2c – 2530, W.B.L.
11	27/02/17	BE2	St. Catherine 16:48	Capt. J.H. McArthur. K.I.A. Pvt. J. Whiteford. K.I.A. No.12 Sqn. RFC. BE2e – 7197, W.B.L.
12	04/03/17	BE2	S. of Berneville 11:30	Sgt. R.J. Moody. K.I.A. 2 Lt. E.E. Horn. K.I.A. No. 8 Sqn RFC. BE2d – 6252, W.B.L. (See Comments.)
13	06/03/17	DH2	Favreuil 16:35	Capt. H.G. Southon. W.I.A., P.O.W. No. 32 Sqn. RFC. DH2 – 7941, W.G.L.
14	11/03/17	FE2	Combles 10:00	2 Lt. L.L. Beal. A/M. F.G. Davin. W.I.A. No. 22 Sqn. RFC. FE2b – 7685, W.B.L.
15	11/03/17	Nieuport	Bailleul (Berthoult) 14:30	Lt. A.D. Whitehead. W.I.A., P.O.W. No. 60 Sqn. RFC. Nieuport 17 – A279, W.G.L.
16	17/03/17	FE2	Mory 12:15	2 Lt. R.W. Cross. P.O.W. Lt. C.F. Lodge. P.O.W. No. 11 Sqn. RFC. FE2b – 7695, W.G.L.
17	17/03/17	DH2	Warlencourt 12:25	Lt. T.A. Cooch. W.I.A. No. 32 Sqn. RFC. DH2 – A2583, W.B.L.

Victory No.	Date	Claimed	Location/Time	Pilot/Crew/Aircraft Flown
18	18/03/17	BE2	Neuville-Vitasse 18:40	2 Lt. C.R. Dougall. W.I.A., P.O.W. 2 Lt. S. Harryman. D.O.W. No. 8 Sqn. RFC. BE2d – 5784, W.G.L.
19	18/03/17	BE2	Boyelles 18:50	Capt. G.S. Thorne. D.O.W. 2 Lt. F.E.H. van Baerle. P.O.W. No. 13 Sqn. RFC. BE2d 5770. (See Comments.)
20	19/03/17	'Sopwith'	St Léger 09:30	Capt. E.W. Bowyer-Bower. K.I.A. Lt. E. Elgey. K.I.A. No. 59 Sqn RFC. RE8 – A4165, W.G.L.
21	24/03/17	FE2	SE. of St Léger 16:10	Sgt. E.P. Critchley. W.I.A. A/M. F. Russell. K.I.A. No. 23 Sqn. RFC. FE2b – A5485, W.B.L.
22	24/03/17	BE2	SE. of Mercatel 16:45	Lt. H. Norton. K.I.A. 2 Lt. R.A.W. Tillett. K.I.A. No. 8 Sqn. RFC. BE2d – 5769, W.B.L.
23	01/04/17	BE2	E. of St Léger 11:45	Capt. A.M. Wynne. W.I.A. Lt. A.S. Mackenzie. K.I.A. No. 15 Sqn. RFC. BE2e – 2561, W.B.L.
24	06/04/17	BE2	S. of Lagnicourt 09:45	2 Lt. A.H. Vinson. W.I.A. 2 Lt. E.C. Gwilt. No. 15 Sqn. RFC. BE2e – A3157, W.B.L. (See Comments.)

Victory No.	Date	Claimed	Location/Time	Pilot/Crew/Aircraft Flown
25	07/05/17	'Sopwith'	Etaing 19:25	2 Lt. R.M. Chaworth-Musters. K.I.A. No. 56 Sqn. RFC. SE5 – A4867, W.G.L.
26	09/05/17	BE2	Havrincourt 14:00	Lt. R.H. Coles. K.I.A. 2 Lt. J.C Day. K.I.A. No. 52 Sqn. RFC. BE2e – 7209, W.B.L.
27	09/05/17	Sopwith	Lesdain 16:45	2 Lt. G.C.T. Hadrill. W.I.A., P.O.W. No. 54 Sqn. RFC. Sopwith Pup – A6714, W.G.L.
28	09/05/17	FE2	Bel-Aise Farm 16:50	2 Lt. C.A.M. Furlonger. P.O.W. 2 Lt. C.W. Lane. P.O.W. No. 22 Sqn. RFC. FE2b – 4991, W.G.L.

POSTED TO JAGDSTAFFEL 5: 28 MAY 1917

Victory No.	Date	Claimed	Location/Time	Pilot/Crew/Aircraft Flown
29	23/05/17	FE2	Havrincourt 14:25	2 Lt. W.F. Macdonald. K.I.A. Lt. F.C. Shackell. K.I.A. No. 18 Sqn. RFC. FE2b – A5502, W.B.L.
30	26/05/17	Sopwith	S. of Gouzeaucourt 15:45	2 Lt. M.B. Cole. W.I.A. No. 54 Sqn. RFC. Sopwith Pup – A6168, W.B.L.
31	28/05/17	FE2	SE. of Douai 14:00	Capt. A. de Selincourt. P.O.W. Lt. H. Cotton. P.O.W. No. 25 Sqn. RFC. FE2d – A6378, W.G.L.

Victory No.	Date	Claimed	Location/Time	Pilot/Crew/Aircraft Flown
32	04/06/17	Sopwith	SSE. of Douai 07:10	Capt. R.G.H. Pixley. K.I.A. No. 54 Sqn. RFC. Sopwith Pup – B2151, W.G.L.
33	05/06/17	FE2	N. of Vaucelles 09:30	Capt. F.P. Don. W.I.A. – P.O.W. 2 Lt. H. Harris W.I.A. – P.O.W. No. 22 Sqn. RFC. FE2b – A857, W.G.L.
34	06/06/17	Nieuport	W. of Graincourt 13:10	Flt. Lt. Fabian Pember Reeves. K.I.A. No. 6 Sqn. RNAS. Nieuport 17 – N3204, W.G.L. (See Comments.)

POSTED TO JAGDSTAFFEL 10: 30 JULY 1917

Victory No.	Date	Claimed	Location/Time	Pilot/Crew/Aircraft Flown
35	10/08/17	Spad	S. of Dixmude 16:25	Capt. H. Rousseau. Escadrille Spa-31. K.I.A. Aviation Militaire. Spad XIII, W.B.L.
36	15/08/17	FE2	Zillebeke Lake 19:10	Pvt. S.E. Pilbrow. K.I.A. No. 20 Sqn. RFC. FE2b – A5152, W.B.L.
37	16/08/17	Sopwith	St Julien 21:00	Capt. N.W.W. Webb. K.I.A. No. 70 Sqn. RFC. Sopwith Camel – B3756, W.G.L. (See Comments.)
38	23/08/17	Spad	SW. of Dixmude 10:10	Capt. A.L. Gordon-Kidd. D.O.W. No. 19 Sqn. RFC. Spad VII – B3528, W.B.L.
39	03/09/17	Sopwith	N. of Houthem 09:52	Lt. A.T. Heywood. K.I.A. No. 45 Sqn. RFC. Sopwith Camel – B3917, W.G.L.

Victory No.	Date	Claimed	Location/Time	Pilot/Crew/Aircraft Flown
40	05/09/17	Sopwith	St. Julien 15:50	2 Lt. C.W. Odell. No. 46 Sqn RFC. Sopwith Pup – B1842, W.B.L.
41	05/09/17	Caudron	Bixschoote 16:30	(See Comments.)
42	06/09/17	FE2	St Julien 16:35	Lt. J.O. Pilkington. K.I.A. A/M. H.F. Matthews. K.I.A. No. 20 Sqn. RFC. FE2d – B1895, W.B.L.
43	10/09/17	Sopwith	Langemarke 17:50	2 Lt. A.J.S. Sisley. K.I.A. No.70 Sqn. RFC. Sopwith Camel – B3927, W.G.L.
44	10/09/17	Sopwith	Langemarke 17:55	2 Lt. O.C. Pearson. K.I.A. No. 70 Sqn. RFC. Sopwith Camel – B3787, W.G.L.
45	10/09/17	'FE or SE'	Langemarke 18:15	Adjt. Pierre Tiberghien. K.I.A. Escadrille Spa – 37. Aviation Militaire. Spad VII, W.G.L.
46	11/09/17	'New Type'	Langemarke 10:30	(See Comments.)
47	11/09/17	Sopwith	St Julien 16:25	Lt. O.L. McMaking. K.I.A. No. 45 Sqn. RFC. Sopwith Camel – B6236, W.G.L.
48	23/09/17	DH4	Roulers 09:30	2 Lt. S.L.J. Bramley. K.I.A. 2 Lt. J.M. De Lacey K.I.A. No. 57 Sqn. RFC. DH4 – A7643, W.G.L.

COMMENTS

2. Aircraft recognition during the Great War was never an exact science and it was common for all sides to loosely categorise types until they became familiar. For example, the Germans applied the generic term Vickers to all pusher types, simply because they were all of strikingly similar configuration. The Vickers Gunbus, the DH2, FE2b and the FE8, with their distinctive lattice tails, were all termed Vickers at some point, and accounts for Voss claiming a Vickers and not an FE as his second victory.

6. Aizlewood was not shot down, he returned safely to base and claimed an E.A. out of control.

8. Although badly shot about, Payn returned to base and landed safely.

12. This 'kill' is often confused in aviation histories with Manfred von Richthofen's twenty-second victory. However, the details given by Richthofen were vague and the location of the crash site was erroneously given as 'one kilometre from Loos, near the German Trenches.' The RFC report on the only BE loss of the day confirms that 'it fell in flames within our lines' which clearly identifies it as the machine flown by Moody and Horn.

19. To the author's knowledge the story of Voss landing beside the downed BE2d flown by Thorne and van Baerle in order to retrieve its Lewis guns has never been thoroughly investigated, though it should be noted that it was not uncommon for pilots to land beside their victims whenever the opportunity presented itself.

24. In earlier victory lists Vinson and Gwilt are not identified as Voss' twenty-fourth victim, the dubious honour fell to Foster of 56 Squadron; and even though there is a very good case for it, Voss was never credited with shooting Foster down. Vinson and Gwilt were originally attacked by six machines from Jasta 2, but the coup de grace was almost certainly administered by Voss.

34. On this day, Voss claimed a Nieuport diving into the lines, and made no mention of it breaking up, as happened to Reeves' machine. It is therefore more likely that Voss was referring to the Nieuport flown by his flight commander, Christopher Draper.

37. At some point, it was thought Voss' thirty-seventh victim was 2nd. Lt. W.R. Fish of 32 Squadron, but there can be little doubt that it was actually Webb; it has now been established that when he went missing Fish was not flying a Sopwith Camel but a DH5.

41. Voss claimed a Caudron two-seater, falling at Bixschoote, but the only Caudron loss of the day fell at Remoncourt on the German side of the lines and was credited to a pilot of Jasta 3.

46. Given as a Spad in the Abschusse, but as a 'New Type' in the War Diary of JG1. There were no RFC losses that fit for type, location or time, so a French Spad is the probable candidate, and if this is true then the controversial possibility that the pilot was Georges Guynemer cannot be discounted without further investigation.

INTELLIGENCE REPORTS
ON FOKKER FI 103/17

Werner Voss was killed at the height of the Third Battle of Ypres, known to the British as the Battle of Passchendaele. The immediate area around Frezenberg Ridge was the scene of fierce land fighting during September and early October 1917. German strong points, (reinforced concrete blockhouses) known as Borry Farm and Beck House, flanked the northern limits of the ruined village and held up the British advance. Plum Farm was adjacent to these strong points on the British side. Although the farm, a heavily fortified redoubt bristling with many machine guns and surrounded by thick belts of wire, had been captured by the 55th West Lancashire Division on 31 July, Frezenberg village and a number of smaller blockhouses nearby remained in German hands until 20 September. British attacks in the area were continued almost on a daily basis, but progress was painfully slow, and the crash site was still within yards of the front line on 23 September. In consequence, little more than cursory examinations of the triplane could be made by RFC intelligence officers whilst the fighting was still going on, and a detailed inspection of the wreckage was not be carried out until 27 October 1917 – more than a month after Fokker FI 103/17 had crashed.

For some time the report reproduced here was thought to be a forgery because of its association with a similar document dreamt up by an over enthusiastic historian who was trying to add substance to an article he had written. In recent times it has been thoroughly investigated and is now widely accepted as genuine. Words in parenthesis are those of the author.

[From report in PRO file AIR/1, Box 1061]

Report on Fokker Triplane.
Allocated RFC No. G72 [captured enemy aircraft].

Brought down by Lieut. Rhys Davis (*sic*) of No. 56 Squadron on 23rd September, 1917 near St Julien.

General

This machine was for a long period in the open before being salved and is therefore in a very bad condition. It is camouflaged green on the upper surfaces and sky blue on the lower.

Pilot's seat is adjusted by releasing two wing nuts which are fastened to two tubes in rear, thus allowing the seat to be raised or lowered. Maker's No. 1730. Fabric is good but the dope is of very poor quality.

Construction

The fuselage is of 2mm steel tubing braced with 18 gauge wire, all the steel work being welded together as in the AEG (G67). The system of fixing the wires to the struts has not been found before; a piece of tubing is welded across the angles made by the struts and longerons and the wire is then bent round these, the ends being made fast to a turnbuckle in the centre of the span. The fuselage is covered with fabric, the top having a plywood fairing which is also covered with fabric; the piece on the bottom is laced.

Main Planes

Only the lowest one was salved. It consists of wooden ribs and one large main spar (box type) built up of seven members $1^1/_{32}''$ x $9/_{16}''$ (average) which taper towards the wing tip. These are covered with three ply on the sides, top and bottom, the last two being reinforced at the fuselage end by a piece of spruce $2'$ x $5/_{16}''$ fixed on the outside.

Span of this plane (approx.)	14' 10"
Chord of this plane (approx.)	1' 11"
Dimensions of span	10cm x 25cm

Tail plane is fixed across the fuselage, which is cut away like Sopwith machine so that the tail plane when in position is flush with the fuselage. It is constructed of steel tubing.

The fabric is fixed on to strips of fabric sewn round the ribs and upper and lower surfaces sewn to the strips.

Chord (average)   3' 9"
Span (average)   6' 9"

The Elevators are on each side of the fuselage, connected by a single axis tube, and balanced in the same way as the tail plane. The two balance pieces are triangular and are 1' 2" x 7$1/2$".

Chord (average)   16$1/2$"
Span (average)   8"

The controls pass down the fuselage and emerge under the tail plane, the one to the top of the kingpost going up through the tail plane itself. These controls are not duplicated.

The Tail Skid. The post is ash and the shoe is steel in the shape of a knife edge bolted to the post. The shock absorber is of black elastic strands covered with thread.

Undercarriage well staggered forward; the 'Vee' struts are of streamline steel tubing. Between the 'Vees' is an aluminium box through which the axle passes and on each end of the box there are two lugs. The shock absorber, which is the same type as the tail skid, is bound round the lugs and over the axle.

Petrol Tank placed in front of pilot had a capacity of approximately 18 gallons.

Engine used was a 110 Le Rhône No. 3247 type J., was missing in an English Nieuport early this year; it had a Bosch Magneto fitted, No. 2070815, type DA, and REV plugs.

Propeller: Axial manufacture, diameter 2600, pitch 2300. Consists of four laminations of mahogany an inch thick.

Armament: Two Spandau guns, Nos. 5848 and 5849, were fitted to fire through the propeller with a direct flexible drive interrupter gear.

Instruments: Among the usual instruments a Le Rhône pattern revolution counter was found.

Advanced Headquarters (I)   G. Barfoot-Saunt
Royal Flying Corps in the Field   2nd Lt. RFC.
27th October, 1917.

The following 'Incident Report' has appeared in a number of Voss related articles over the years, but it has never been authenticated.

Incident Report
To Lieut. Barfoot-Saunt, Wing Intelligence, Area HQ.
Subject – Fokker Triplane which was shot down by a flight of SE5s.
Total wreck. Number 103/17. Date – September 1917.

Details: Little of this machine is intact to enable a fully detailed description at this time but the following points are worthy of note. The machine is one of the new Triplane 'Scouts' which have been reported active in the Sector during the past four weeks. The fuselage is of alloy tubing covered with fabric, whilst the wings are of wood, fabric covered. The Le Rhône engine is covered with a cowling, or rather partly covered as the cowl is not a full one possibly to assist cooling as are the two holes in the front/top of same. The machine features a new attempt by the enemy at camouflage. The entire upper and side surfaces are doped in various shades of green, blue and grey which takes the form of streaks applied at various angles – vertical on the fuselage and slanted on the tail. The upper and second wing have not been salved but the streaks on the bottom wing are just off the vertical, slanting slightly to the left. Lower surfaces are greyish blue. Upper surface dope is of poor quality but fabric is good.

[This report is usually accompanied by what purports to be a 'Fabric and Dope Report' that has a drawing of FI 103/17, attached to which are coloured samples of fabric supposedly cut from the wreck, but this must be discounted as it is unsigned and almost certainly a 1960s forgery.]

APPENDIX VI

WHERE WERE THE GERMAN TRIPLANES?

As demonstrated throughout the text, there is no real conundrum surrounding the death of Werner Voss, or his final aerial combat, but there are intriguing questions concerning other matters connected to the Voss saga: one that has developed into a lively debate stretching back to the 1960s and beyond concerns the actual deployment of Fokker Triplanes on the Western Front between 25/28 August and 13 October 1917. The question was, and still is, were there more than two? There are of course opposing views on the subject: (A) there were only two in service, and (B) there were more than two. Eminent historians in camp 'A' can produce much documentary evidence to argue their corner: Fokker factory records, movement orders for the triplanes, and witnesses who only ever saw two. Historians no less eminent in camp 'B' have for the most part remained silent about their suspicions, because there has been very little documentary evidence unearthed to support a view that is primarily based on simple logic and controversial sightings. My own research led me to conclude this latter argument deserved a proper airing, and by examining what evidence there is, introducing a little known statement made by Karl Bodenschatz and notes found in the recently discovered papers of Friedrich Rüdenberg, I hope to persuade at least some of the dyed-in-the-wool doubters to re-evaluate the question. But in order to put my arguments into perspective it is, perhaps not necessary but desirable, to first consider the historical events around which the matter revolves.

At the time of its introduction the Fokker Triplane, like all experimental types, was something of an unknown quantity. It was not a direct copy of the successful Sopwith Triplane that had been at the Front with the Royal Naval Air Service since November 1916, yet the concept lies therein. German pilots that met the Sopwith in the skies over Flanders and northern France were most impressed with its amazing performance, for it completely out-classed the Albatros variants in

153

almost all respects, and proved a tricky customer to tangle with in a dogfight. As part of an arrangement to support the hard pressed RFC during the bitter air fighting of 'Bloody April' 1917, the RNAS, who were virtually a law unto themselves, were allowed first pick of the most up to date aircraft the Allies were able to produce at the time, and had plumbed for the Sopwith Triplane. It was fast, very agile, and capable of a spectacular evasive manoeuvre in which this very strong, though often fickle, machine was rolled onto its back; once inverted, the pilot had simply to pull the stick back sharply into the pit of his stomach and the machine nose dived like a meteor. On one notable occasion, while chasing an Albatros, Flight Sub-Lieutenant E.D. Crundall of Naval 8, became so intoxicated by the adrenaline rush experienced in such a power-dive, he forgot to pull out until almost down to ground level. When it came to opening the throttle, a procedure employed to pull out of a dive, Crundall found it was already wide open. Incredibly, he had dived the Sopwith through 7,000 feet on full power. This extremely lucky pilot had pushed his triplane to its very limits: speeds approaching 200 m.p.h. No German fighter in service at the time was capable of mirroring such a dive without tearing its wings off.

Anthony Fokker inspected a captured Sopwith in April 1917, and no doubt this inspired him to produce his home-grown tri-wing fighter. But, apart from the fact that his baby was an adaptation of a biplane design, it did incorporate a revolutionary concept: the cantilever wing, which improved the strength to weight ratio of thicker airfoils and afforded greater lift. Again this was not an original Fokker idea, it was the brainchild of the aircraft designer Dr. Hugo Junkers, who developed an all-metal cantilever wing for his J-1 monoplane back in 1915. Fokker simply studied the idea and adapted it. Throughout his life the Dutchman was renowned for drawing freely on the inspirations and thoughts of others but, invariably, whenever he presented his projects to the military, borrowed ideas or not, they usually had a touch of Fokker genius about them. The Germans had originally rejected the triplane concept as a passing fad that would have little impact on the air war, but pilots like Voss and Richthofen who had encountered British triplanes in combat realised the idea had considerable potential. The 'Red Baron' was a supporter of Fokker, and during the sluggish months of 1916 and early 1917, when all Fokker D-type fighters were being withdrawn from service due to disproportionate unreliability factors, Richthofen was among the few who kept the faith; he firmly believed the Dutchman could produce war-winning machines. Manfred von Richthofen desperately wanted triplanes for JG1, and it is thought that he and Fokker discussed the possibilities at some point. Be this as it may, Fokker's imagination was certainly fired by the prospect of regaining grace and favour with Idflieg: he saw triplane construction as not just another challenge to his engineering ability but also the answer to a looming problem: Fokker had not produced a winner since the heady days of his acclaimed E-type monoplanes, and by early 1917 the cupboard was almost bare. He now desperately needed new orders for his aviation products; accordingly, he lost no time getting the triplane project off the ground.

In early June 1917 an existing biplane demonstrator, being prepared for the Austro-Hungarian Air Service, was converted into a triplane at the Schwerin works by the simple expedient of adding an extra wing. This was the original V4 prototype. Fokker calculated that the enormous strength afforded by the cantilever wing assemblies negated any need for interplane struts and bracing wires, but in the event this proved to be a bad idea: it didn't look right, and during flight tests there was a perceptible degree of wing flutter. The designer overcame the problem by fitting wings of greater-span and chord, thus increasing their surface areas, and for the sake of conformity added interplane struts, but there were still no bracing wires. This became the modified V4, soon to be flight tested by Werner Voss. To this day, whenever a new aircraft design is appraised by test pilots they apply an old aviation maxim: if it looks right it will almost certainly fly right. This was never truer than in the case of what was to become the most celebrated of all German fighting Scouts, the very agile, aerodynamically clean, Fokker V5 triplane, better known to aficionados as the Fokker Dr I (Driedecker I). It looked right, and it flew like a demon.

As noted above, opinions differ, but many historians have long adhered to the notion that only two Fokker Triplanes were in service during the months of August and September 1917, both of them V4s, and that deliveries of later V4s and V5 production models did not commence until mid-October. This is an understandable hypothesis based on Fokker factory records for the period and official movement orders of the triplanes. All evidence indicates that normal procedures were followed as for all new types destined for front line service: once accepted by Idflieg new machines were first dispatched to Flieger Lager West at Aachen, thence to Flugparks, the holding grounds or depots situated close to the areas of operation, from where they were delivered to the Jastas when called for. But this did not happen in the case of the two V4s, they were rushed into service and delivered directly to Jagdeschwader Nr. 1 at Marckebeke in occupied Belgium on or about 25-28 August 1917.

The first two triplanes delivered were fitted with captured 110 h.p. Le Rhône rotary engines. Later production models were fitted with Fokker's standard 110 h.p. Oberusel UR.II engine, an almost exact copy of the French Le Rhône unit made under licence by the Thulin Company in

Sweden. Although providing more than sufficient power to out-climb anything else on the Western Front, triplanes fitted with the UR.II could only manage around 90 m.p.h. in level flight. When deliveries of the V5s commenced in mid-October a few examples were fitted with more powerful 160 h.p. Goebel Goe III units, which did improve performance to a maximum speed of 118 m.p.h. in level flight. This extra power knocked vital seconds off important zooms and turns, but did little to improve the overall performance: the Fokker was never to match the diving capabilities of the Sopwith Triplane, or indeed its sister aircraft the Sopwith Camel.

The two prototype V4s, designated Fokker FI 102/17 and FI 103/17, were earmarked for evaluation by Richthofen and his 'Gentlemen' of Jagdgeschwader Nr. 1. Richthofen made several flights in 102/17, and scored two victories before commencing a period of leave on 6 September. In his absence Oberleutnant Kurt Wolff had use of the machine, but Wolff was shot down on 15 September over Wervicq. Werner Voss had sole use of 103/17, and was shot down near to the ruins of Frezenberg village on the 23rd; yet reports of engagements or sightings of other triplanes by RFC pilots are rife throughout September. Fokker records, which are notoriously unreliable, indicate that although twelve machines were actually accepted for service by Idflieg in September, none were delivered during that month. In all, JG1 took delivery of nineteen triplanes in October, and records indicate the twelve machines accepted in September were included in this batch. These were given military serial numbers 104/17 through 127/17. However, a quick calculation reveals there must be five omissions from this sequence. Model numbers 105, 120 and 124 through 126 were not included in the delivery, and although it is of course entirely possible that they were held back for final adjustments or modifications, none of the five are subsequently recorded as being accepted or delivered to other Jastas, so what became of them?

Second Lieutenant F.H. Bickerton of 70 Squadron claimed he shot down one of two triplanes he engaged on 10 September in flames, when documentary evidence suggests he was wrong; Captain Norman Macmillan of 45 Squadron reported three triplanes encountered on the 11th, one of which he mentioned as falling out of control, but didn't see it crash; RNAS Flight Sub-Lieutenant MacGregor, who killed Kurt Wolff, reported being attacked by five Albatros Scouts and four triplanes on the 15th; and finally, both Arthur Rhys Davids and Richard Maybery noted two triplanes in action on the 23rd. Could it be possible that these RFC pilots all made the same mistake, and confused the distinctive configuration of triplanes with ordinary biplanes? This seems very unlikely. For one thing, there are several reports relating to different camouflage schemes used on these machines; they range from all grey to all green, an earthy brownish-yellow, silvery blue, and drab streaky green: a variety of colours that could not possibly have been found on just two models. It is well known that at the time, and because of severe economic constraints, the Germans were experimenting with cheap cellulose shrink dopes, and that various dyes and other paint forms were being tried out for camouflage schemes. It is logical to assume that Fokker was among those experimenting with these dyes and dopes, and that he employed a number of base coats and not too dissimilar camouflage schemes on the early triplanes in order to come up with the best effect. Therefore the combat reports of these RFC men, all submitted on the day of the event when encounters were still fresh in the mind, cannot be dismissed as the ravings of nervous or fatigued pilots: all were battle hardened veterans. Their documented testimonies positively reveal that engagements with two, three, and even four triplanes did take place at a time when all records indicate they could not possibly have done so. Chances are they encountered all four early model V4s and one or two of the later V5s, all from the batch of twelve officially accepted in mid-September, which were being evaluated under battle conditions, and no doubt sported a variety of colour schemes.

It has been suggested, that throughout September several machines identified by British pilots as Fokker Triplanes were in fact captured Sopwith Triplanes that were involved in a number of dogfights. This is supported by the fact that the Germans, and indeed the Allies, used captured or repaired enemy aircraft. National markings were simply changed and the prize was occasionally used in combat, which could account for the several sightings, but the use of captured machines in combat was something of a rarity: although the number of aircraft brought down intact, or only slightly damaged was considerable, obtaining spare parts for them was a major problem. Moreover, when used in combat there was ever present the very real danger of being shot at by an eagle-eyed comrade who recognised a distinctive enemy type. More often, captured machines were only ever employed in non-operational roles, such as practice air fighting or for transporting personnel around the back areas. Just how many intact Sopwith Triplanes fell into German hands has never been clearly established, but there could not have been many, as only 150 were ever built. What is more, by the autumn of 1917 British triplanes were steadily being withdrawn from front line service, the majority being returned to England for home defence.

Considered analytically, it is entirely possible that Bickerton saw two V4s operating together on 10 September, and in the excitement of a dogfight he may have mistaken another type shot down in flames, perhaps the Camel flown by his own squadron mate Smith Sisley, so his report adds little weight to argument 'B'. But Norman Macmillan was no novice; he was an experienced pilot and had been in France for almost a year, so his claim that his Flight ran into three triplanes on the 11th cannot be rejected out of hand. On paper, the shooting down of FI 102/17 on the 15th would have left only one triplane in service, FI 103/17, yet MacGregor reported seeing four triplanes in the vicinity during the fight with Wolff. This again is perhaps a questionable sighting, but not an impossible one. Werner Voss had gone on leave immediately after the encounter with Macmillan and he took his triplane with him – evidenced by a little known cine film of Voss and Anthony Fokker taken at Schwerin during the period of this leave. It shows the two celebrities examining and perhaps discussing the origin of the painted face design on the cowling of FI 103/17. This film proves beyond all doubt that Voss flew his machine back to Germany, which on the face of it would have left only Wolff's FI 102/17 at the front, but McGregor was convinced he saw four triplanes on the 15th. Finally, Rhys Davids and Maybery both noted two triplanes on the scene during the Voss fight: Rhys Davids in a letter home to his mother, and Maybery to Maurice Baring, personal secretary to Hugh Trenchard, GOC the RFC. Over the last thirty odd years, these reports and comments have all appeared in articles or books that touch on the subject. At some time or other, all have been rejected as spurious by respected historians who consider the two triplane theory inviolate, but there is now German evidence to support the claims of these RFC pilots – evidence that has never before appeared in print.

As previously mentioned, in one of the letters from Karl Bodenschatz, Douglass Whetton was told that a second triplane was in action on the evening of 23 September, and that it had been delivered to Marckebeke on the 5th. Evidence to support this statement has also been found in the papers of Friedrich Rüdenberg. Rüdenberg, who joined Jasta 10 as a Vizefeldwebel on 7 September, wrote: 'Only three test models of the Fokker triplane were flown on our front, one by Richthofen, the other by Voss, and the third by a pilot whose name I forgot'. Bodenschatz clearly identified this pilot as Oskar von Boenigk, who in absentia of Rittmeister Kurt-Bertram von Döring, was acting commander of Jasta 4 during September. Bodenschatz would not have offered this unsolicited information to Whetton unless he knew the truth of the matter. After more than forty years, he could not remember the model number of the third machine, but this was almost certainly FI 104/17. Evidence suggests that these three triplanes were placed at the disposal of the Staffelführers of Jastas 11, 10 and 4. So what about Jasta 6, was its newly appointed commander Hans Ritter von Adam obliged to wait? This seems very unlikely.

Model number 105/17 was almost certainly earmarked for Jasta 6, but was it delivered in September? Chances are the answer is yes, and even though official records say no other triplanes were delivered to JG1 until 13 October, we now have two separate sources indicating that at least one other machine did arrive in September. Bodenschatz could only recall more triplanes being delivered on October 8th, 9th and 10th, all dates notably earlier than those promulgated by supporters of camp A, and over a month later than the machine flown by Boenigk. So what was happening at Schwerin? It is extremely unlikely aircraft production came to a halt for the summer vacation! So it may be assumed with some degree of confidence that of the twelve triplanes accepted by Idflieg in early September, a few were indeed delivered during that month, and Fokker FI 105/17 was among that number. Yet this machine was never taken on to the strength of any Jasta, and its fate has never been determined. This raises interesting questions: could it have been the machine shot down by Bickerton or Macmillan, could it have been the triplane McCudden saw crashing north of Zonnebeke, or was it wrecked in an accident?

In summation, evidence to support advocates of camp B is based on the integrity of a handful of hard-pressed British pilots, the evidence of Bodenschatz and Rüdenberg, and simple logic. Some cynics would say that even this is not enough to go on, but there are other clues that add weight to this view. In *The Fokker Triplane*, Alex Imrie notes that the first order for twenty triplanes was placed with Fokker's Flugzeugwerkes on 14 July 1917. He also notes that experimental and new-type machines were often attached to operational units for evaluation, but not taken on to the strength of a Jagdstaffel until rigorously flight-tested, and this would have included several combat sorties over the front. Richthofen was keen to re-equip JG1 with the wonder machines and badgered Kogenluft for deliveries to commence as soon as humanly possible. Two V4s were already available and delivered to Marckebeke on or between 25-28 August. Anthony Fokker, labouring under an unrealistic work schedule, was then put under greater pressure to complete the first order, and did so in record time. It can therefore be assumed with a fair degree of certainty that several machines were finished and arrived at the Front for evaluation in September, and there can be little doubt these were pressed into service almost before the first coat of paint was dry: as usual with Fokker products minor defects in construction were overlooked. But towards the end of October a series of crashes grounded the triplanes, and experienced pilots began pulling the wings off machines in seemingly innocuous dives and little more than gentle turns. Shoddy workmanship at the Fokker factory proved to be the cause and like wraiths in the night the 'minor' defects again came home to roost. In consequence all triplanes were grounded and returned to Schwerin for complete wing replacements. The work, which included strengthening wing-tip ribs and horn balances on the ailerons, was again completed in record time and deliveries recommenced in December, though by then the office of Kogenluft had conceded that the relatively slow German triplane had been outclassed by the much faster, highly manoeuvrable SE5 and F1 Camel. In all the Dr I enjoyed but a brief career; 320 models were ordered, but the accidents of October 1917 interrupted delivery schedules and production ceased in May 1918, when just over 170 were still in service.

THE VOSS COWLING AND TRIPLANE CAMOUFLAGE SCHEME

Barfoot-Saunt's report failed to touch on what has become the most contentious of all issues concerning Fokker Triplane FI 103/17: he makes no mention of the engine cowling, its colour, or whether it was salvaged. In consequence, arguments as to whether it was coloured red, green, black or yellow continue to this day. At the time of writing, June 2003, the subject is still prompting a lively exchange of views on the Internet, often involving some very salubrious names among aviation historians and academics. The facts of the matter are that no one knows for sure what the colour really was. Save for a few pioneer historians dedicated to researching the subject between the two world wars, there was little interest in the first conflict in the air until the early 1960s, when happily it enjoyed a tremendous revival. But by then many surviving ex-pilots were already in their 70s and 80s, and although most never forgot life or death experiences minor details usually escaped them. The colour scheme of enemy aircraft they encountered in the skies over Flanders and northern France, often only for a few brief seconds, was understandably not of paramount importance. Mechanics and riggers, men that serviced aircraft on a day-in day-out basis, became quite blasé about their charges. At the time their first concern was with a machine's fighting readiness; what kind of paint job they had completed on a particular type was less of an issue. Moreover, it is a fact that memories of colour are one of the first things to fade with the passing of time. Accordingly, when asked, old-timers rarely remembered these finite details.

The colour of the Voss cowl is a classic case, there is little or no hard evidence to go on and no official record or description of its colour scheme has ever come to light, leaving aviation enthusiasts to make what are in fact little more than educated guesses as to what it could have been. However, we do know that after its formation Richthofen issued a command that the Jagdstaffeln of JG1 should each adopt an identifying unit colour on engine cowlings or forward fuselage sections; this order was carried out, and it has long been established that Jasta 4 used off-white and, according to Bodenschatz, a black snake-like line along the fuselage; Jasta 6 black, with zebra stripes on the tailplane and elevators; Jasta 10 chrome yellow on engine cowlings, and Jasta 11 red. Alex Imrie, among others, researched the question of the Voss cowling in the 1960s and came to the conclusion that it could only have conformed to the unit colour of yellow. Werner Voss made whimsical use of the cooling holes on the cowling of 103/17 by adding the Japanese style, moustachioed face picked out in white seen in contemporary photographs, and although it can be argued that white on yellow does not stand out well at all, Voss may not have had any choice in the matter. Karl Timm, Voss' mechanic who was interviewed by Imrie in 1968, stated that when received 103/17 was coloured all grey. To use his own words: 'A very dark earthy grey on the engine cowl but with a lighter shade on the fuselage aft of the cockpit.' He further maintained that no other colours were added and that the machine was flown as delivered. However, this cannot possibly be correct. After more then forty years, Timm's powers of recall were not so sharp, he made no mention of the streaky green stripes or the distinctive moustachioed face evidenced in several photographs published in books and journals over the intervening years – which he must surely have seen from time to time.

By 1917 the Germans were suffering from a serious shortage of raw materials, not least of which were good quality colour pigments for the paints industry. The Allied blockade of Central Powers ports and points of entry had by then begun to bite hard. In particular the German aircraft industry suffered badly. Relying heavily as it did on a wide range of imported commodities, manufacturers were reduced to experimenting with a number of synthetic materials and products in order to keep aircraft flying operationally, notably castor oil, rubber, high-grade benzene, and colour pigments that could not be produced domestically. Castor oil, for example, was used almost exclusively throughout the aircraft industry for lubricating rotary engines. Obtained from the seeds of the *Ricinus communis* plant, which at the time grew only in hot climates, this essential commodity was difficult to obtain and was substituted by a product known as Voltol, a blend of oils derived from fish, rape seed, and minerals. Likewise, synthetic rubber compounds, used for tyres and shock cord on aircraft, were produced from the polymerised chemical Butadiene. In fact, the ingenuity and resourcefulness of the Germans knew no bounds and they were able to overcome many technical difficulties of substitution for a considerable period of time, but good red pigments were always scarce, and this may explain why the extensive use of red colours was often reserved for the elite Jastas or star pilots.

Varnishes were not too much of a problem, but by 1917 the Germans were making every effort to use dopes made only from cellulose for shrinking airframe fabrics. Cellulose, derived from abundant plant matter, was cheap; it was also effective, but of poor quality. On the triplanes delivered to JG1, Fokker used a variety of grey dopes for the base coats: the linen covering was first washed over in light or dark grey, sometimes a combination of both, but always sparingly. It was then thinly over-painted with dark or olive green stripes, which also varied in shade, again often on the same machine. The brushed-out streaky effect was achieved by applying the colour until the loaded brush was positively exhausted. Successive applications and brush strokes over the same area thus resulted in a greater depth of colour on the upper portion of a stripe and degradation at the extremities. Photographic evidence of early V4s, and British intelligence reports on FI 103/17, suggest brush strokes were applied in lines at varying widths and angles to all upper and side surfaces, vertical on the fuselage with a slight bias to the left on the top planes and almost diagonal on the tail unit. It is thought the stripes were applied while the base coat was still wet, causing the dope to seep into the fibres of the linen and spread. A final dark linseed oil varnish was then applied. Once dry, the varnish may well have given the greys a deepish blue hue, whilst the olive greens turned to an earthy brown. The final varnish resulted in the entire machine taking on a silvery sheen in the right light, and this could be one explanation for why Geoffrey Bowman and James McCudden both said 103/17 was silvery or sky blue. Keith Caldwell was of the same opinion, he also said the triplane flown by Voss appeared to be blue.

In the 1960s Ian Huntley, AMRAes, was a leading light of the Historical Aircraft Maintenance Group at Hendon in London, and a recognised authority on first war German camouflage schemes. Over a period of many years he analysed how shrink dopes were produced and applied, and his study has relevance to the curious variations of colours reported by British pilots who met and fought Fokker Triplanes in the skies over Flanders between 1917 and 1918. In the course of his work Huntley noted that an alternative, though similar, method of camouflage was used on some of the early models. The effect was achieved by applying the olive green stripes directly onto the un-bleached airframe fabric, which had first been proofed against the elements with one or two clear dope base coats. Again this caused the colours to seep into the material and spread, but when the final linseed varnish was applied, it not only turned olive greens to brown, it also gave the linen a yellowish, almost ochre tint. The use of such varying shades undoubtedly accounts for why British pilots described the V4s and early Dr Is they encountered as being of such diverse colours.

The yellow and brown colour scheme of the triplane encountered by Second Lieutenant R.H. Sloley of 56 Squadron, seen on 6 September over Houthulst Forest, is a good example of this diversity. He also noted that although the pilot of this machine was in a very favourable position to attack, he fired on him from extreme range before smartly turning east; this was never the stamp of Voss, who would have pressed home the attack and taken it to its final conclusion. Sloley was much bemused by this behaviour and recorded it in his combat report. Chances are this was the machine delivered to Marcke on 5 September and its pilot, identified by Bodenschatz as Oskar von Boenigk, was probably familiarising himself with its handling and simply chose to avoid a potentially dangerous combat. In a letter to Douglass Whetton, Bodenschatz described this machine as dirty grey, green-brown in colour, and this ties in with the triplane seen by Lieutenant Maybery on the evening of 23 September going east. Not surprisingly, over the years, there has been considerable debate on the actual colours used on the early V4s, and indeed the Dr Is, but it is now generally agreed that as they were all hand-painted the colour schemes were in fact multifarious, and as alike as two sets of fingerprints.

The actual colour of the engine cowling on FI 103/17 is a recurring theme, so it is advisable to tread carefully when considering all the possibilities. Contemporary photographs appear to show the cowling as black, but this was almost certainly due to the film in use and photo-processing techniques of the time. During a lengthy discussion with the historian Alex Revell, a former RFC photographer explained that orthochromatic film tended to reverse the polarity of certain light colours, resulting in tonal graduations on the monochrome scale that varied from light greys to midnight-black. As an old experienced hand, the photographer was able to clearly identify many original colours by the degree of graduation that appeared on old wartime prints. Even after more than fifty years, and without any knowledge of the study made by Alex Imrie, when shown a famous photo line-up of Jasta 10 Pfalz D IIIs at Heule in the autumn of 1917, all sporting what appeared to be black engine cowls, the elderly RFC photographer unhesitatingly revealed the original colour was yellow: this was the testimony of someone charged with making like evaluations throughout the war. In recent times advanced chromo-spectrographic analysis has been used on the Pfalz line-up and many other old prints of the period, proving the photographer was correct about the polarity reversal.

Previously, the consensus among historians of the early 1960s was that the cowling on 103/17 lent more towards an olive or dark green, which, like yellow, also fared badly in photo-processing techniques of the day, and is just as difficult to distinguish from black in old prints. And yet, despite a mountain of research being carried out, not one shred of incontestable evidence has ever been produced that settles the argument one way or another. Interestingly, and notwithstanding the photographic evidence, none of Voss' contemporaries, Heldmann and Rüdenberg, Bodenschatz or even Richthofen himself, ever noted the famous moustachioed face or its colour scheme in reports or memoirs, and nor did any allied pilot that met Voss and the triplane in action. Barfoot-Saunt failed to report anything unusual about the cowling, which suggests he saw nothing out of the ordinary; no striking colours or the stylised face, yet every photograph of 103/17 in existence shows the face picked out in white. Despite being badly damaged in the crash, what remained of the wreck was salvaged by the RFC, which means it was removed from the crash site for inspection and must have been picked over by many specialist and intelligence officers – it was after all the very first German triplane to fall into Allied hands – the streaky camouflage scheme was new, and so described, but there was never any mention of a bespoke paint job on the engine cowling.

Alex Revell offered a very plausible explanation for this, suggesting that the original decorated cowl may have been replaced by Voss' mechanics before his final combat due to damage sustained in an earlier engagement, or some other mishap that has gone un-chronicled. The unsubstantiated story that, with other items, the cowl was recovered from the wreck and sent to 56 Squadron as a war trophy should also be considered. The cowl is said to have been hung on a wall in the squadron Mess and used as an ersatz dartboard by pilots who regularly took to aiming paper darts at the cooling holes after a dram or two in the evenings. However, if there was any truth in this tale, and 56 were sent the original painted cowl, somewhere along the line someone would surely have mentioned the moustachioed face in a letter or memoir, but this is not the case. Unwittingly, even Raymond Collishaw added to this particular debate: in one of his letters to Evan Hadingham he claimed that Wendelmuth told officers at Heule the triplane he saw over Frezenberg had a plain engine cowl. Unfortunately, as with many of Collishaw's nebulous assertions, he never offered any corroboratory evidence to support the statement. On the face of it, it seems no one ever noted the stylised face, either before or after Voss' final combat. This aside, there is in existence a little known piece of cine-film, taken at Schwerin in mid-September 1917, that features Voss standing before 103/17 pointing out the grotesque face to a studious Anthony Fokker. This unique footage is undeniable evidence that Voss must have flown his triplane back to Germany the day after he wrote out his final leave warrant on 11 September, and if the cowling had been changed at all it must have been carried out on this visit to Schwerin or on Voss' immediate return to the Front. But was it changed?

No analysis from any quarter positively answers the question beyond reasonable doubt, but there are two factors that seem to have been overlooked by almost every historian who has ever tackled the cowling issue. According to Bowman the Voss triplane turned over onto its back seconds before it crashed, an observation given credence by Barfoot-Saunt who reported the upper and middle wings could not be salved as they were just too badly smashed, clearly damage consistent with an aircraft ploughing into the ground in an inverted position. In a crash of this nature the soft aluminium cowling would have been severely buckled and bent, possibly beyond all recognition, and this may be why Barfoot-Saunt never mentioned the cowling – it had simply ceased to be an engine cowling at all. A second factor to consider is that the wrecked triplane remained out in the open, exposed to the elements and shellfire for more than a month before a detailed inspection was carried out. The weather during most of this period remained cold and wet and the adverse conditions had taken their toll, as noted in the RFC intelligence report. This leads to the possibility, however outrageous it may seem, that even if the cowling had not been too badly damaged the inferior quality paints then in use by the Germans may have simply flaked off or been washed away before what remained of the machine was removed from the shell-torn field at Plum Farm. This may sound far-fetched, but there is an interesting parallel that may shed light on the matter: at the height of the Battle of Britain in 1940, the author's aunt recalled seeing a yellow-nosed ME-109 crash land in a Kentish field, where it remained for more than two weeks before being removed by the RAF. She had to pass the wreck every day on her way to work on the land, and although it was high summer, it rained a good deal. Over a period of less than ten days she noticed the bright yellow paint on the engine cowling had been completely washed off. This indicates that the Germans still had paint problems more than twenty years after Voss fell.

Whatever the truth concerning the Voss cowling it is the nature of aviation historians to disregard all speculative and controversial theories until positive, incontestable proof is presented to them, and as it now seems very doubtful that proof will ever come to light as to what became of the famous cowl, or its actual colour scheme, the subject will undoubtedly remain one of the central issues of debate for perhaps another eighty years or more.

GLOSSARY

Abschusse   Kogenluft War Book detailing German victory claims. See Kogenluft.

Ace   Originally a French term first used in 1915 for any pilot of the Aviation Militaire who had destroyed five enemy machines. The term was later adopted by the Americans, but not the British. See Kannon.

Airco DH   Aircraft Manufacturing Company – de Havilland. Its chief aircraft designer and major shareholder was Geoffrey de Havilland who produced a number of types accepted by the RFC and RNAS during the war. Most notable was the single-seat DH2 pusher biplane that was brought into service in 1915. This type, together with another de Havilland design for the Royal Aircraft Factory, the FE2b, was a match for the Fokker E.1 monoplanes and brought the period known as the 'Fokker Scourge' to a close.

AMRAes   Aircraft Maintenance Group, Royal Aeronautical Society.

AM   Air Mechanic.

Archie   Purely British euphemism for anti-aircraft fire. Derived from a popular music-hall song of the time that included the line 'Archibald, certainly not!' implying the substantial ineffectiveness of early aerial artillery. See Flak.

Art-Obs   Artillery-observation.

Ausweis   Leave Warrant or Pass.

Aviatik   The Aviatik was one of the first German recon-naissance machines to be noted by the Allied Press and became well known to the general public during the war. Built by Automobile und Aviatik A.G., their C.I and C.III class machines were virtually on a par with the British BE2c and suffered similar shortcomings.

Aviation Militaire The French Army Air Service.

Avion de Chasse French term for fighting Scouts often called chaser aircraft. The Americans later changed this designation to 'pursuit aircraft'.

BAM & BAO German acronyms for Brieftauben Abteilung Metz and Brieftauben Abteilung Ostende, two early bombing sections known as the 'Carrier Pigeons'. Brieftauben, literally Pigeon-Post, was simply a cover name intended to fool the Allies into believing these units were assigned to simple intelligence gathering.

BE Blériot Experimental, two-seater reconnaissance machines designed and built by the Royal Aircraft Factory at Farnborough. Examples range from the BE1 to the BE12. Almost all were slow but inherently stable, which made them vulnerable to the fighting Scouts. Further RAF series followed the BE, including the FE, RE and SE. See below.

Blériot Generic term applied to early monoplanes, named after Louis Blériot who flew the English Channel in 1909 in a monoplane of his own design. See BE and Taube.

Bloody April Generally referring to the period of late March, April and early May 1917 when the Germans secured air supremacy on the Western Front. In the month of April alone the RFC lost 315 pilots and observers.

Blue Max See Pour le Mérite.

Brieftauben
Abteilung See BAM and BAO.

Brisfit An affectionate term for the acclaimed two-seater Bristol Fighter.

Caudron A French biplane manufactured by the René Caudron Company. Very few Caudron types saw operational service with the RFC. Thought to be unreliable as an aircraft, the only thing of value was its 80 h.p. Le Rhône engine which the British stripped out for use on other types.

CC
Constantinesco
Synchronising
Gear An interrupter gear invented by the Romanian George Constantinesco who worked for the Vickers Aircraft Company. Connected to a machine gun, the gear was operated by hydraulic fluid being pumped through metal tubing in a series of pulses synchronised with the revolutions of the engine crank-shaft, and thus the propeller. Generally acknowledged as the most

efficient interrupter mechanism used during both world wars and long after.

GOC the RFC   General Officer Commanding the Royal Flying Corps.

Ground Attack   Strafing enemy ground troops and defences from low altitudes.

Dawn patrol   The first scheduled duty flight of the day. Usually the least active, since the Germans were notoriously late risers.

DFW   Deutsche Flugzeug-Werke. The DFW CV was possibly the most successful German two-seater reconnaissance machine of the war. It was produced in large numbers, not only by the parent company, but also by sub-contractors such as LFG, Halberstadt and Aviatik.

Dogfight   A wild aerial mêlée in which numbers of aircraft participate and fight at very close quarters. As a result many aircraft were lost in mid-air collisions.

Drachen   The German word for kite balloon.

EA   Enemy aircraft.

Einsitzerschule   German single-seater training school.

Elevator   The horizontal control surface set on the tailplane to control the up-and-down direction of the nose of the aircraft.

Escadrille   French term for squadron.

Escadrille de
Chasse   French term for a fighter or pursuit squadron.

FE   Farnborough Experimental, a designation assigned to aircraft types designed and built by the Royal Aircraft Factory. Includes the two-seat fighter-reconnaissance FE2b pusher biplane which, when brought into service in 1915, together with the DH2, outclassed the Fokker E.1 and brought the 'Fokker Scourge' to an end.

FEA   Flieger Ersatz Abteilungen. Aviation Replacement Unit, where German aircrews underwent training, followed by a posting to an active service unit. During the war there were 12 main FEA depots, the most important of these being at: 1. Johannisthal, 3. Gotha, 5. Hannover, 6. Grossenhain, and 7. Cologne.

Feldflieger-
Abteiling   German Field Aviation Unit, the basic unit of organisation in the Fliegertruppe, normally equipped with six aircraft and attendant personnel.

Feldwebel   Sergeant Major.

FLAK   Acronym of Flugabwehrkanonen, German anti-
                   aircraft gun. The term flak was not adopted by the
                   Allies until the Second World War. See Archie.

Flaming Onions   Familiar term used by British airmen to describe
                   particularly nasty anti-aircraft fire which came up in a
                   cluster of what appeared to be fiery green balls
                   chained together. In fact these were five separate
                   tracer shots fired by an automatic 37mm flak canon.

Flieger   The lowest rank air mechanic or private in the German
                   Army Air Service.

Flieger Lager   The main German aviation storage depot for the
West   Western Front situated at Aachen, close to the frontier
                   with Belgium.

Fliegertruppe   German Military Aviation or Army Air Service under
                   the direct control of the Army's Chef des
                   Feldflugwesens (Chief of Field Aviation). An Army
                   order dated 25 November 1916 then established the
                   Luftstreitkräfte, which came under the autonomous
                   control of the Kommandierenden General der
                   Luftstreitkräfte. The office of Chef des
                   Feldflugwesens was then abolished. See Kogenluft
                   and Luftstreitkräfte.

Fliegerschule   Flying school.

Flight   A RFC unit of six aircraft. A squadron was generally
                   composed of three Flights – A, B, and C. See Kette.

Flugpark   Aircraft holding ground, situated close to areas of
                   operation.

Flying Circus   Purely British term applied to Jagdgeschwader Nr. 1
                   commanded by Manfred von Richthofen. The wing
                   consisted of four elite Jagdstaffel Nos. 4, 6, 10 and 11.
                   When encountered en-mass, JG1's multi-coloured
                   aircraft reminded RFC pilots of a circus.

Fokker Scourge   The period between late summer 1915 and the spring
                   of 1916, when the Germans achieved air supremacy
                   for the first time. This principally came about with the
                   introduction of the Fokker and Pfalz E-type
                   monoplanes. Fitted with an effective interrupter
                   mechanism, that allowed a machine gun to be fired
                   directly through the arc of the propeller, the E-types
                   reigned supreme until the introduction of the FE2b,
                   DH2, and French Nieuport Scouts.

Fokker Triplane   A tri-winged fighting Scout designed by the Dutch

	aircraft manufacturer Anthony Fokker. Introduced in late August 1917, the prototype and, it is believed, four pre-production models were given the factory designation V4s, later production models were desigdnated V5s. When accepted into service the V5s were given the military designation Dr I (Driedecker I).
Freiherr	Literally Freeman or Master, a lower order of German aristocracy, usually translated as Baron in most dictionaries; yet the rank is in fact more on a par with the English Lord of the Manor or Country Squire than anything else.
Gefreiter	Lance Corporal or Private First Class.
Halberstadt	A highly manoeuvrable German fighting Scout produced by the Halberstadt Flugzeug-Werke in Saxony. Introduced in 1916 the Halberstadt replaced the ageing Fokker monoplanes. Werner Voss is thought to have scored his first four victories whilst flying the type.
Hauptmann	German rank equivalent to a Captain.
Hun	A fatuous term for the Germans used chiefly by the British. It was also used in British flying schools and applied derisively to heavy-handed students who broke up more than their fair share of training aircraft.
Hunland	A purely British euphemism for territory held by the Germans.
Husarren-Regiment	Hussar Cavalry Regiment.
Idflieg	See Inspektion der Fliegertruppen.
Immelmann Turn	A manoeuvre used in aerial combat, erroneously attributed to Max Immelmann, that results in a spectacular turn effected by a sudden zoom followed by a half roll off the top. Once on its side, control surfaces on an aircraft are effectively reversed (the rudder at once becomes the elevator, and the elevator becomes the rudder). When flown in this attitude the elevators whip the machine around very fast. The turn was in general use as a stunt or exhibition manoeuvre in France and England before the outbreak of World War I. In combat it was widely used to quickly recover from a diving attack on an opponent.
Inspektion der Fliegertruppen	German Inspectorate of Military Aviation abbreviated to Idflieg.
Jagdgruppe	A non-permanent grouping of Jagdstaffeln, normally

	under the command of an experienced commander. The number of Jastas within the group could vary according to requirements, but none were under permanent secondment.
Jagdgeschwader	A permanent grouping of four Jagdstaffeln under the command of an experienced commander. Roughly equivalent to a RFC Fighter Wing.
Jagdstaffel	A fighting unit roughly equivalent to a RFC fighter squadron, though generally consisting of ten aircraft and not twelve. Commonly referred to as Jasta or Staffel by the Germans.
Jasta Boelcke	Jagdstaffel Nr. 2. Renamed Jasta Boelcke in honour of its famous leader Oswald Boelcke, often referred to as the Father of the German Air Service.
Jastaschule	School of air fighting.
KEK	German acronym for Kampfeinsitzer-Kommando. Single-seat Fighter Detachment. KEKs were the precursors to the Jagdstaffeln. The first two units were originally stationed at Fort Vaux near St. Quentin and at Metz in Lorraine.
Kaghol	German acronym for Kampfgeschwader der Obersten Heeresleitung. Fighting Squadron or Battle Group of the Army High Command.
Kameradengrab	Literally the Comrades Grave, sited at Langemarck, Belgium. It is in fact more of an ossuary than a mass grave, in which the bones and other remains of some 45,000 German soldiers were interred.
Kampfgeschwader	See above.
Kampfstaffel	Fighting section. Commonly referred to as Kasta, usually equipped with six aircraft.
Kannon	German pilots who had destroyed ten enemy aircraft were referred to as a Kannon. See Ace.
Kette	German term for a Flight of aircraft – usually three to four.
KIA	Killed in Action.
King post	The short lever above or below a movable surface to which the control cable is attached to the elevators or ailerons.
Kogenluft	See next.
Kommandierenden General der Luftstreitkräfte	Office of the General in Command of the German Air Force, generally abbreviated to Kogenluft.
Landing wires	All wires or cable supporting the plane when it lands

	or stands on the ground. Flying wires take over the support of the plane in the air.
Landstrum	Third-line reserve troops. Commonly composed of men who had completed their conscription or regular service in the German army; accordingly their average age was well above thirty-five years.
Leading edge	The front edge of a wing or airfoil. The rear edge is known as the trailing edge.
Leutnant der Reserve	Second Lieutenant of the Reserve. A temporary rank.
Leutnant	Second Lieutenant. A permanent rank.
Longerons	The main structural members of an aircraft running the length of the body or fuselage.
Luftstreitkräfte	The German Army Air Service.
LVG Roland	Luft-Verkehrs Gesellshaft GmbH. The company's Roland reconnaissance aircraft were among the most successful German two-seater designs of the war. Though slower than the Rumpler, the LVG was immensely strong and very stable, attributes which lent themselves readily to medium bombing, photo-reconnaissance and artillery-observation.
Main spar	Chief structural member of a wing to which all ribs and bracings are attached.
Monocoque	A type of fuselage or aeroplane body in which the main loads of the structure are taken by the skin covering: thin sheets of pliable plywood wrapped around fuselage ribs and the longerons. Widely used on Albatros variants and later the Pfalz D III.
Nacelle	A body that encloses either the crew or the engine.
Nieuport	One of the most famous of all French designed fighting aircraft. Variants 12-24 were widely used by the RFC, of which the Nieuport 17 was the best loved.
Oberleutnant	First or full Lieutenant.
OOC	Out of Control.
Pfalz D III	Manufactured by Pfalz Flugzeug-Werke GmbH of Speyer am Rhein. The Pfalz D III and the D IIIa were highly manoeuvrable fighting Scouts. Although overall performance was good they were mainly employed by Bavarian Jastas; for some unknown reason Prussian Jasta pilots preferred the Albatros, which in some respects was inferior.
Pfalz Dr I	The Pfalz Triplane stemmed from the company's D VII biplane Scout, and was in fact a D VII fitted with

triplane wings. Overshadowed by the success of the Fokker Triplane, the Pfalz design saw little service and not more than ten examples were delivered to the Front.

Pour le Mérite   The highest Prussian award for gallantry instituted by Kaiser Friedrich II in 1740. The order was given a French name because Friedrich only spoke French. It was known to German airmen as 'The Blue Max.'

PRO   Public Record Office, Kew, London.

Pusher type   A machine in which the engine and propeller are mounted behind the crew compartment. Examples of which are the FE2b, DH2, the early Vickers Gun Bus and variants. The Germans used very few pusher type machines on the Western Front.

RAF   Royal Aircraft Factory, responsible for British aircraft production between 1914-19. Not to be confused with:

RAF   Royal Air Force, formed in April 1918 by the amalgamation of the RFC and RNAS.

RFA   Royal Field Artillery.

RFC   Royal Flying Corps, formed out of the Aeroplane Section of the Royal Engineer's Balloon Company in May 1912. Combined with the RNAS in 1918 to form the Royal Air Force.

RNAS   Royal Naval Air Service, a completely independent arm of the Royal Navy. Originally intended to operate in co-operation with shipping and in defence of naval shore stations. Combined with the RFC in 1918.

RE   Reconnaissance Experimental. A generic term for a series of aircraft designed for reconnaissance work. Produced by the Royal Aircraft Factory, the series ended with the RE8, intended to replace the ageing BE variants. The RE8 was better armed but its inherent stability prevented tight manoeuvring and it was prone to spinning at low altitudes. First introduced in November 1916.

Radial Engine   An aircraft engine with its cylinders arranged radially around a master crankshaft. The cylinders are stationary and the crankshaft revolves. See Rotary Engine.

Reichsarchiv   The German Military Records Office at Potsdam, southwest of Berlin. Functional between and during the two World Wars.

Ritter	Knight.
Rittmeister	Cavalry Captain.
Roving Commission	Pilots who elected to fly lone patrols after regular duties were completed were said to have Roving Commissions.
Rotary Engine	An aircraft engine in which the cylinders are set radially around its crankshaft, but in this case all cylinders and the engine shell revolve around the crankshaft.
Rumpler Taube	Taube-type aircraft produced by Rumpler Luftfahzeugbau GmbH. One of the first reconnaissance machines used by the Germans in the early months of the war. Rumpler two-seaters saw service on all fronts throughout the conflict and few Allied Scouts could catch the fast C IV variant at altitudes exceeding 15,000 feet.
SE	Scout Experimental, a designation assigned to a series of aircraft designed and built by the Royal Aircraft Factory that ended with the SE5 and SE5a. The SE5 and the F1 Sopwith Camel were more than a match for the Albatros variants, which formed the backbone of the German Air Service in the autumn of 1917.
Scarff Ring	A machine-gun mounting used on many British two-seaters. Invented by Warrant Officer Scarff of the RNAS. Scarff also invented a machine-gun interrupter gear, but it was not so successful. See Constantinesco.
Sopwith Camel	The F1 Sopwith Camel was the most successful Allied fighter of the war, as by the end of hostilities in November 1918 the Camel had accounted for almost 2,000 enemy aircraft. It was also the first RFC fighting Scout to be fitted with two synchronised forward-firing machine guns. Heavy on the controls, the Camel was most unforgiving to novice pilots: at low altitudes the tremendous torque of its huge rotary engine had a preponderance to throw the aircraft into a right-hand spin unless the fine adjustment fuel control lever was not set correctly; this resulted in many fatal accidents in the early days of training and even in operational use.
Sopwith Pup	The Pup was the forerunner of the Camel and entered service with RNAS in September 1916. Its ease of handling and ability to maintain height in a dogfight made it a firm favourite of pilots that flew the type,

though its single synchronised forward-firing Vickers gun was its main shortcoming.

Sopwith 1¹/₂ Strutter — A small, two-seater fighter-reconnaissance machine used in large numbers by both the RFC and RNAS. It came into service in May 1916 and was deployed on all fronts. Fitted with a single synchronised forward-firing Vickers gun and one, sometimes two, Lewis guns for use by the observer, the 1¹/₂ Strutter was no easy meat for German Scouts. Many later examples were converted to single-seat bombers and night fighters.

Sopwith Triplane — The Sopwith Triplane, evolved out of the basic design of the Pup, was one of the most manoeuvrable British fighters on the Western Front. Used almost exclusively by the RNAS, its incredible agility in combat inspired the Germans to design their own triplanes, the most famous of which was the Fokker Dr. I.

Spad — Société pour Aviation et ses Dérives, responsible for producing very successful fighting Scouts, notably the Spad 7 and 13. Fairly manoeuvrable, and with a very good turn of speed, Spads were a match for the ubiquitous Albatros variants. Three RFC squadrons were equipped with Spads during the war, but the intermediate Spad 12, fitted with a 37mm Hotchkiss cannon, that fired an explosive shell weighing approximately one pound through the hollow crankshaft of its 150 h.p. Hispano-Suiza engine, was never employed by the RFC.

Staffelführer — Commander of a Jadgstaffel.

Taube — German word for Dove. Applied erroneously to many early German machines that had a swept back curvature to the wing tips which gave them a bird-like appearance.

Tractor type — An aircraft in which the engine and airscrew (propeller) are mounted in front of the crew compartment.

Unteroffizier — Corporal.

Vizefeldwebel — Sergeant Major.

Zoom — A sudden climb, more usually proceeded by a dive to gain air-speed.

THE FINAL COMBAT OF WERNER VOSS

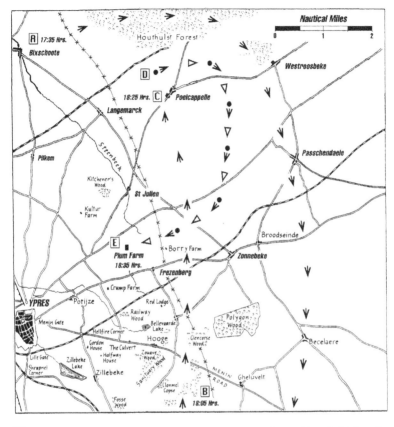

A	Approximate course flown by McCudden's 'B' Flight after crossing Lines at Bixschoote (17:35 Hrs. 23/09/17).
B	Approximate course flown by 'B' Flight after McCudden shot down DFW 2-seater N.E. of Houthem (18:05 Hrs.)
C	'B' Flight, joined by 'C' Flight, attacks Voss & red nosed Albatros scouts W. of Poelcappelle (18:25 Hrs.)
D	The running fight drifts east, then south towards Zonnebeke and Frezenberg (18:30 Hrs.)
E	Voss crashes approximately 125 yards N.W. of Plum Farm after final attack by Rhys Davids (18:35 Hrs.)
	Approximate position of Front Line following Battle of the Menin Road (20/09/1917)

LOCATIONS OF THE VOSS VICTORIES
IN THE ARRAS SECTOR
27/11/1916 – 6/6/1917

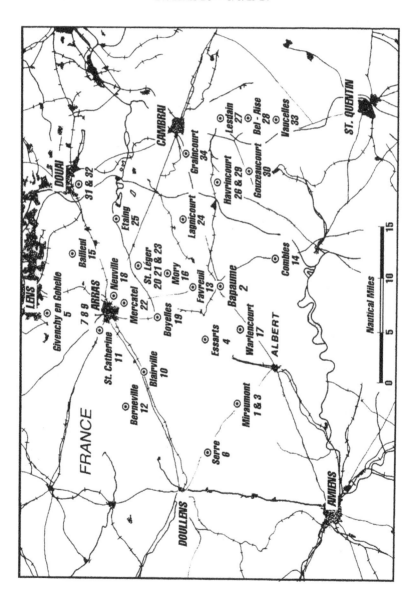

LOCATIONS OF THE VOSS VICTORIES
IN THE YPRES SECTOR
10/8/1917 – 23/9/1917

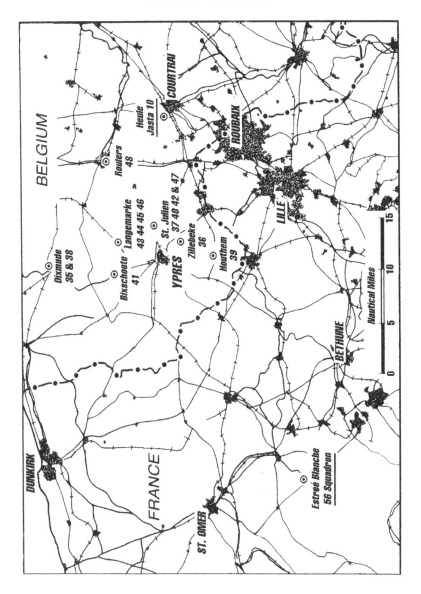

A SELECT BIBLIOGRAPHY

ANGELUCCI, ENZO & MATRICARDI, PAOLO. *World Aircraft: Origins – World War 1*, London, Book Club Associates, 1977.

BAKER, DAVID. *Richthofen: The Man and the Aircraft he Flew*, London, Outline Press Ltd., 1990.

BARING, MAURICE. *Flying Corps Headquarters 1914-1918*, London, G. Bell & Sons, 1920.

BARRAT, WILLIAM E. *Sky Fighters of World War 1*, Greenwich, CT, Fawcett Publications, 1964.

BARTLETT, C.P.O. *In the Teeth of the Wind: The Story of a Naval Pilot on the Western Front 1916-1918*, London, Leo Cooper, 1994.

BICKERS, RICHARD TOWNSHEND. *The First Great Air War*, London, Hodder & Stoughton, 1988.

BODENSCHAZ, KARL. *Jagd in Flanderns Himmel – Aus den sechzehn Kampfmonaten des Jagdgeschwaders Freiherr von Richthofen*, Munich, Knorr & Hirth, 1935. (English translation by Jan Hayzlett, London, Grub Street, 1996 as: *Hunting with Richthofen: The Bodenschatz Diaries*).

BOELCKE, OSWALD (Translated by Robert Reynold Hirsch). *An Aviator's Field Book: Being the Field Reports of Oswald Boelcke, from August 1st 1914, to October 28th 1916*, Nashville, The Battery Press, 1991.

BORDEAUX, HENRY (Translated from the French by Louise Morgan Sill). *Guynemer Knight of the Air*, New Haven, CT., Yale University Press, 1918.

BOWYER, CHAZ. *Sopwith Camel – King of Combat*, Falmouth, Glasney Press, 1988.

BOWYER, CHAZ. *Albert Ball, VC*, London, William Kimber, 1977.

BOWYER, CHAZ, (Editor). *Royal Flying Corps Communiqués 1917-1918*, London, Grub Street, 1998.

BOYLE, ANDREW. *Trenchard, Man of Vision*, London, Collins, 1962.

BRUCE, J.M. *The Aeroplanes of the Royal Flying Corps: Military Wing*, London, Putnam, 1992.

CLARK, ALAN. *Aces High: The War in the Air over the Western Front 1914-18*, London, Weidenfeld & Nicolson, 1973.

COLE, CHRISTOPHER, (Editor). *Royal Flying Corps Communiqués 1915-1916*, London, William Kimber, 1969.

COLLISHAW, RAYMOND & DODDS, R.V. *Air Command: a fighter pilot's story*, London, William Kimber, 1973.

CRUNDALL, E.D. *Fighter Pilot on the Western Front*, London, William Kimber, 1975.

DOUGLAS, SHOLTO. *Years of Combat*, London, Collins, 1963.

DREW, Lt. Col. GEORGE A. *Canada's Fighting Airmen*, Toronto, Maclean, 1930.

DUDGEON, JAMES M. *'Mick': The Story of Major Edward Mannock VC DSO MC RFC RAF*, London, Hale, 1981.

DUVAL, G.R. *War in the Air 1914-1918: A Pictorial Survey*, Truro, Bradford Barton Ltd., 1975.

VON EBERHARDT, W. (Editor). *Unsere Luftstreitkräfte 1914-1918*, Berlin, Vaterlandisce Verlag, 1930.

FRANKS, NORMAN L.R. & BAILEY, FRANK W. *Over the Front: A Complete Record of the Fighter Aces and units of the United States and French Air Services 1914-1918*, London, Grub Street, 1992.

FRANKS, NORMAN; BAILEY, FRANK W. & GUEST, RUSSELL. *Above the Lines: A Complete Record of the Fighter Aces of the German Air Service, Naval Air Service & Flanders Marine Corps, 1914-1918*, London, Grub Street, 1993.

FRANKS, NORMAN & GILBIN, HAL. *Under the Guns of the German Aces*, London, Grub Street, 1997.

FRY, Wing Commander W.M. *Air of Battle*, London, William Kimber, 1974.

FUNDERBURK, THOMAS R. *The Fighters: The Men and Machines of the First Air War*, New York, Grosset & Dunlap, 1966.

GANN, ERNEST K. *In the Company of Eagles*, New York, Simon & Schuster, 1966.

GIBBONS, FLOYD. *The Red Knight of Germany: Baron Von Richthofen, Germany's Great War Airman*, London, Cassell, 1938.

GRAY, PETER & THETFORD, OWEN. *German Aircraft of the First World War*, London, Putnam, 1992.

GRINNEL-MILNE, DUNCAN. *Wind in the Wires*, London, Hurst & Blackett, 1933.

HADINGHAM, EVAN. *The Fighting Triplanes*, London, Hamish Hamilton, 1968.

HARE, PAUL R. *The Royal Aircraft Factory*, London, Putnam, 1990.

HARTNEY, HAROLD E. (Edited by Stanley M. Ulanoff). *Wings Over France*, Folkestone, Bailey & Swinfen, 1974.

HAWKER, Lt. Col. TIRREL M. *Hawker, VC: The Biography of the late Major Lanoe George Hawker, VC DSO*, London, The Mitre Press, 1965.

HEGENER, HENRE. *Fokker – The Man and The Aircraft*, Letchworth, Harleyford, 1961.

HOEPPNER, ERNST WILHELM von. *Deutschlands Krieg in der Luft*, Leipzig, Hase & Koehler, 1921.

HYLANDS, DENNIS. *Werner Voss. Aces and Aeroplanes Series*, Berkhamsted, Albatros Publications, 1986.

IMMELMANN, FRANZ, (Editor). *Max Immelmann 'The Eagle of Lille'*, London, John Hamilton, 1935.

IMRIE, ALEX. *Pictorial History of the German Army Air Service 1914-1918*, London, Ian Allan, 1971.

IMRIE, ALEX. *The Fokker Triplane*, London, Arms & Armour Press, 1994.

ISHOVEN, ARMAND van. (Translated by Chaz Bowyer). *The Fall of an Eagle: The Life of Fighter Ace Ernest Udet*, London, William Kimber, 1979.

ITALIAANDER, ROLF. *Pour le Mérite-Flieger mit 20 Jahren*, Berlin, G. Weise, 1939.

JACKSON, ROBERT. *Fighter Pilots of World War I*, London, Arthur Barker, Ltd., 1977.

JOHNSTONE, E.G. (Editor). *Naval Eight: A History of No. 8 Squadron RNAS, (afterwards No. 208 Squadron RAF) From its Formation in 1916 Until the Armistice in 1918*, London, Arms & Armour Press, 1972.

JONES, H. [Based on the notes of Walter A. Raleigh]. *The War in the Air, Vol. II-VI*, Oxford, The Clarendon Press, 1928-1937.

JONES, IRA. *King of Air Fighters: The Biography of Major 'Mick' Mannock VC DSO MC*, London, Ivor Nicholson & Watson, 1934.

JONES, IRA. *An Air Fighter's Scrapbook*, London, Ivor Nicholson & Watson, 1938.

KÄHNERT, M.E. *Jagdstaffel 356*, Stuttgart, Berlin, Leipzig, Union, 1936.

KIERNAN, Capt. R.H. *Albert Ball: A Historical Record*, London, The Aviation Book Club, 1939.

KILDUFF, PETER. *Germany's Last Knight of the Air: The Memoirs of Major Carl Degelow*, London, William Kimber, 1979.

KILDUFF, PETER. *Germany's First Air Force 1914-1918*, London, Arms & Armour Press, 1991.

KILDUFF, PETER. *Richthofen: Beyond the Legend of the Red Baron*, London, Arms & Armour Press, 1994.

KILDUFF, PETER. *The Red Baron Combat Wing: Jagdgeschwader Richthofen in Battle*, London, Arms & Armour Press, 1997.

LAMBERTON, W.M. *Fighter Aircraft of the 1914-1918 War*, Letchworth, Harleyford Publications, 1961.

LEE, ARTHUR GOULD. *No Parachute: A Fighter Pilot in World War I*, Letters written in 1917 by Lieutenant A.S.G. Lee, *Sherwood Foresters, Attached Royal Flying Corps*, London, Jarrolds, 1968.

LEE, ARTHUR GOULD. *Open Cockpit: A Pilot of the Royal Flying Corps*, London, Jarrolds, 1969.

LEWIS, CECIL. *Sagittarius Rising*, London, Peter Davies, 1936.

[MACLANACHAN, WILLIAM] *Fighter Pilot*, by 'McSCOTCH' [pseud.]. London, George Routledge & Sons, Ltd., 1936.

MACMILLAN, Capt. NORMAN. *Into the Blue*, London, Duckworth, 1929.

McCUDDEN, JAMES THOMAS BYFORD. *Five Years in the Royal Flying Corps*, London, The Aeroplane & General Publishing Co., Ltd., 1918.

McKEE, ALEXANDER. *The Friendless Sky, the Story of Air Combat in World War I*, London, Souvenir Press, 1962.

MEIJERING, PIET HEIN. *Signed with Their Honour: The Story of Chivalry in Air Warfare 1914-45*, Edinburgh, Mainstream Publishing, 1987.

MUNSON, KENNETH. *The Pocket Encyclopaedia of World Aircraft in Colour: Fighters, Attack and Training Aircraft 1914-19*, Poole, Blandford Press, 1976.

MUSCIANO, WALTER H. *Werner Voss: Germany's Greatest Teenage Ace*, New York, Hobby Helpers Publications, 1962.

NEUMANN, GEORG PAUL. *The German Air Force in the Great War*, Bath, Cedric Chivers Ltd., 1969.

NEUMANN, GEORG PAUL, (Editor). *In der Luft unbesiegt*, Munich, Lehmanns, 1923.

NOBLE, WALTER. *With a Bristol Fighter Squadron*, London, Andrew Melrose Ltd., 1975.

NOFFSINGER, JAMES P. *World War I Aviation: A Bibliography of Books*, London, Scarecrow Press, 1997.

PHELAN, JOSEPH A. *Aircraft and Flyers of the First World War*, [Originally titled *Heroes & Aeroplanes of the Great War 1914-1919*.] Cambridge, Patrick Stephens, 1974.

PUDNEY, JOHN. *The Camel Fighter*, London, Hamish Hamilton, 1964.

RALEIGH, SIR WALTER. *The War in the Air Vol. I*, Oxford, The Clarendon Press, 1969.

REVELL, ALEX. *Brief Glory: The Life of Arthur Rhys Davids DSO, MC & Bar*, London, Kimber, 1984.

REVELL, ALEX. *High in the Empty Blue: The History of 56 Squadron RFC/RAF 1916-1920*, Mountain View, Flying Machine Press, 1995.

REYNOLDS, QUENTIN. *They Fought for the Sky: The Story of the First War in the Air*, New York, Bantam Books, 1958.

VON RICHTHOFEN, M. (Translated by P. Kilduff). *The Red Baron*, Garden City, Doubleday & Co., 1969.

RICKENBACKER, CAPTAIN EDDIE V. *Fighting the Flying Circus*, Folkestone, Bailey & Swinfen, 1973.

ROBERTSON, BRUCE, (Editor). *Air Aces of the 1914-1918 War*, Letchworth, Harleyford Publications Ltd., 1959.

SCHRÖDER, HANS, (Translated by Claud W. Sykes). *An Airman Remembers*, London, John Hamilton, Ltd., 1936.

SMITHERS, A.J. *Wonder Aces of the Air: The Flying Heroes of the Great War*, London, Gordon & Cremonesi, 1980.

STARK, RUDOLPH (Translated by Claud W. Sykes). *Wings of War: A German Airman's Diary of the Last Year of the Great War*, London, Greenhill Books, 1989.

STRANGE, Lt. Col. L.A. *Recollections of an Airman*, London, John Hamilton, 1935.

STUART-WORTLEY, ROTHESAY. *Letters from a Flying Officer*, London, Oxford University Press, 1928.

[SYKES, CLAUD W.] 'VIGILANT'. *German War Birds*, London, John Hamilton, 1933.

[SYKES, CLAUD W.] 'VIGILANT'. *French War Birds*, London, John Hamilton, 1937.

[SYKES, CLAUD W.] 'VIGILANT'. *Richthofen – The Red Knight of the Air*, London, John Hamilton, 1934.

TITLER, DALE M. *The Day the Red Baron Died: Final Proof that Ground Fire Brought Von Richthofen down*, New York, Ballantine Books, 1970.

TREADWELL, TERRY C. & WOOD, ALAN C. *The First Air War: A Pictorial History 1914-1919*, London, Brassey's, 1996.

TREADWELL, TERRY C. & WOOD, ALAN C. *German Knights of the Air 1914-1918: The Holders of the Orden Pour le Mérite*, London, Brassey's, 1997.

UDET, ERNST (Translated by K. Kirkness). *Ace of the Black Cross*, London, Newnes, 1937.

WERNER, PROFESSOR JOHANNES (Translated by Claud W. Sykes). *Knight of Germany: Oswald Boelcke German Ace*, New York, Arno Press, 1972.

WINTER, DENIS. *The First of the Few*, London, Allen Lane, 1982.

WOODMAN, H. *Early Aircraft Armament – The Aeroplanes and the Gun up to 1918*, Washington D.C. Smithsonian Institution Press, 1989.

YEATES, W.M. *Winged Victory*, London, Jonathan Cape, 1961.

INDEX OF PERSONS

GENERAL INDEX